The A

Garden Directory
Containing Practical Directions For The Culture Of Plants, In The Hot-House, Garden-House, Flower Garden And Rooms Or Parlours, For Every Month In The Year

Robert Buist

Alpha Editions

This Edition Published in 2021

ISBN: 9789355116352

Design and Setting By
Alpha Editions
www.alphaedis.com
Email – info@alphaedis.com

TABLE OF CONTENTS

PREFACE	- 1 -
INTRODUCTION	- 3 -
OMITTED IN MARCH	- 5 -
ERRATA	- 6 -
HOT-HOUSE JANUARY	- 7 -
GREEN-HOUSE JANUARY	- 15 -
FLOWER GARDEN JANUARY	- 19 -
ROOMS JANUARY	- 21 -
HOT-HOUSE FEBRUARY	- 24 -
GREEN-HOUSE FEBRUARY	- 28 -
FLOWER GARDEN FEBRUARY	- 32 -
ROOMS FEBRUARY	- 39 -
HOT-HOUSE MARCH	- 41 -

GREEN-HOUSE
MARCH - 42 -

FLOWER GARDEN
MARCH - 91 -

ROOMS
MARCH - 115 -

HOT-HOUSE
APRIL - 117 -

GREEN-HOUSE
APRIL - 119 -

FLOWER GARDEN
APRIL - 124 -

ROOMS
APRIL - 149 -

HOT-HOUSE
MAY - 151 -

GREEN-HOUSE
MAY - 179 -

FLOWER GARDEN
MAY - 185 -

ROOMS
MAY - 188 -

HOT-HOUSE
JUNE AND JULY - 190 -

GREEN-HOUSE
JUNE AND JULY - 191 -

FLOWER GARDEN
JUNE AND JULY - 192 -

ROOMS
JUNE AND JULY - 198 -

HOT-HOUSE
AUGUST - 199 -

GREEN-HOUSE
AUGUST - 200 -

FLOWER-GARDEN
AUGUST - 206 -

ROOMS
AUGUST - 209 -

HOT-HOUSE
SEPTEMBER - 210 -

GREEN-HOUSE
SEPTEMBER - 212 -

FLOWER GARDEN
SEPTEMBER - 217 -

ROOMS
SEPTEMBER - 219 -

HOT-HOUSE
OCTOBER - 220 -

GREEN-HOUSE
OCTOBER - 221 -

FLOWER-GARDE
OCTOBER - 225 -

ROOMS
OCTOBER - 229 -

HOT-HOUSE
NOVEMBER - 231 -

GREEN-HOUSE
NOVEMBER - 232 -

FLOWER-GARDEN
NOVEMBER - 233 -

ROOMS
NOVEMBER - 237 -

HOT-HOUSE
DECEMBER - 238 -

GREEN-HOUSE
DECEMBER - 240 -

FLOWER GARDEN
DECEMBER - 242 -

ROOMS
DECEMBER - 243 -

PLANTS DESCRIBED OR MENTIONED
IN THIS WORK - 250 -

PREFACE

This volume owes its existence principally to the repeated requests of a number of our fair patrons, and amateur supporters, whose enquiries and wishes for a practical manual on Floraculture, at last induced us to prepare a work on the subject. That now offered is given unaffectedly and simply as a plain and easy treatise on this increasingly interesting subject. It will at once be perceived that there are no pretensions to literary claims—the directions are given in the simplest manner—the arrangement made as lucidly as was in our power—and the whole is presented with the single wish of its being practically useful. How far our object has been attained of course our readers must judge. Nothing has been intentionally concealed; and all that is asserted is the result of minute observation, close application, and an extended continuous experience from childhood. We pretend not to infallibility, and are not so sanguine as to declare our views the most perfect that can be attained. But we can so far say, that the practice here recommended has been found very successful.

Some very probably may be disappointed in not having the means of propagating as clearly delineated as those of culture; but to have entered into all the minutiæ connected therewith, would have formed materials for two volumes larger than the present. We might have described that branch, as it has already been done in works published both on this continent and in Europe. In one of the former it is said, "You may now propagate many kinds (*Exotic Plants*) by suckers, cuttings, and layers, which should be duly attended to, particularly such as are scarce and difficult to be obtained." And the directions given in one of the most extensive works in Europe on the propagation of an extensive genus, varied in character and constitution, run thus: "Cuttings of most kinds will strike root. From the strongest growing kinds, take off large cuttings at a joint, and plunge them in a pot of sand under a hand-glass in the bark bed. Of the smaller kinds take younger kinds, and put them under a bell-glass, also plunged in heat. The sooner the plants are potted off after they are rooted the better."

Such instructions to the inexperienced, are imperfect and unavailing, which, we flatter ourselves, is not the character that will attach to the present work. We are well aware that there are persons, who, to show their own superior abilities, may cavil and say that there is nothing new. To such critics it may be answered, if arranging, simplifying, digesting, and rendering Floraculture attainable by the humblest capacity, with useful lists and tables on a plan quite novel, as we believe—offer nothing new, it may at least be called an improvement. However, we submit all to a generous public, to whom we are already under many obligations.

HIBBERT & BUIST.

Philadelphia, April 18th, 1832.

INTRODUCTION

In presenting this work, constructed as a monthly calendar, which is the most simple and easy method to convey the necessary operations of the year, considerably more labour has been expended, than was at first expected, to render it as accurate as possible. Some verbal mistakes may have been overlooked in the botanical names. Where such occur, the list of names at the end of the volume will enable the reader to correct them; as well as the accentuation. For such other errors as may be discovered, the indulgence of the reader is solicited.

Frequently, in the description of plants, there are Botanical and English names compounded, in order the more clearly to elucidate their several parts to those who are not fully acquainted with scientific terms. The description of the colour of flowers and habits of plants will be useful to such as are at a great distance from collections, in enabling them to make selections judiciously.

Those plants described and recommended have all, with a few exceptions, passed under our own observation, and are generally such as are most worthy of attention, either for beauty of flower, foliage, or habit, together with those celebrated in arts and medicine. Many may possibly have passed unobserved, either from their being very generally known, or difficult to obtain; but in no case has there been suppression from selfish motives. Where the words "our collections" occur, it is meant for those of the country generally, and especially those immediately in the vicinity of Philadelphia. In all our observations, no regard has been paid to what has been written by others, either in the way of depreciation, or of particular appreciation. Perhaps some other cultivators may differ from us respecting culture and soil; however this may be, we rest satisfied, as our work is designedly and professedly given as the result of our own experience, the plan laid down is our own routine of culture, and the soils are those which we adopt. We do not say that there is no soil in which the plants will not grow better, fully aware that every art and profession is subject to improvement. The table of soils has been constructed at the expense of much labour, and condensed as much as possible; to every one that has a single plant it will be found invaluable. Many are the publications in Europe on Gardening and Floraculture, the directions in which, when practised in the United States, prove almost a perfect dead letter. A work adapted to the climate must be the guide in this country, and not one which is foreign to us in every respect. On this account a work like the present has been a desideratum, considering the rapidly increasing and interesting advancement of the culture of flowers amongst the fair daughters of our flourishing republic.

To aid them and others seeking information in this instructive and delightful pursuit—to enable them to examine more minutely, and judge more correctly of the qualities, properties, and beauties of plants—have been prominent objects in this publication. Here, as knowledge is increased, the warmer will be the devotion of the delighted student; and as the mind correspondingly expands, the desire for further information will keep pace—advancing constantly in the development of nature, the mind will participate in the enjoyment, and become meliorated and purified—as the study of nature's works inevitably lead to the contemplation of nature's God, and the result of the whole prove a harmonious combination of personal gratification and mental improvement.

OMITTED IN MARCH

Jasmìnum, Jasmine. A few species of this genus are celebrated either for the Green-house or Rooms. *J. odoratíssimum*, Azorian, has very sweet-scented yellow flowers, blooming from April to November. *J. revolùtum* is the earliest flowering one, and of the same colour; it is apt to grow straggling, and should be close pruned as soon as done blooming, which will be about June. *J. grandiflòrum* is frequently called Catalonian, and should be pruned early in spring to make it bloom well, especially old plants. *J. officinàle* is a hardy climbing plant for arbours, walls, &c. There are several varieties of it, and it is reported there is a double one.

ERRATA

Page 104, *dele* "*L. Silaifòlia* has leaves bipinnatifid and smooth; segments wedge-shaped and cut; *L. dentáta* and *L. ilicifòlia*, are the finest;" and place it to "*Lomàtia*," page 103.

Page 321, ninth line from top, *dele* "*Pèdulis*."

Hot-House

JANUARY.

At all times be very careful of the temperature of this department, and more especially at this season of the year, as a few minutes' neglect might materially injure many of the delicate plants. The thermometer ought to range between 58° and 65°. In fine sunshine days, admit a little air by having some of the top sashes let down, one, two, or three inches, according to the weather, and let it always be done from eleven to one o'clock; but by no means in such a manner as to cause a draught in the interior of the house, which would be very prejudicial. Therefore be always cautious during cold weather, in administering that necessary element to vegetation, which is so conducive to health.

OF FIRING AND FUEL.

The Hot-house ought never to be left entirely to inexperienced persons, because they are not aware of what might be the result of inattention even for an hour. Attention to the following observations will obviate every difficulty. About this season of the year, frost generally sets in very severe in the middle states. Suppose the day may have all the clemency of spring, the night may be directly the reverse. Every precaution is necessary to guard against extremes. According to what was said last month, it is understood that the shutters are put on every night at sundown, and in severe weather, they must be put on as soon as the sun goes off the glass. If the shutters are omitted till late in severe frost, it will so reduce the heat of the house, that you cannot overcome it by fire until near midnight; and when done, the fire or fires have been made more powerful than they ought to be, proving uncongenial to the plants that are near the flues. The air, as above directed, having been taken off the house at one o'clock, as soon as the mercury begins to fall in the thermometer, kindle the fire, and supposing it is anthracite coal, in twenty minutes, with a good drawing furnace, the heat will operate in the house. If a coal fire, kindled about four o'clock, it will require an addition about six, and then may be made up again about nine or ten, which will suffice until morning. The quantity must be regulated by the weather. If the fuel is wood, it must be attended to three or four times during the evening; and when the mornings are intensely cold, one fire in the morning is requisite. When there are bad drawing furnaces the fires must be made much earlier, perhaps by two or three o'clock, which will be easily observed by the time the fire takes effect upon the air of the house. The temperature ought never to be under 55° of Fahrenheit.

OF WATERING THE PLANTS.

To do this judiciously, is so necessary to vegetation, and so requisite to understand, and yet the knowledge so difficult to convey to others (being entirely acquired by practice,) that if the power was in man to impart it to his fellow-men, he would possess the power of perfecting a gardener by diction. However, the hints on this important point of floraculture, will be as clear and expressive as can at present be elicited. All plants in this work that are aquatic, shall be specified as such; and those that are arid shall be duly mentioned. All others will come in the medium.

All the plants must be looked over every day, and those watered that appear to be getting dry on the top. It must be strictly observed not to give water to any but such as are becoming dry, and let it be given moderately at this season. Two or three days may perhaps elapse before it need be repeated. There is not so much liability to err at present in giving too little, as in administering too much. Vegetation amongst the stove or Hot-house plants will soon begin to show, and the soil will prove uncongenial if it is impregnated with stagnant moisture. Small plants should always be watered with a pot, having what is termed a rose upon it. The surface of the rose, that is, where it is perforated with small apertures, ought to be level, or a little concave, which would convey the water more to a centre, and make neater work, by preventing any water from being unnecessarily spilt in the house. The size of the pot will be regulated by the person to suit the conveniences of the place. Water, when applied either to the roots or foliage of the plants, should be about the medium temperature of the house. The cistern, built on the plan herein recommended, will always give this, and sometimes more, which can easily be reduced by adding cold water. Where there are no cisterns, a tank or barrel might be in the house, in which the water could stand for one night or more, as is most suitable. When water is given without being thus aired, it chills the roots, prevents a luxuriant growth, injures the fresh and healthful appearance of the foliage, and too frequently gives to all the plants a sickly hue.

OF INSECTS, THEIR DESTRUCTION, &c.

In this department, insects begin to increase by hundreds, and too frequently their ravages are very obvious before their progress is arrested. We will treat of those which are most common, under their respective heads, with their nature and cure, as far as has come under our observation.

Aphis rosæ, of the natural order of Hemiptera, or what is commonly known by Green Fly, Green Lice, &c. infect plants in general, and are particularly destructive in the Hot-house to *Hibíscus ròsa-sinénsis*, *Asclèpias*, *Crássula coccínea*, *Alstræmèria*, and many other plants of a free growing nature. They attack the young and tender shoots at the point, leaving a dark filthy appearance on the foliage. Many remedies for their destruction have been offered to the public by various writers, each equally secure in his own opinion. Extensive practice alone can show the most easy and effectual cure. Fumigating with tobacco is decidedly the most efficacious, and in the power of any to perform. Take a small circular furnace, made of sheet iron, diameter at top twelve inches, and at bottom eight; depth one foot, having a grating in it to reach within three inches of the bottom, which will leave space for the air to pass, and where the ashes will fall and be kept in safety, having a handle like a pail to carry it with. This, or any thing similar, being ready, put in it a few embers of ignited charcoal; take it into the centre of the house, and put on the coals a quantity of moist tobacco stems. If they attempt to blaze or flame, sprinkle a little water over them; and as they consume, continue to add tobacco until the house is entirely full of smoke, observing always to do it in still, cloudy weather, or in the evening. If it is windy, the smoke is carried off without having half the effect, and requires more tobacco. The house must be closely shut up. There are several plants whose foliage is of a soft downy nature, such as *Helitròpiums*, *Callacárpas*, *Sálvias*, and many of the *Lantànas*, *Víncas*, with several others, that cannot stand, without danger, strong fumigation. These should be put low down in the house, or under the stage. These fumigations will have to be repeated frequently, the time for which will easily be perceived; and, when required, ought not to be delayed. Several species and varieties of the same genus, *Aphis*, can be destroyed in the like manner.

Acaris tellurius, or red spider, is caused by a dry atmosphere, and its havoc generally is obvious before it is arrested. With its proboscis, it wounds the fine capillary vessels; and if the leaves are fine, they will appear as if probed with a needle, and yellowish around the wound. If they have farther progressed in their destructive work, the leaves will prematurely decay. On this appearance, turn up the leaf, and you will see them running about with incredible swiftness. Their body is of a blood colour, and their feet, eight in number, light red. When very numerous, they work thick webs on the under side of the leaf, and frequently all over it, forming a mass of half dead plants, decayed leaves, and thousands of spiders. The most effectual remedy is a thorough syringing with water, and profusely under the foliage. This being done every evening, will subdue and eventually banish them. Had the house been syringed two or three times per week, these intruders would not have appeared. It is said by some writers, that watering only reduces them to a temporary state of inaction, and will not destroy them. Laying aside the many prescribed nostrums, we assert that the pure element is the most effectual cure, as well as the most easy to be obtained.

Thrips, order *Hemiptera*, are insects so minute as scarcely to be perceptible to the naked eye. They generally lurk close to the veins of the leaves of plants, and frequently attack esculents. When viewed through a glass, they are seen, when touched, to skip with great agility. The larva is of a high brown, or reddish colour. The thrip has four wings, and walks with its body turned upwards. It frequently attacks the extremities of tender shoots, or young leaves, which become shrivelled, brown, and will rub to dust easily between the thumb and finger. When any leaves or shoots are perceived to be so, if you do not observe the green fly, expect the thrips. They may be destroyed by a fumigation of tobacco, in the same manner as the green fly. By the simple and expeditious method of fumigation, these insects and several others may be destroyed effectually at any time they appear.

Cocus hesperidus, or mealy bug, has appeared in the Hot-houses about Philadelphia within these few years, and, if not instantly destroyed, increases rapidly. It is of a white dusty colour, when broken, of a brownish red, generally covered with down, under which it deposits its eggs; and they, in a few months, come forth in great numbers. The cocus generally is of a dormant nature, but, in warm weather, they may be seen moving rapidly up the stems of the plants. Fumigating has no observable effect on these insects; therefore, as soon as they appear, recourse must be had to other means. The liquid made from the following receipt, is death to any of the *Cocus* tribe: Take two pounds of strong soap, one pound flour of sulphur, one pound of leaf tobacco, one and a half ounce of nux vomica, with a table spoonful of turpentine, which boil in four gallons of river water to three; then set aside to cool. When boiling, stir it well with a stick, continuing to do so until it is reduced as above. In this liquor immerse the whole plant, drawing it to and fro gently, that the liquor may penetrate every where.

This done, lay the plant on its side, until it begin to dry, then syringe well with clean water, and put it in its respective station. Where a collection of plants is free from any insects of the kind, every plant that is introduced, ought to be minutely scrutinized, that the unclean may be kept from the clean: the above insect will feed almost on any plant, but indulges on *Cráss ulas*, any of the bristly *Cáctus*, *Gardènias*, and in fact whatever is in the way.

Cocus————, or brown scaly insect, is frequently found on many plants, but we never could perceive that it does any other material injury, than dirtying them. We have always observed, that it is found in winter to abound most in those situations which are most excluded from air; therefore is of less importance than the other species, which eat and corrode the leaves of tender plants. A washing with strong soap suds will destroy them, or the above liquid will do it more effectually. Tie a piece of sponge on the end of a small stick, and scrub every leaf, stem, and crevice. Fumigating destroys the larvæ of this species.

Cocus————, or small white scaly insect, which generally infests *Cycas revolùta* and *circinàlis*, the varieties of *Nèrium oleánder*, *Oleas*, and several species of *Acacias*, may be destroyed by washing as above with a sponge, and a strong decoction of tobacco, using the liquid about the warmth of 100°. Being thus heated, it irritates the insect, when, by easing itself from its bed, the fluid passes under it, and causes immediate death. If it is not thus irritated, it adheres so closely to the foliage, that it will keep you at defiance. The under, or dark side of the leaves is its residence; and we have observed a plant in a house where there was only light on one side, with the dark side literally covered, while the light side was clean. So much for having houses with plenty of light. The effects of this insect are of a corroding nature, extracting all the juices from the leaf under it, even straining to the other side; and where they have got to the extremity, the foliage is completely yellow, and of a decayed appearance.

Cocus————, or turtle insect. We have never observed this insect arrive to any extent, but think that the *Datura arborea* is most infested with it. It is the largest of any genus known amongst us, and very like a turtle in miniature. On lifting it from the wood, to which it generally adheres, there appear to be hundreds of eggs under it, but fumigating completely destroys the larvæ. In our opinion this turtle insect is no other than the old female of the brown scaly insect, which swells to a large size before depositing its eggs. We have frequently observed the insect dead in this enlarged state, and question if this is the last stage of its transmigration. The male insect is winged, and very active in its movements.

OF SHIFTING PLANTS.

At this period of the season very little is required to grow *Calceolàrias* to perfection. They require a few months of the Hot-house, and if the directions given last month were followed up, some of these will have advanced a little in growth. The herbaceous kinds, when grown about one inch high, ought to be divided, and put into four inch pots, sprinkled gently, and kept in the shade until they begin to grow; after which, keep them near the glass, to prevent them from becoming spindly and drawn. Their farther treatment will be observed as they require. This is a beautiful genus of plants, flowering very profusely all summer, and some of them early in spring.

Alstrœmèrias, about the beginning or middle of the month, will have made their appearance above ground. When shot about one inch, turn them out, and carefully shake them clear of earth; and if required, divide the crowns, and put them in as small pots as possible, taking care not to break any of the strong fleshy roots. (For Soil, see Table.) To flower these plants well, they require to be frequently shifted, during their active stage of growth, which must be duly observed. The most of the species of this genus will more than repay the attention, by their abundantly and beautifully spotted flowers. *A. flòsmartìna*, *A. Pelegrìna*, *A. pulchélla*, and *A. atrópurpurea*, are the most splendid. The former flowers very freely. All natives of South America.

Where bulbous roots, such as *Hyacinths*, *Jonquils*, *Narcissus*, *Ixias*, *Lachenàllas*, &c. are required to be early in flower, they may, about the beginning or end of the month, be put in the front of the Hot-house, giving very little water until they begin to grow; then water freely, and tie up the flower stems as they advance.

OF CLEANSING PLANTS, HOUSE, &c.

This subject ought to be kept constantly in view. However correct every thing may be executed, without that adorning beauty, cleanliness, all will appear only half done. Therefore let all the dead leaves be picked off every day, and with dust and other litter swept out of the house, and when necessary, the house washed, which will be at least once a week. That the foliage of the plants may always appear fresh, syringe them in the evening, twice or three times per week; (when the weather is very cold, do it in the morning.) At present this will in a great measure keep down the insects, and will prove a bane to the red spider.

A hand engine is certainly the best. Milne's patent hand engine surpasses any that we have used. Nevertheless a hand syringe is very effectual. Some of these engines are powerful, throwing the water above forty feet. Read's patent of London is excellent. At the store of

D. & C. Landreth, Phila., there is a very good kind, which answers admirably in small houses. Tie up neatly with stakes, and threads of Russia mat, all the straggling growing plants; let the stakes be proportionate to the plants, and never longer, except they are climbing sorts. Do not tie the branches in bundles, but singly and neatly, imitating nature as much as possible. If any of the plants are affected with the *Cocus* insect, let them be cleaned according to the plan already mentioned, taking particular care also in washing the stakes to which they had been previously tied, and burning all the old tyings, which contain the larvæ of the insect in many instances, especially of *Cocus hesperidus*. It is premised, when any of these things are done, that they will be well done, and not half doing, and always doing. Cleanliness, in every respect, promotes a pure air, which is congenial to vegetation, and will, with other attention, always ensure a healthful and vigorous appearance in the house.

Green-House

JANUARY.

This compartment requires particular attention, in order to preserve the plants in good health, and carry them through this precarious season of the year. A little air must be admitted at all convenient times. An hour or two at mid-day will be of the utmost importance in drying up damp, and clearing off stagnated air, which is a harbour for every corruption. The top sashes being let down, or turned a few inches, in mild days (that is, when it is not high and cutting winds) from ten or eleven o'clock to two or three, according to the intensity of the frost, will renovate the interior air of the house, and harden the plants. When the weather will permit, let the front sashes be opened about one inch or more. An assiduous, experienced hand will never omit an opportunity.

With regard to fire heat, the temperature must be regulated to suit the nature of the plants in a general sense; so let the mercury, or spirits of wine, of Fahrenheit's thermometer, be from 34° to 43°; if it begins to fall, give a little fire heat. No doubt we have seen the thermometer much lower in the Green-house, than the above, even as low as 24°, without any immediate injury; but it was in an extensive collection, where the most hardy of the plants were selected into one house. Many boast how little fire they give their Green-house, and how cold it is kept, not observing the miserable state of their plants,—inexperience causing them to think, that the least fire heat will make them grow, and would rather look on naked stems than healthy plants. The above temperature will not, in exotics, cause premature vegetation, but will cause the plants to retain the foliage requisite to vegetative nature. A high temperature is not necessary for the generality of Green-house plants; on the contrary, it might very much injure them.

OF WATERING.

In this month very little is requisite, and must be given with great caution. Few plants will require much, and some hardly any; but all must be attended to, and have their wants supplied. Some will need it twice, some once a week, and some in two weeks, according to their shrubby and woody nature. Herbaceous and deciduous plants will seldom need water. Perhaps, from the throwing of the foliage, to the commencement of vegetation, three or four times will be sufficient. Particular attention should be paid to the state of health and of growth, in which the plants respectively are, in the application of water; otherwise much mischief may be done, and many entirely ruined.

Green-house plants, being now in an absolutely inactive state, require little more water than merely to keep the earth about their roots from becoming perfectly dry, by occasionally applying a very small quantity at the root; and, if done with a watering pot, as described under this head in the Hot-house of this month, very little will be spilt in the house to increase dampness, which, if it does appear, by any of the leaves of the plants becoming musty, they must be instantly picked off; and, if it increases, give a little fire and air. Succulent plants will not need any water during this month, unless omitted in December.

CAMELLIA JAPONICA.

This magnificent and attractive flower, with all its splendid varieties, will, about this time, begin to open its beautiful flowers. But for this admired genus of plants, our Green-houses, at this season, would be void of allurement. It is, in this country, subject to mildew and red spider, and more especially in the city, which appears to be from the nature of the air. The effects of mildew on these plants, if not prevented, would prove fatal; as, from appearance, many have died by it in our city. If it has reached a great extent, the leaves are brownish, having the appearance of being decayed, or scorched with the sun. In taking hold of the leaf, it feels soft, and altogether seems to have lost its nutritive substance; and, when the young foliage expands, it becomes covered with dark brown spots, and finally very much disfigured; and, when in this state, it is attacked by red spider, and, ultimately, death ensues.

If any of the plants are affected as above described, take a sponge, and wash every leaf minutely with soft water, and syringe them with water three or four times a week, which will clean them. All the young foliage will be healthy, and that which has been affected will fall off. However, prevention is better than cure; and if the *Camellias* are properly syringed every evening during summer, and once or twice a week during winter, they will never be subject to the ravages of mildew or of red spider.

Tie up any of the flowers that are expanded to stakes, in case of accident; and, in syringing, observe not to let any water fall on the flowers, as it causes premature decay, and change of colour.

The mildew first appears like small particles of very fine flour, around the under edge of the leaves, and visible to the naked eye; so that, syringing, sponging, &c. under the leaf is most requisite; but, as the mildew extends, both sides of the leaves are covered with these white particles.

OF ORANGES, LEMONS, &c.

As there will perhaps be more leisure in the Green-house this month than in any other during the winter, it is presumed that there will not be a moment lost. If any of the trees are infested with insects, these, being now in their inactive state, may be more easily destroyed than at any other time. It is the brown scaly insect that generally infests them. For treatment, see *Hothouse, January*. The plant, or tree, after being washed, before it becomes dry, will require to be syringed with water, otherwise the dust will adhere to the glutinous particles of the soap. Set the plant in an airy situation to dry, in case of damp. There are several others subject to this insect, such as *Myrtles*, *Oleas*, *Oleanders*, &c. which treat in the same manner. Be careful that these trees are not over watered; if the soil is moist, it is sufficient.

OF CAPE BULBS, &c.

If there are any out of the ground, it is time that the whole were potted, such as *Lachenàlia*, *Wachendórfia*, *Eùcomis*, *Ixia*, *Gladìolus*, with several others. Keep them in the shade until they begin to grow; then put them on shelves near the light. Those that are growing must be kept in front of the house, to prevent them being weak. *Wachendórfia* has a beautiful large red tuber root; and, as the new root descends, give it a pot about six or seven inches.

OF HYACINTHS AND OTHER BULBOUS ROOTS.

All these roots must be carefully examined. In case slugs or snails are preying upon the embryo of the flower, some of those that are farthest advanced, may be put for a few weeks in the Hot-house. It will greatly accelerate their flowering, but they must be brought out again before the florets expand, and carefully tied up, leaving room for the increase and extension of the flower stem. Give them plenty of water, and if saucers can be placed under them to retain it, it will be of advantage. Change the water every week on those that are in glasses, and keep all the growing bulbs near the light. *Narcissus*, *Jonquils*, &c. may be similarly treated.

Flower Garden

JANUARY.

If the covering of the beds of choice bulbs, herbaceous plants, or tender shrubs, has been neglected last month, let it be done forthwith. The season is now precarious, and delays are dangerous. For particular directions, see *December*. Any bulbous roots that have been kept out of the ground, should be planted immediately, according to directions in *October*. Some writers have recommended keeping some of the bulbs until this month, in order to have a continued succession. Experience will prove the inefficacy of the plan, and will satisfactorily show that the difference is almost imperceptible, while the flowers are very inferior and much degenerated; and in place of having "a long continued succession of bloom," there appear, along with your finest specimens, very imperfect flowers, calculated to discourage the admirers of these "gaudy" decoratives of our flower gardens. Whereas every art employed should be to the advancement and perfection of nature.

OF FRAMING, &c.

The plants and roots that are in frames, should be protected with straw mats, and the frame surrounded with litter, or leaves, or what is more advisable, banked with earth—the former being a harbour for mice and other vermin. For full directions, see *December*. Under this head the plants, such as *Auriculas*, *Polyanthus*, *Daisies*, *Carnations*, *Pinks*, *Gentianellas*, *Campanula pyramidalis*, *Double rocket*, *Double stock*, *or Stockgillys*, *Double Wall-flower*, *Anemone*, *Ranunculus*, &c. as previously enumerated as frame plants, will require very little water, and be sure to give none while they are in a frozen state. If snow should cover them, the plants will keep in a fine state under it, so never remove snow from covering cold frames, even suppose it should lay for months,—nature will operate here herself.

All the above plants except *Anemone* and *Ranunculus* are kept in perfection in the Green-house; but where neither this nor framing can be obtained, they will, in most winters, keep tolerably, if well covered with litter—the roughest from the stable, straw or hay, or such like, using means to secure it from being blown over the whole garden.

OF PRUNING AND PREPARING FOR SPRING.

It is not advisable to carry on a general pruning in this month, in whatever state the weather may be. The severest frosts generally are yet to come, and too frequently in this operation, what is done now has to be repeated on the opening of spring, causing at that time work to a disadvantage; because, if pruning, when done just now, is accomplished judiciously, whatever more on the same bush is requisite to be done in spring, from the effects of frost, will be injudicious. Hence it is far preferable to delay it until the frost is over, when all can be done to advantage.

There are, undoubtedly, some shrubs that may be pruned any time, from the end of November to the first of March, such as *Hibíscus syrìacus* (*Althea*), and all its varieties, except the *Double White*, which is in some instances entirely killed by our severe winter, and certainly, for precaution, would be the better of some simple protection.

In many seasons, the beginning of this month is open, and admits of the operation of digging, which if it is not all done as advised last month, ought not to be delayed. The fruits of it will appear in the mellowed state of your soil in spring.

If there is any spare time, straight sticks or stakes may be prepared for summer. Tie them up in neat bundles, which will be of great service during the hurried period of the year. An opportunity of this kind should always be laid hold of; the beneficial results will in season be displayed.

ROOMS.

JANUARY.

Plants that are kept in rooms generally are such as require a medium temperature, say 40°. Sitting rooms or parlours, about this season, are, for the most part, heated from 55° to 65°, and very seldom has the air any admittance into these apartments, thus keeping the temperature from 15° to 25° higher than the nature of the plants requires, and excluding that fresh air which is requisite to support a forced vegetative principle. Therefore, as far as practicable, let the plants be kept in a room adjoining to one where there is fire heat, and the intervening door can be opened when desirable. They will admit sometimes of being as low as 33°.

If they be constantly kept where there is fire, let the window be opened some inches; two or three time a day, for a few minutes, thereby making the air of the apartment more congenial, both for animal and vegetable nature.

WATERING, &c.

There are very few plants killed for want of water, during winter. All that is necessary is merely to keep the soil in a moist state, that is, do not let it get so dry that you can divide the particles of earth, nor so wet that they could be beat to clay. The frequency of watering can be best regulated by the person doing it, as it depends entirely upon the size of the pot or jar in proportion to the plant, whether it is too little or too large, and the situation it stands in, whether moist or arid. Never allow any quantity of water to stand in the flats or saucers. This is too frequently practised with plants in general. Such as *Cálla Æthiòpica*, or African Lily, will do well, as water is its element, (like *Sagittària* in this country;) and the *Hydrángea horténsis*, when in a growing state, will do admirably under such treatment. Many plants may do well for some time, but it being so contrary to their nature, causes premature decay; a fœtid stagnation takes place at the root, the foliage becomes yellow, and the plant stunted; and in the winter season, death will ensue.

OF CAMELLIA JAPONICA.

In rooms the buds of Camellias will be well swelled, and on the Double White and Double Variegated sorts, perhaps they will be full blown. While in that state the temperature should not be below 34°; if lower they will not expand so well, and the expanded petals will soon become yellow and decay. If they are where there is fire heat, they must have plenty of air admitted to them every favourable opportunity, or the consequence will be, that all the buds will turn dark brown, and fall off. It is generally the case, in the treatment of these beautiful plants in rooms, that through too much intended care they are entirely destroyed. In the city, they do not agree with confined air, and they cannot get too much of pure air, if they are kept from frost or cutting winds. To sponge frequently will greatly promote the health of the plants, and add to the beauty of their foliage, as it prevents the attacks of mildew. In this season they do not require much water at root, which may be observed in the slight absorption by the soil. See this subject under the head of *Watering*.

When the flowers are expanded, and droop, tie them up neatly, so that the flower may be shown to every advantage.

OF INSECTS, &c.

Insects of various kinds will be appearing on your plants. For method of destruction see *Hot-house, January*. It will not be agreeable to fumigate the room or rooms, or even to have the smell of tobacco near the house from this cause.

Many ingredients have been compounded, and prescriptions recommended, for the destruction of these nefarious pests. Many of them are altogether ineffectual. Of receipts specified in works of this kind, not a few of them (though eagerly sought for) by men of extensive practice, have been rejected. We shall give the most simple, and in part effective receipt for the destruction of the Green fly.

Take a large tub of soft water, (if the day is frosty, it had better be done in the house,) invert the plant, holding the hand, or tying a piece of cloth, or any thing of the kind, over the soil in the pot, put all the branches in the water, keeping the pot in the hand, drawing it to and fro a few times; take it out, and shake it. If any insects remain, take a small fine brush, and brush them off, giving another dip, which will clean them for the present. As soon as they appear again, repeat the process—for nothing that we have found out, or heard of, can totally extirpate them.

OF BULBOUS ROOTS IN GENERAL.

If you have retained any of the *Cape bulbs* from the last planting, let them be put in, in the early part of the month. For method, see *September*. Those that are growing must be kept very near the light, that is, close to the window, or they will not flourish to your satisfaction. The fall-flowering oxalis may be kept on the stage, or any other place, to give room to those that are to flower.

Hyacinths, *Jonquils*, *Narcissus*, *Tulips*, &c. will keep very well in a room where fire heat is constantly kept, providing that they are close to the window. A succession of these, as before observed, may beautify the drawing room from February to April, by having a reserved stock, in a cold situation, and taking a few of them every week into the warmest apartment.

Wherever any of the bulbs are growing, and in the interior of the room, remove them close to the light, observing to turn the pots or glasses frequently to prevent them from growing to one side, and giving them support as soon as the stems droop, or the head becomes pendant. The saucers under the Hyacinth and Narcissus especially may stand with water, and observe to change the water in the glasses, as already mentioned.

Every one that has any taste or refinement in their floral undertakings, will delight in seeing the plants in perfection; to have them so, they must be divested of every leaf that has the appearance of decaying—let this always be attended to.

Hot-House.

FEBRUARY.

In the early part of this month the weather generally is very cold and changeable in the middle states, and strict attention, with the greatest caution, will require to be paid to the management of the Hot-house. Most of the tropical plants commence an active state of vegetation; and if checked by temperature or otherwise, they will not recover until midsummer. The thermometer may be kept two or three degrees higher with fire heat than last month; the sun will be more powerful, and this will, in a great degree, increase the vigour of the plants. Air may be admitted when the thermometer rises to 75° or 80°, not allowing it to rise higher than the latter. In giving air, let it be done by the top sashes. It is improper to give it in any way to cause a current, for the external air is very cold, although the sun is more powerful. An inch or two on a few of the sashes, as has been previously observed, will be effectual in keeping the temperature low enough, except the weather is very mild.

With regard to firing, what was said last month may suffice for this. Always recollect that it is preferable to keep out the cold than to put it out. It will frequently happen in the time of intense frost, that the weather is dull. In such cases fire in a small degree is requisite all day.

Heavy snows ought never to be allowed to remain on the shutters while they are on the house. If the snow lies on the sashes one day, the internal heat will dissolve some of it; night coming on will freeze it to the wood work, when it will become a solid mass, and too frequently cannot be separated without much damage. If allowed to remain on for two days, the plants are very much weakened, and the foliage discoloured. Therefore let the snow be cleared off instantly, that no inconvenience may take place.

It will be observed that plants absorb more water this month than last. The quantity given will require to be increased, according to the increase of vegetation and the advancement of the season; but never give it until the soil begins to get dry, and then in such proportion as will reach the bottom of the pot. After the sun has got on the house in the morning is the best time to water, observing all the directions given in January.

OF INSECTS, &c.

Perhaps sufficient observations were given under this head last month; but the importance of keeping these disagreeable visitors out of the house, constrains us to make a few more remarks, and perhaps it may be necessary every month. Man cannot be too frequently guarded against his foes, more especially when they are summoning all their forces, and no profession has more than that of the Horticulturist. Let a strict examination be made about the end of the month for the Red spider; they will be in operation some weeks before their depredations are observed on the foliage. The under side of the leaf is their resort in the first instance, and on such plants as have been already mentioned.

Observe daily the young shoots, in case the Green fly becomes numerous. They give the foliage a very disagreeable appearance, and with most people it is intolerable, before their career is arrested. It also takes a stronger fumigation, which has frequently to be repeated the following day to the same degree, much to the injury of many of the plants, and adding to the disagreeableness of the continued vapour in the house.

OF SHIFTING PLANTS.

The *Calceolàrias* that were put in small pots about the beginning or middle of last month, will, if they have done well, require, about the end of this, to be put in pots a size larger.

If any of *Lilium longiflòrum*, *Speciòsum*, or *Japónicum*, are wanted to flower early, and were put in the Hot-house in December, without dividing, those that are to flower will have pushed their flower stems, and can be separated from those that will not flower, and put singly into pots; the two former into five or six inch pots, while the latter require six or seven inch pots. Of those that do not flower, three or four can be put into one pot.

About the end of the month, some of the plants of *Eurcúma*, *Amómum*, *Kæmpféria*, *Glóbba*, *Phrynium*, *Cánna*, *Zíngiber*, *Hedychium*, and others that are on the dry shelf, will be offering to grow. Let them be taken out of their pots, some of their weakest shoots or tubers taken off, and the strong ones repotted: give gentle waterings until they grow freely, then give an abundance.

Dionæa mucípula, or Venus fly trap, grows best in the Hot-house, and will, about the end of the month, stand in need of being repotted. This plant is very seldom grown in any degree of perfection, having been always considered a delicate plant in collections. The operator has never had courage to treat it according to its nature in a cultivated state. If it is taken out of the pot, just when beginning to grow afresh, and divested of all the soil, leaving only a few of the young roots, (it is a bulb, and will receive no injury by so doing,) put it in new soil; when potted, place the pot in a saucer with one inch of water in it, giving always a fresh supply, when necessary. A shady and moist situation is best adapted to it; this being repeated every year, it will grow, flower, and seed in perfection.

Gesnérias, if in small pots, give larger as they advance in growth. This genus requires to be well attended to make them flower well. *G. bulbósa* ought to have a situation in every Hot-house. It is remarkable for its many brilliant crimson flowers, and continues in flower for a length of time. When the bulb begins to push, shake it out of the earth, putting it into a small pot; and, as soon as the roots reach the side of the earth, which will be in about one month, put it in a larger pot, and continue to do so until flowering, which will be about the first of June, observing always to keep the ball of earth entire.

Gloriósas must be repotted in the beginning of this month. Etymologists have said that this *genus* is named from the glorious appearance of its flowers. *G. supérba* is the most beautiful and curious. The roots ought to be planted one and a half inch deep, taking care not to break them; if there is a bark bed, place the pots in it. Do not water much until they begin to grow. Where there is no bark bed, put the pots into others three inches larger, filling all round with sand, and place them in the warmest part of the house. Keep the sand moist, which will assist to keep the soil in a moist state. The earth must not have much water. As the plants grow, they will require a more liberal supply; yet it is necessary, at all times, to be moderate in giving it. If well treated, the superb flowers will appear in June or July.

OF CLEANSING PLANTS, HOUSE, &c.

With regard to cleaning the plants. Sprinkling, or syringing, is at all times, to a greater or less degree, necessary. The plants will, in this compartment, be in their first stage of growth, and, if dust or foulness be permitted to lodge on their foliage, the pores will be obstructed, the plants will become unhealthy, and the growth of insects increased.

Let all moss, litter, decayed leaves, or weeds, be cleared out of the house, the earth in the pots stirred up with a round pointed stick, and fresh earth given where required, that the air may operate therein freely.

The house ought always to be sprinkled before being swept, to prevent the dust rising.

Attend to the bulbous roots as directed last month, such as *Hyacinths*, *Narcissus*, &c.

Green-House.

FEBRUARY.

The directions given last month respecting the airing and temperature of the house, may still be followed, differing only in admitting air more freely as the season advances, and according to the power the sun has on the glass, which now begins to be considerable.

If the weather is tolerably mild, air may be admitted in time of sunshine, so as to keep the mercury as low as 45°, but be cautious in cold, cloudy, frosty weather. It is a practice with many in such weather to keep the shutters on the house night and day, for the space of a week, and sometimes more, never entering it; and, when the weather has induced them to look in, they find that the frost and damp have made many lifeless subjects; whereas, had the house and plants been attended to, in taking off the shutters, and giving a little fire when requisite, all would have been in safety, and many that cannot be replaced still in the collection.

When watering, strictly adhere to the directions of last month, except with *Geraniums*, and other soft wooded plants, which require a little more water toward the end of the month. If the days are mild and sunny about eight or nine o'clock in the morning, all the plants would be benefited by a gentle syringing, which retards the progress of insects, and accelerates vegetation.

Succulents, such as *Cáctus*, *Mesembryánthemum*, *Aloes*, *Furchræas*, *Crássulas*, *Cotylèdons*, &c. will very seldom need water, at the same time keep them from getting as dry as powder.

OF ORANGES, LEMONS, &c.

Similar treatment to that recommended last month will do for this. Where the soil in the tubs or pots requires to be enriched, take of bone dust or shavings, and fresh sheep dung, equal quantities; put the mixture into a large tub or barrel, until one third full; and fill it up with water. Stir it well two or three times every day for a week, then give each tree one good watering with the compound. Continue to mix up afresh, and let it stand another week, and so on until all the trees requiring it are watered. This watering will greatly enrich the soil, and invigorate the roots.

OF CAPE BULBS, &c.

The bulbs, of *Ferrària undulata* and *F. antheròsa*, that were taken out of the pots in October, will now require to be planted. Five inch pots will be large enough for good roots. The grand criterion for planting bulbs is when there is a protuberant appearance about the bottom, or root part of the bulb, showing, by a principle of nature, the true time for transplanting. When bulbous roots of any description appear above ground, they ought to be placed in an airy situation. They are very frequently placed under other plants, by the inexperienced, until they show their flowers, and then brought to the light, having weak flowers, and comparatively of momentary existence.

Hyacinths, *Narcissus*, *Gladìolus*, *Ixia*, &c. having flower stems, ought to have support, to prevent accident, especially the two former; keep them nigh the glass, and water freely. Change the water regularly in the bulb glasses, observing that their roots are never allowed to become matted with fœtid water. Any of the above plants that are in flower, might, if desired, be taken into the drawing room or parlour, washing the pots clean, and putting saucers under them, keeping therein a little water. Twice a week the decayed ones can be taken out, and supplanted with those that are coming into bloom.

CAMELLIA JAPONICA

Will, in this month, show a profusion of flowers; and, where there is a variety, they have truly a magnificent appearance. From a good selection, endless varieties, by seed, of exquisite beauty, might be obtained by attention to the following rule. The best to select for bearing seed are *Single white*, *Atoniana*, *Grandiflora*, *Waratah*, *Carnation Waratah*, *Fulgens*, and, in many instances, the pistil, or pistillum of *Variegata*, *Pompone*, *Pæoniflora*, and *Intermedia*, are perfect, with several others. When any of the above are newly expanded, (*Waratah* is most perfect about one day before expansion,) take a fine camel hair pencil, and put it gently on the farina or pollen, which is a yellow substance on the anthers, and, when ripe, appears in thousands of small particles.

Take the finest double kinds, then, with this on the pencil, rub lightly the stile of those intended to carry seed. Between the hours of ten and twelve in the forenoon, is the most proper time for the operation; the seed will be ripe in September or October, which will be taken notice of, and directions given. For other particulars on cleaning and syringing, see *January* under this head.

OF SHIFTING &c.

The best time to repot *Camellias*, is just when they are done flowering, which will be before they begin to grow. There are, though not frequently, some flowers after the young foliage begins to appear, and probably it would be better to discriminate the time by the buds offering to push, which will answer to those that have no flowers, as well as those that have. The most general time in shifting *Camellias* is in August and September, indiscriminately with other plants; and, if then not very gently handled, bad roots eventually are produced. Frequently very fine plants have been killed by probing, and breaking the young fibrous roots, thus causing mortification.

In the process, do not, by any means, break, or bruise any of the roots: and do not give large pots, with the idea of making them grow fast: it acts on most plants diametrically opposite to what is intended. A pot one or one and a half inches wider and deeper than the one they have been in previously, is sufficient. Healthy plants under five feet will not require shifting oftener than once in two years; from five feet upwards in three or four years, according to the health of the plants. This treatment, in the opinion of some, will appear not sufficient: it will be found enough with a top-dressing every year to keep them in a healthy, flowering condition, the soil being according to our description.

On turning the plant out of the pot, it may easily be observed if the soil has, in any degree, been congenial to it; for if so, the roots will be growing all round the ball; if otherwise, no roots will appear.

Therefore, with a blunt pointed stick, probe away all the bad earth, until you come to the roots; then put the plant in the pot about one inch in diameter, larger than the combined roots, previously putting a few small pieces of broken pots, or clean gravel, to drain off the superabundant moisture, and give light waterings, as the roots in this case will grow but slowly.

Top dress all that requires shifting, probe out the soil down to the roots, and by the side of the pot, taking care not to break the fibres; then fill up with fresh earth, watering gently with a rose on the watering pot to settle it.

OF CLEANING, &c.

If any of the plants require cleaning, either by fumigation or otherwise, let it be done before the young foliage appears, according to directions heretofore given. Likewise tie neatly all that require it, clean and top dress those that will not be shifted, having every plant and all in the Green-house, in perfect order, before the throng of spring commences. The weather will now admit, in very fine mornings, of the plants being syringed, which may be done between half past seven and half past eight: and the path or pavement should be washed out once a week, which is a great improvement to the appearance of the whole interior.

In winter whenever any glass is broken it should be immediately mended. Broken glass in cold nights causes a very destructive current of air. It should always be made water tight, for if the drops fall into the pots upon the roots, they will frequently prove fatal to the plants; therefore care ought to be taken during rain to remove those that stand in any manner exposed.

Flower Garden.

FEBRUARY.

Where the borders and beds were dug in the fall, and compost or a thin coating of well decayed manure given, the advantage will now in part be experienced. If the weather is open about the end of the month, the pruning should be done with the utmost despatch; that all may be prepared for a general dressing next month, and let nothing be delayed which can now properly be accomplished, under the idea that there is time enough.

OF PRUNING, &c.

Generally about the end of the month the very severe frosts are over; and when none need be apprehended that would materially injure hardy shrubs, they may freely be pruned of all dead branches, and the points cut off such shoots as have been damaged by the winter. Most of shrubs require nothing more than to be pruned of straggling, irregular, and injured branches, or of suckers that rise round the root, observing that they do not intermingle with each other. Never trim them up in a formal manner. Regular shearing of shrubs and topiary work have been expelled as unworthy of a taste the least improved by reflections on the beauty, simplicity, and grandeur of nature. In fact, the pruning of deciduous hardy shrubs should be done in such a manner as not to be observable when the plants are covered with verdure. It may frequently be observed in Flower-gardens, that roses and shrubs of every description are indiscriminately cut with the shears, the *Amórphas* and *Althèas* sharing the same fate.

Robínias, *Colùteas*, *Cyticus*, *Rhús*, *Genístas*, with several of the *Viburnums*, and many others, bear their flowers on the wood of last year, and when thus sheared afford no gratification in flowering. And those shrubs that thus flower on the shoots of last year are perhaps worse to keep in regular order, than those to which the knife can be freely applied; but good management while young will ensure handsome free flowering plants.

Climbing shrubs, and others that are trained against outbuildings, walls, or such as are sheltered thereby, and not now in danger of suffering by frost, may be pruned and dressed. These should be neatly trimmed, and the branches moderately thinned out, tying in all the shoots straight and regular. Avoid at all times, if possible, the crossing of any shoots.

There is not a shrub in the garden that agrees so well with close cutting, as the *Althèa*, and all its varieties. These can be made either bushes or trees, and kept at any desired height. Where the wood of last year is cut to about two or three inches from the wood of the former year, the young shoots of this year will produce the largest and finest flowers, and likewise more profusely. When they have attained the desired height, let them be kept in the most natural and handsome shape that the taste of the operator can suggest. They will bear cutting to any degree.

Honeysuckles of every description may with all freedom be trimmed, providing the frost is not very severe. These are very frequently allowed to become too crowded with wood, and then superficially sheared or cut. The flowers would be much finer, and the bush handsomer, if they were regularly thinned out, divesting them of all naked and superfluous shoots. Of those that remain, shorten the shoots of last year. Where any of the honeysuckle kind has become naked at the bottom, and flowering only at the top of the trellis, or extremities of the shoots, one half of the bush should be cut to within four inches of the ground. It will throw out plenty of fine young wood, which give room for, and train them straight, and to the full extent, during summer. These shoots will flower profusely the following season, and in like manner, when thought proper, the other half can be cut.

Roses of the hardy kinds (termed garden roses) that were not attended to in November, should, if the weather permit, be dressed and pruned forthwith. In small gardens, where these are generally attached to the walls and fences, neatness should be a very particular object. If any of such bushes have got strong and irregular, the most proper method to bring them to order, will be to cut down each alternate shoot of the bush to within a few inches of the surface, thereby renovating it, and, in part, preserving the flowers. Those that are cut down will put out several luxuriant shoots, which must be regularly tacked in, spreading them in a fan shape. These, in another year, will flower well, when the others may go through the same operation. Thus, in two or three years, the bushes will have resumed a different, and more agreeable aspect. By the above treatment, these ornaments of the garden will always have a neat and healthful appearance, and the roses will be much finer. Where they are intended for the borders, they should never be allowed to get too high. In a border from four to six feet, they ought never to exceed four feet at the back of the border, and in front, one foot, after being pruned; they can be kept down by the above method. It is not advisable to cut down rose bushes all at once, unless no regard is paid to flowering. The roses that are in grass plats would have a superior appearance in every respect, if they were kept and trimmed like small trees. They may be of different sizes and heights, according to the extent of the grass plat or clump. A single stem may arise from six inches to six feet, with a head in proportion to the height of the stem. Where it is necessary to have them above two feet, and likewise to carry a good head, inoculation must be resorted to, which, in the months of June and July, will be fully treated of. All under two feet (except the weak growing kinds) will do on their own stems, taking care not to allow shoots to arise from the bottom during the summer. For directions for pruning climbing roses, see March and April.

OF PLANTING SHRUBS, &c.

As soon as the frost is out of the ground, these should be planted if the soil is not too wet. Where soil is binding, upon no consideration plant in it while wet, rather defer it until the end of March.

Shrubs, if they are well arranged, are the chief ornament, give the most pleasure, and afford the greatest delight that we enjoy in our gardens. Although they give no sort of nourishment, nor produce any edible fruits, yet they are particularly grateful and conducive to our enjoyments. Our walks in summer would be oppressive, but for their agreeable shade; in the fall and winter, we would be left exposed to the chilling winds, but for the shelter they afford.

Likewise they produce a great variety of flowers; a varied foliage, and are standing ornaments that give no great trouble. In the character of screens they are particularly useful, whether to hide disagreeable objects, or as a guard against the weather; and for either of these purposes, they can be planted nearer to the house than large trees. Or, if they are planted in masses at a distance, they soon become agreeable objects, frequently very much improve the scenery of the place, become objects of utility as well as ornament, and, in such case, afford the highest satisfaction. When formed so as to exclude offices from the view of the house, or for sheltering the latter, or for connecting the house with the garden, orchard, or any similar purpose, shrubs are both useful and interesting.

Where many shrubs are to be planted, the disposing of them properly is a matter of considerable importance to the future welfare of the whole; and, whether deciduous or evergreens be mixed or grouped, that is, indiscriminately planted together, or the evergreens planted by themselves, as is frequently done, a regular and natural arrangement is indispensable for establishing ornament.

Arranging, no doubt, depends very much on fancy; still, there ought always to be plenty of evergreens planted, that the whole may be more cheerful in winter.

If shrubberies were made to a great extent, the scenery would be much more varied and characteristic by grouping judiciously than by indiscriminately planting.

However, in small flower gardens and shrubberies, the latter has to be adopted. In such places, tall growing kinds should never be introduced, unless merely as a screen from some disagreeable object, for they crowd and confuse the whole. The dwarf and more bushy sorts should be placed next to the walks, or edges, in order that they may conceal the naked stems of the others. Generally when shrubs are planted, they are small; therefore, to have a good effect from the beginning, they should be planted much thicker than they are intended to stand. When they have grown a few years, and interfere with each other, they can be lifted, and such as have died, or become sickly, replaced, and the remainder can be planted in some other direction. Keep them always distinct, one from another, in order that they may be the better shown off. But, if it is not desired that they should be thicker planted than it is intended to let them remain, the small growing kinds may be four or five feet apart; the larger, or taller sorts, six or eight feet, according to the condition of the soil.

Thick masses of shrubbery, called thickets, are sometimes wanted. In these there should be plenty of evergreens. A mass of deciduous shrubs has no imposing effect during winter; and, as this is not the proper season for planting evergreens, (April and October being best,) small stakes can be placed in the destined spot. Planting in rows, or in any plan of a formal character, should at all times be avoided.

In planting at this season, observe that the roots are not much exposed to the air, especially if the wind be high and sharp; but it is always better, if possible, to defer the business until good, mild weather. According to directions in November, the ground will be well prepared, and only requires a hole dug for the reception of the roots, which must be considerably larger, that the roots may not be in the least confined. Break the earth well at bottom, put in as much as will receive the plant from one to two inches (according to its size) lower than it has previously been in the Nursery. If any of the roots are bruised or broken, cut them off; then place the plant in the centre of the hole, breaking fine all the soil that is put in, at the same time shaking the stem a little, that the earth may mix with the roots when full up; press all the soil down with the foot, that it may, in some degree, consolidate about the roots, and support the plant. If it is tall, or top heavy, put in a good stake for a support, and place a small, bandage between the stake and stem of the plant, shrub, or tree, where the tie is to be made, to prevent the bark from suffering by friction. Observe always before planting, if the soil is not suitable, to supply that which is congenial to the nature of the intended plant.

When shrubs or trees are to be carried to any distance, the roots should be carefully kept from air, by tying damp moss, straw, or Russia mats about them, as circumstances will admit; their success greatly depends on due attention being paid to this.

OF HYACINTHS AND OTHER BULBOUS ROOTS.

It sometimes occurs that *Hyacinths* and other bulbous roots that were planted in the fall, are thrown above ground by the frost. This will take place if the soil is inclined to moisture, and they not being deep enough planted. If such is the case, cover them with wood earth, old decayed tan, or soil, whichever is most convenient; if not done, the sun and air overpower the bulbs, and, although the fibres have hold of the ground, the flowers will be miserably weak. *Hyacinth* bulbs, and many others of Holland, are very hardy. Even exposure to our severest frosts would not kill them, but they would be much weakened.

OF FRAMING, &c.

Where a frame or hotbed is wanted to grow some of the finest and more tender annuals, it is time, about the 20th of the month, to collect and prepare manure for the desired hotbed. And, as that operation, in many instances, is very imperfectly performed, a few observations on the subject may be useful.

Take three parts of fresh hot stable manure, with one part of fresh oak leaves. Have a sufficient quantity to make the intended bed or beds from three to four feet high. Shake and mix up both together in a compact conical heap, in order to encourage fermentation. If the weather is cold and windy, cover it with straw or leaves and boards, which is necessary to produce the desired effect. If fermentation soon takes place, it will need to be thoroughly turned over in eight or ten days. If any of it has become dry and musty from excessive heat, as you proceed, water the affected parts, pile all up neatly, and leave it protected in part as before. In five or six days more, it will have to be turned again, repeating it until the first extreme heat has been over. In neglect of this, the heat, after making up the bed, will be vehement for a week or two, frequently destroying the vegetative purity of the soil, and proving destructive to the seeds.

Allowing the manure to come to a lively heat, having no unpleasant, rancid smell, proceed to mark off your intended bed, running it east and west as nearly as possible, measure your frame, and allow the site of the bed eight inches each way larger than the frame: at the corners place a stick or rod perpendicularly. The ground ought to be higher than that around it, to prevent water from getting into the bed, which, if low, must be filled up; or, if supposed that water may lodge there, a little Brushwood might be put under the manure, which would keep it from being inundated. The manure must be built up square and level, shaking, mixing, and beating it regularly with the back of the fork. When you have it to the desired height, (three feet will be sufficient for annuals,) leave the centre of the bed a little higher than the sides, thus allowing it more to subside. When finished, put on the frame and sash or sashes, keep them close until the heat arises, covering them at night with mats and shutters. As soon as you feel the heat increased, give air by tilting the sashes a few inches to let off the steam and stagnated air, observing to close in the afternoon, and cover at night. If the heat is violent, about an inch of air might be left during the night. In about three days, if all has been properly attended to, the bed will be what is termed sweet. Then put in about six inches of fine garden soil; if heavy, mix a little sand with it. Spread it level, and, when the soil is heated through, sow in small drills from one eighth to an inch deep, according to the size of the seeds. Some very small kinds do best when sown upon the surface. When sown, give gentle sprinklings of water until they come up, when it will be necessary to give air to prevent them from being weak, or damping off, which many of them will do if they have not air regularly admitted. When they begin to crowd, thin them out, to allow those that remain to grow strong. It is better at all times to have one strong, healthy plant, than two weak and sickly objects.

Rooms.

FEBRUARY.

At this season, the plants call for the most assiduous attention. If the stage has been made according to our description, in very cold nights it should be drawn to the centre of the room, or at least withdrawn from the window, observing every night to close the window tight by shutters, or some substitute equally as good. And, if the temperature begins to fall below 34°, means should be adopted to prevent it, either by putting a fire in the room, or opening any adjoining apartment where fire is constantly kept. This latter method is the best where it is practicable, and ought to be studied to be made so.

Some, very injudiciously, in extreme frosts put into the room, where there is no chimney, amongst the plants, a furnace of charcoal, in order to heat the room. The effect is, that the foliage becomes dark brown, and hardened like, and many of the plants die, the rest not recovering until summer.

Watering may be attended to according to the directions of January, only observing that those that begin to grow will absorb a little more than those that are dormant.

Roses, especially the Daily, if kept in the house, will begin to show flower buds. Use means to kill the Green-fly that may attack them.

Hyacinths and other bulbs must have regular attendance in tying up, &c. Take care not to tie them too tight, leaving sufficiency of space for the stem to expand. Give those in the glasses their necessary supplies, and keep them all near the light. Never keep bulbous roots while growing under the shade of any other plant.

Camellias, with all their varied beauties, will, in this month, make a splendid show. Adhere to the directions given in the previous month, and so that new varieties may be obtained, (see *Green-house*, *February*, under the head of *Camellia*,) which directions are equally applicable here. When the flowers are full blown, and kept in a temperature between 34° and 44°, they will be perfect for the space of four, five, and frequently six weeks, and a good selection of healthy plants will continue to flower from December to April.

Be sure that there is air admitted at all favourable opportunities. Give a little every day that there is sunshine, if it is only for a few minutes.

MARCH.

If this department has been regularly attended to, the plants will be in a fresh healthy state. Where there is any sickly appearance, heat has been deficient, or insects of a destructive character are preying upon them. Too much water at the root frequently causes the foliage to become yellow. It will add greatly to their general improvement, to syringe the whole twice or three times a week, observing to do it in the morning about sunrise; and it is highly necessary that the water that is used should be of the same temperature as the house; and at all times, whatever water is given to the roots, the same must be observed. For airing, see last month, observing, as the season advances, to increase the quantity.

Continue to fumigate when any of the Green-fly appears, (see *January* for directions,) and where there are any of the plants infected with the white scaly insect, clean them as there directed. If overlooked for a few months, they will be increased tenfold. Very frequently, where there are only a few, they are neglected until the plant is overrun with them, and then it may be said, it is impossible to dislodge them entirely. Clear off all decayed leaves from the plants. These will have made fresh shoots, and the decayed leaves very much disfigure the whole collection. We would not have repeated this observation, if it was not an essential point, and one which is so frequently neglected.

OF SHIFTING PLANTS.

Those *Alstrœmèrias* that are growing freely, and in small pots, should be put into pots of a larger size. This genus of plants will not flower except they are encouraged with frequent shifting: they are all beautiful.

Green-House.

MARCH.

The plants in this compartment will begin to assume a different aspect, and air must be admitted every day if practicable, giving large portions in sunshine by the sashes regularly over all the house, opening those of the front a little, and likewise the doors in fine mild days. To perform this judiciously, give a little about eight or nine o'clock, more at ten, and the whole from eleven till twelve o'clock, shutting again by degrees.

Fire heat will now be dispensed with, but in frosty nights have the shutters on about sundown. The sun is now powerful, and the house can be early shut up in the afternoon, and will gain as much natural heat as will keep up the required temperature, viz. 36° to 40°. Perhaps there may be uncommonly cold weather; at such times be attentive to ward off danger by applying artificial heat.

OF WATERING.

Look over the pots and tubs at least every alternate day, to see where water is wanted. In watering, too much caution cannot be used, especially during winter and the commencement of spring. It was observed last month what would be the effect of too much water. It may be remarked, that if the exterior of the pot is very damp, the soil inside is too wet, and in that state is uncongenial to vegetation, which now begins to start, and ought by all possible means to be encouraged. People may be frequently observed watering all plants indiscriminately, not taking the trouble to look into or feel the state of the soil in the pots or tubs, and by going over them three or four times in this manner will be sufficient to put the plants in such a state, that they will not be recruited for some months. Hence the reason of so many sickly plants.

Caméllias, where there are collections, will continue to flower. Treat them according to the directions given last month.

OF ORANGES, LEMONS, &c.

Be sure they are not too wet, as too much humidity as well as aridity causes their foliage to have a yellow appearance, with this difference, that in the former case the foliage is the same to the touch as when green; but in the latter, it is soft and dry. We have observed trees in tubs and half barrels, with holes all round their sides. This is a ludicrous idea, having the appearance of keeping the water from reaching the bottom of the tub or barrel. For the best kind of tub for large trees, see *August* under this head. If any of the trees have stunted, straggling, or irregular heads, about the end of this month, or beginning of next, head or cut them down to the shape desired The old wood will push fresh shoots. You may cut close, or shorten less or more, according as you desire young shoots to arise; at the same time observe that you do not cut below the graft or inoculation. Trees thus headed down should be kept until May, and then planted in the garden, (see *May*,) or if that cannot be done, turn it out, and reduce the ball of earth by probing with a pointed stick all round the sides and bottom of the ball, cutting off any very matted roots. If any of the roots are decayed, cut them into the sound wood. By being thus reduced, it will go into the same pot or tub if not a less one. Having a good supply of fresh earth ready, put a few inches in the bottom of the pot or tub, place the tree therein, and fill all round, at the same time pressing it down with the hand or a stick. Give very little water until there are signs of vegetation.

MYRTLES, OLEANDERS, &c.

These, with similar exotics, may be treated as above. If any of them have been infected with the scaly insect, after heading down, &c. scrub the remaining stems with a strong decoction of tobacco, heated to about 100°. Afterwards clean with soap and water.

GERANIUMS.

These will be growing freely. Keep them in airy situations, so that they may not grow too weak, and flower imperfect. To flower these plants strong, and of good colour, they must not be too crowded together, neither far from the light, and have plenty of air admitted to them, when the weather is favourable. Keep them free from the Green-fly by fumigating frequently.

HERBACEOUS PLANTS.

Plants of this character will, by the first of the month, begin to grow. The best time to divide and fresh pot them is when the young shoots are about one inch above ground. See under the head *Shifting* in this month.

OF CAPE BULBS, &c.

Cape Bulbs, such as *Lachenàlias*, *Oxalis*, *Ixias*, *Gladìolus*, *Watsònias*, *Babiànas*, &c. will in many of the species be showing flower. Keep all of them near the glass, to prevent them from being weak and unsightly.

Hyacinths, *Tulips*, *Narcissus*, &c. Those that have been kept in the Green-house during winter will be in great perfection. Have all the flower stems tied up neatly to small stakes, (which, if painted green, will look much better,) and keep them from the direct rays of the sun. In the front of the house perhaps will be the best situation. They must be freely watered while in flower. Where there is convenience, it will be essential to keep the pots in saucers containing water; it will strengthen both stems and flowers, and likewise preserve them longer in perfection. Those that are blooming should be put aside, and watered sparingly, until the foliage begins to decay, when the pots may be laid on their side to ripen the bulbs.

REPOTTING.

If you have any of the following plants that you are desirous of encouraging, they should be repotted this or next month at the latest. Large plants will not require it, if they were done in August. Pots one size larger than those that they are in, are sufficient. *Acacias and Mimòsas* being now united into one genus, there are above two hundred species. About one hundred and thirty belong to the Green-house. Amongst such a beautiful family, both for elegance of flower and beauty of foliage, it will be difficult to specify the most handsome and desirable for this department. *A. móllis*, *A. glaucéscens*, *A. verticilàta*, *A. florabúnda*, *A. diffùsa*, *A. armàta*, *A. verniciflùa*, *A. decúrrens*, *A. armàta*—weeping variety, *A. púbescens*, *A. leucolòbia*, *A. decípiens*, *A. fragràns*, *A. pulchélla*, *A. lophántha*, *A. myrtifòlia*, &c. These will afford a great variety of foliage, and are very desirable, flowering principally in winter, or early in spring. The flowers of those belonging to the Green-house are of a yellow or straw colour; the most of those that are red or purple, with the celebrated medicinal species, belong to the Hot-house, for which see *May*. There are some of the species very subject to the white scaly insect, which must be attended to, that they may not get to any extent.

Agapánthus, three species. They are all blue flowers. *A. umbellàtus* is very celebrated, and well known in the collections of the country. There is a variegated variety of it highly desirable, the foliage being white striped, and frequently the flower stem and the flower are as good as the species. They have very strong roots, and require plenty of freedom. Plants are always large before they flower, and when the pots, by frequent shifting, become inconvenient, the plant should be divested of all the earth, and, if too large, divide it, cutting off the strongest of the fibres; then they will admit of being put into smaller pots. If the above operation is performed in August or September, it will not retard their flowering, which, when well grown, is very handsome, the flower stem arising about three feet, and crowned with twenty or thirty brilliant blue blossoms, continuing to bloom successively.

Alonsòas, five species, all soft wooded, small, shrubby plants, with scarlet flowers. *A. incisifòlia* is known amongst us under the name of *Hemímeris urticifólia*, and *A. lineàris* as *H. lineàris*. If well treated, they form very handsome plants, and flower freely. They will not bear strong fumigation; and, when the house is under that operation, they must be put on the floor of the Green-house, where they will not be so much affected. They flower from May to August.

Aùcuba japónica is the only species. The flowers are small and almost insignificant, colour purple; but the foliage is a desirable object, being yellow spotted, or blotched. It is tolerably hardy, and withstands our winters. It prefers shade, and, if the situation was such when planted out, it would grow more freely. The hot rays of the sun are very prejudicial to its growth. It is an evergreen shrub, and very desirable.

Anagyris, three species, evergreen, pea flowered shrubs, flowers yellow, nothing very attractive in either of the species. A. *fœtida* is found in many collections, and we have no doubt but it may prove, in this country, a hardy shrub.

Azàleas, seven of the China species, which are those we shall enumerate here. The one that has been longest known in the collections of this country is *A. índica*, a most splendid shrub, with scarlet cup flowers and dark spots. *A. índica àlba*, flowers of the purest white, and rather larger than the former. *A. índica purpùrea pleno*, double purple. This variety is not so fine as any of the others. Properly it is not purple, or, if it may be termed so, the colour is very light; the flower irregular. *A. índica phœnícea* is magnificent. The colour is darker, and the flower larger than *A. índica*, and a free grower. *A. sinénse*, flowers large, yellow. The wood is much stronger than any of those previously mentioned. It bears a very high character in Europe. It has not yet flowered in our collection, but appears as if it would in the ensuing season (1832). All the above ought to have a situation in every Green-house. They flower from March until May. There are two other varieties which have not come under our observation. Do not shift or repot them, if they are in flower, until the flowering is over. The pots must be well drained; and the plants require a shaded situation. If they are properly treated, they will be completely covered with their showy flowers every year.

Aòtus, two species, both fine leguminose plants. *A. villòsa*, is a native of Van Dieman's Land; and *A. virgàta*, is from New Holland. The former is preferable. Both have yellow flowers, and are small evergreen shrubs.

Andersónia sprengelioídes, is the only species, and closely allied to *Epácris*, flowers small, and of a pale yellow colour. Drain the pots well; flowers from March to August.

Arbutus, eight exotic species, and six varieties. They are generally hardy in England; but we question if they stand out in the middle states. *A. unìdo rùbra* has the finest crimson flowers; *A. serratifólia*, the largest panicles; and *A. Andráchne*, the finest foliage. They flower in nodding panicles; the flowers are principally white, tinged with green, and wax-like. They bear a pretty fruit similar to a strawberry; hence it is called strawberry tree, and the fruit will remain on the bush a long time. They are very fine evergreens, and if any of them become acclimated, they will be a great acquisition to our gardens.

Bánksias. There are about thirty-two species, all curious in flower, and handsome and various in foliage; flowers in large heads and cone-shaped anthers, mostly green, and continue a considerable time in flower; produces a cone in shape of a pine, but not imbricate. The substance is as hard as bone, and contains many seeds. A cone of *B. grándis* in our possession weighs one pound twelve ounces, and contains about 107 seeds. Those most admired for the foliage are *B. dentata*, *B. æmula*, *B. serràta*, *B. latifòlia*, *B. grándis*, which is the largest. *B. speciòsa* has the longest foliage. *B. Cunninghámii*, *B. spinulòsa*, *B. palludòsa*, and *B. rèpens*, these will afford a good variety. *B. verticillàta* is entirely different in appearance from the others.

They should be well drained, and placed in an airy part of the Green-house. Great care should be taken that they do not get too dry, for they seldom recover if allowed to flag for want of water. This genus is named in honour of Sir Joseph Banks, a distinguished promoter of the study of natural history.

Bignònias. Those of this genus belonging to the Green-house have been divided to *Tecòma*, and there are only three for this department. *T. austràlis* known as *B. Pandòræ*; *T. grandiflòra*, known as *B. grandiflòra*, and has large and magnificent clusters of orange-coloured flowers, flowering from May to October.

Tecòma capénsis is a very pretty climbing shrub, a free grower, and flowers abundantly; flowers in dense panicles, colour orange and red, continues for several weeks in succession from April to August, greatly esteemed in Europe where it is known; being now in a few of our collections, will soon be generally admired.

Blètia hyacinthìna is the only species belonging to the Green-house, once known as *Cymbídium hyacinthìnum*. It is herbaceous, and when it begins to grow divide the root, putting the best into five inch pots. The spike of flowers are hyacinth-like, and of a beautiful purple, flowering from April to July.

Boronia is a beautiful genus of New Holland plants, contains about nine species; most of them have been universally admired; the flowers are star-like, and rose-coloured, and some of them sweet-scented. *B. pinnàta* grows and flowers freely. *B. serrulàta*, foliage serrated and very crowded, bearing the flowers on the extremity of the shoot. *B. alàta* has a fine appearance, and grows handsomely. The foliage is winged and pinnate, of a hardy nature, and easy culture, flowers freely. They are in flower about April and May, and continue a considerable time; are subject to mildew if not frequently syringed; drain the pots well.

Bouvárdias, two species. *B. triphylla* is well known amongst us, has brilliant scarlet flowers, and when well grown, will flower beautifully from May till September. To keep the plants, they should be frequently renewed; otherwise they are liable to grow straggling, and become subject to the small white scaly insect. *B. Jacquìnæ* we suspect has got confounded with the former, being very little different, except the foliage, which is more pointed. They flower from the young wood, and often throw their foliage in winter.

Brachysèmas, two species, both evergreen climbers. *B. latifòlium* has the best foliage, and large purple leguminose flowers. *B. undulàtum*, flowers yellow, and more plentiful than the former, continuing in long successions. The pots require to be well drained; very few plants of either in the country.

Burchéllias, two species. *B. capénsis* is a beautiful dwarf evergreen shrub, with tubular scarlet flowers in large terminate clusters; when well treated, grows and flowers freely, and highly deserving of attention. *B. parviflòra* differs from the above in the flowers being smaller and paler, and the foliage more pointed.

Beaufórtias, only two species. *B. decussàta* is splendid; the flowers come out of the wood with stamens in fine parcels, colour bright scarlet, foliage decussate, oval, and many-nerved, bloom persistent, and much esteemed. *B. spársa*, in flower similar to the other, colour light pink, foliage scattered, both easy of culture, and flower abundantly.

Brùnias, about ten species, have heath-like foliage, very fine, generally, on close observation, found to be three cornered. The flowers are white and globular, the plants when young are very handsome; the finest are *B. nodiflòra*, *B. lanuginósa*, *B. comòsa*, *B. abrotanoídes*, and *B. formòsa*. They require an airy situation, and in summer to be protected from the powerful rays of the sun. Drain the pots well.

Bósea yervamóra, Golden rod tree, leaves large, alternate, ovate, acute, with purple veins and nerves, flowers brown, in axillary dense panicles, grows strong and freely.

Bæckias, above twelve species, of heath-like appearance, and except for variety, are not otherwise desirable. *B. camphoràta* is camphor-scented; *B. pulchélla* is very neat; and *B. virgàta* flowers freely. Pots should be well drained. The flowers of all the genus are white.

Billardiéras, about five species, are desirable as climbers, being of rapid growth, and abundant in flower. *B. longiflòra*, fruits freely, and has fine blue berries which look handsome. *B. mutábilis* is changeable from purple to scarlet. The fruit of *B. scàndens* is covered with down, flowers straw coloured. *B. fusifórmis* differs in colour from the others, the flowers being blue. They require to be well drained.

Calceolàrias, about fourteen species, besides many hybrid varieties. *C. angustifòlia*, and *C. integrifòlia* are the best of the shrubby species. *C. plantagínea*, *C. corymbósa*, *C. purpùrea*, and *C. hopiána*, and of the hybrid varieties, *C. micàns* and *C. hybrìda* are very fine; but we understand they are numerous, and some of them very splendid.

To grow any of these properly, they should be divided a few weeks after they begin to grow; put them in small pots at first, and enlarge them gradually. Where there is a hot-house, after dividing them, it will greatly promote their growth to keep them in it a few weeks near the glass, until the weather gets mild, when they may be removed to the Green-house. The flowers are principally yellow. *C. Fothergíllii*, *purpùrea*, and *archnoidea* are purple; the hybrids are spotted with red and brown, and some of them streaked many colours. They continue a long time in flower.

Calothámnus, four species. This genus is named in allusion to the splendid appearance of the branches, covered with scarlet flowers of curious construction, which come out of the old wood. All the species are of easy culture, and very like dwarf pines. *C. quadríffida* has the largest flowers; *C. clavàta* the most abundant. They are all evergreens, and flower from April to November.

Caméllias. There are about nine species, celebrated over the known world as furnishing the domestic drug called tea, in universal use, besides many flowering trees and shrubs as universally admired. Oil may be expressed from the seeds of all the species, and used as that of hemp and poppy in cookery. *C. víridis* and *C. bohèa* are said to be the species which supply the tea. Some have asserted that there is only one shrub used, but by examination it may be easily perceived that there are leaves of various shape and texture, some of them similar to *C. sasanqua*. Dr. Abel gives an explicit detail of the growing and manufacturing process of tea, from which, in compliment to our fair patrons, we give a few extracts:

"The tea districts of China extend from the twenty-seventh to the thirty-first degree of north latitude. It seems to succeed best on the sides of mountains. The soils from which I collected the best specimens consisted chiefly of sand-stone, schistus, or granite. The plants are raised from seeds sown where they are to remain. Three or more are dropped into a hole four or five inches deep; these come up without further trouble, and require little culture, except that of removing weeds, till the plants are three years old. The more careful stir the soil, and some manure it, but the latter practice is seldom adopted. The third year the leaves are gathered, at three successive gatherings, in February, April and June, and so on until the bushes become stunted or slow in their growth, which generally happens in from six to ten years. They are then cut in to encourage the production of fresh roots.

"The gathering of the leaves is performed with care and selection. The leaves are plucked off one by one: at the first gathering only the unexpanded and tender are taken; at the second those that are full grown; and at the third the coarsest. The first forms what is called in Europe imperial tea; but as to the other names by which tea is known, the Chinese know nothing; and the compounds and names are supposed to be made and given by the merchants at Canton, who, from the great number of varieties brought to them, have an ample opportunity of doing so. Formerly it was thought that green tea was gathered exclusively from *C. víridis*; but that is now doubtful, though it is certain that there is what is called the green tea district and black tea district; and the varieties grown in the one district differ from those of the other. I was told by competent persons that either of the two plants will afford the black or green tea of the shops, but that the broad thin-leaved plant (*C. víridis*) is preferred for making the green tea.

"The tea leaves being gathered, are cured in houses which contain from five to twenty small furnaces, about three feet high each, having at top a large flat iron pan. There is also a long low table covered with mats, on which the leaves are laid, and rolled by workmen, who sit round it: the iron pan being heated to a certain degree by a little fire made in the furnace underneath, a few pounds of the fresh-gathered leaves are put upon the pan; the fresh and juicy leaves crack when they touch the pan, and it is the business of the operator to shift them as quickly as possible, with his bare hands, till they cannot be easily endured. At this instant he takes off the leaves with a kind of shovel resembling a fan, and pours them on the mats before the rollers, who, taking small quantities at a time, roll them in the palm of their hands in one direction, while others are fanning them, that they may cool the more speedily, and retain their curl the longer. This process is repeated two or three times, or oftener, before the tea is put into the stores, in order that all the moisture of the leaves may be thoroughly dissipated, and their curl more completely preserved. On every repetition the pan is less heated, and the operation performed more closely and cautiously. The tea is then separated into the different kinds, and deposited in the store for domestic use or exportation.

"The different sorts of black and green arise, not merely from soil, situation, or the age of the leaf; but after winnowing the tea, the leaves are taken up in succession as they fall; those nearest the machine being the heaviest, are the gunpowder tea; the light dust the worst, being chiefly used by the lower classes. That which is brought down to Canton, then undergoes a second roasting, winnowing, packing, &c. and many hundred women are employed for these purposes." Kæmpfer asserts that a species of *Caméllia* as well as *Olea fràgrans* is used to give it a high flavour.

C. oleíferia is cultivated principally in China for the oil which is expressed from its seeds, which is much used in the domestic cookery of the country; flower single white.

C. Sesánqua, Lady Banks's. The foliage of this species is very small, and paler, and the green not so fine, as any of the others. It seeds freely, and is often used as the female parent in producing new varieties; flowers small white and single, with many anthers. There are a Semi-double, and Double variety of it of the same colour.

C. maliflòra is figured in the Botanical Register, under the name of *C. Sesánqua rósea*. The foliage is about the same shape as *C. Sesánqua*, but the appearance and habit of the plant are completely different, growing very freely and quite erect; flowers very abundant. A large plant of it will continue in bloom for the space of three months. The flowers are of about six weeks' duration, colour and shape of *Rose de meaux*; has been highly esteemed. One plant of it has been sold for one hundred and eighty dollars.

C. Kíssii. We believe it is single white, has not come under our observation, the only species that is a native of Nepaul.

C. reticuláta was brought from China by Capt. Rawes. The foliage is very characteristic, being rougher than any of the other flowers, about five inches in diameter, brilliant scarlet, and semi-double. It was introduced into Europe in 1822, and is still very scarce. Twenty-five dollars are paid for a small twig of it. From present appearance, it will never be so plenty as many of the others, being tardy of propagation; only a few eyes on the extremity of each shoot make young wood, and if these are cut off, the plant does not seem to push afresh.

C. *japónica*, the original of many splendid varieties, probably to the amount of one hundred. The true one is in very few collections; it is single striped.

C. *japónica rùbra* is the single red of our collections, and used as stocks to enarch, graft, or inoculate the other varieties upon, being easily struck by cuttings. It seeds very freely, when the stile is impregnated, and the seedlings make the strongest and best stocks.

C. *japónica álba*, single white. It is mentioned in some of our catalogues, as being very sweet-scented, though not very perceptible to us. The foliage and wood are very strong, being a free seeding variety, consequently particularly desirable, as a stock to grow new varieties from. Its flowers are large and abundant.

C. *semidúplex*. This is a flower with two rows of petals. Some good varieties might be got from it, if properly impregnated.

C. *rùbro-plèno* is a strong growing and free-flowering variety. The flowers are large, double red, petals irregular, with the anthers in bunches amongst them; flowers are of long duration and showy.

C. *cárnea*, frequently known as Middlemist's blush. Colour pink, one of the original varieties, and frequently produces seeds; grows freely.

C. *myrtifólia*, known in some collections as *involúta*. There are two varieties of it, major and minor; the former is certainly the best, and has a very handsome, large, and regular red flower; the centre frequently is pink and purple; it is much the shape of *Double white*, only the petals are more cupped. The flower is of considerable duration. It is not properly named. The foliage, though the smallest of the variety, is much larger than that of any of our common myrtles, which might make many mistake its character; and another prominent feature is, the leaves are much recurved and shining.

C. *hexanguláris*. The flower is six angled, very compact, and dark red. It is an esteemed variety, and there has unfortunately been another inferior, substituted for it, in some of our collections. The foliage is similar in shape to *anemoniflòra*, with the nerves more sunk; the flowers are of an ordinary size.

C. *atro-rùbens*, Loddiges' red, is a very fine variety; colour dark red outside, petals large inside, small and irregular, forming a very distinct character; foliage stiff; grows freely and flowers well; and of long duration. We have seen a flower stand fresh on the plant two months; however, that cannot be a rule, as it depends on the situation.

C. *anemoniflòra*, or *Waratah* (from the central petals, having the appearance of the Waratah plant, *Telopìa speciosissima*.) This variety is very characteristic, both in flower and foliage. The flower is dark crimson, with five or six regular large outside petals; those of the centre are very small, and neatly plaited, with the stile (female organ) prominent; the foliage is large and oblong, nerves very smooth, and the wood strong, bark light. Had this kind not been found, we would have been deprived of many most splendid varieties, which have originated from it, and we have no doubt they may become as diversified as the roses of the garden. This variety in a collection for that alone is invaluable. It seeds freely, and the pollen of any of the others applied to the style of this, will produce a new variety, which seldom fails of being double, provided the pollen is from a double variety. It must be applied the first day that the flower is expanded, for the flower is only of a few days' duration. Those that are not acquainted with the buds of this *Camèllia*, will take them to be dead, because, before expansion, they are very dark brown.

C. dianthiflòra, or Knight's *carnation Waratah*, is, when well grown, a very beautiful flower; shape and size same as *anemoniflòra* (and a seedling from it by Mr. Knight, King's Road, Chelsea, London,) seemingly the stamens are crowned with small petals, red and white striped, appearing like a fine large carnation. The style appears fertile, and there is no doubt but some splendid varieties may be obtained from it.

C. blánda, or blush Waratah, flower in shape similar to *anemoniflòra*, rather larger, and of considerable duration.

C. pompónia, or Kew blush, flowers very large, white, with a tinge of blush at the bottom of the petals, which has a good effect in setting off the flower. They frequently bloom all blush, which appears rather curious on the same plant; shape one or two rows of guard or outside petals; those of the inside are short, stubby, and generally irregular, continues long in flower, yellow anthers among the short petals, and seeds when the female organ is perfect; foliage narrower than any of the others, a very fast grower, and flowers freely.

C. pæòniflora. The foliage, shape, and size of the flower of this, is similar to the last mentioned, colour a rich pink; we have never seen any of them vary from this; and have seen it seed very double.

C. Walbánkii, has a very large white irregular flower, by some called poppy-flowered. It is not so pure as the common double white; the anthers show amongst the petals, and the buds before expansion are very round, inclining to flatness; the foliage long and shining. The flowers are of considerable duration. We question with lutea-alba.

C. alba-plèna, common double white, is admired by the most casual observer, and is generally considered a very superior flower, from the purity of its whiteness, and the abundance of its large flowers, which are thickly and regularly set with round petals. The foliage is large, and the plant grows freely; we have seen one shoot grow two feet in one summer. It was imported into Europe from China, amongst the first of the varieties, about eighty years ago.

C. flavéscens, Lady Hume's blush, and by some called *buff*. It is a very double flower, and frequently hexangular; the bottom of the petals are most delicately tinged with blush; on looking into it, it shows more like a blush vapour than nature, and is a great favourite, and deservedly so, with the ladies: flowers and grows freely, foliage rhomboid, elongate, nerves very visible, surface smooth and pale green, distantly serrate.

C. fimbriàta. The size, shape, and set of the flower same as *alba-plena*, and the white as pure, with the edges of the petals deeply serrated, or rather fringed; is equally as free in flowering and growing. It is universally admired, and in great demand. Its character is unique, foliage very like *alba-plèno*. [See Frontispiece.]

C. imbricàta, said to be a very double red, with imbricated petals, and very handsome. We have not seen it in flower.

C. variagàta, is one of the old standard varieties, and very much esteemed. It is striped with red and white; sometimes the ground is red, with white streaks or blotches, and *vice versa.* The flower when well grown is large, and very abundant; foliage very fine dark green, similar to single white. We have had seed from it. The petals are regular, with the anthers showing amongst them; the flower double, though not so much so as many of the others.

C. crassinérvis. We have not the smallest doubt but this is the same as *hexangularis*, and in confirmation of our opinion, we have lately had the best authority in Europe to that effect.

C. conchiflòra, shell flowered, double, a very handsome shape, petals round, stiff set, and in the centre quite erect, red with occasional splashes of white.

C. rubricáulis, Lady Campbell's, very double, colour very rich dark red, with stripes of pure white, beautifully contrasted. The richness of this flower is very striking, and much esteemed; flowers freely.

C. longifòlia is a single red, the foliage is large, and longer than the generality of them.

C. chandlrerii, or versicolor, colour vivid scarlet with occasional splashes of pure white; the flowers vary, and are of long duration, from six to eight weeks; foliage large and dark glossy green.

C. aitònia. This variety is a beautiful specimen of a single flower affording a developement of the organ of fructification; the petals are delicately penciled, and the anthers very bold, colour pink, and the flower very large; grows freely, and, in our opinion, is surpassed by none of the single sorts, for raising fine new varieties, if impregnated with the pollen from double flowers.

C. althæiflòra, hollyhock-flowered, is a great beauty, with large double dark red flowers, the veins are very prominent, petals frequently irregular; foliage large, and approaches to the foliage of single red; and is much esteemed.

C. corallìna, coral-flowered, a very deep scarlet double flower, and bears a high character.

C. insígnis, a most splendid double flower, large dull red colour; a very free grower, and highly estimated.

C. anemoneflòra álba. Those that have seen the common *anemoneflòra* will be disappointed in the appearance of this, not being pure white, neither properly anemone-flowered, though a very good flower, and very distinct from any other; the petals are irregular, anthers abundant, shape resembling *pompone*; flower not so large.

C. heterophylla. The foliage of this varies very much, a character that none of the others possess; flower double red; and merits a place in collections.

C. Woódsii, flower fine double, rose colour; and much has been said in its favour.

C. bícolor, a single flower, with a rose ground and white streaks, very pretty, but not so large as many of the single ones.

C. speciosa is a most splendid variety, has been called *China striped Waratah*. The guard petals are large, round, and bold; colour red with stripes of white; the centre is full of small petals, (like *anemoneflòra*.) and spotted; the foliage large and more heart-shaped than any of the others; grows freely, flower persistent, highly esteemed, and considered one of the finest of the coloured *Caméllias*.

C. fúlgens, flower large, and very bright double red, approaching to *C. atro-rubens*, but more brilliant; foliage a lucid green, very smooth, young wood and wood buds have a red appearance. We have no doubt but it will seed; if so, it will be a first rate breeder.

C. grandiflóra, a very large single rich red flower, foliage very large; a most splendid single variety, and grows freely. It is recommended to all who wish to improve their collections by raising new varieties.

C. rósa sinénsis, a very large double flower, colour bright pink, petals long and full, a very distinct variety, with a beautiful dark green shining foliage, grows and flowers freely, and is highly esteemed.

C. *intermédia*, a very large flower, shape of *C. pompònia*, outside petals streaked to the extremity with a rich blush, ground colour pure white, and is in high estimation; grows and flowers freely. It is in very few collections in Europe, and only in three in the United States.

C. *rose Waratáh*. The description of this flower is the same as *anemoneflòra*, but differs in colour, and being of longer duration, the foliage is uncommonly large.

C. *Pressíi's invincible*. It has been asserted that it is the same as that known by *C. punctata* and *C. Pressíi*. We have not seen it flower, but have seen a drawing of it, the flower equally as large as *double white*, and same shape, with the petals as regular; the ground colour brilliant red, and spotted with pure white. It is one of the newest varieties, and much valued for its unique beauty; hence called *Invincible*; foliage large.

C. *Rose Mundií*, is like the garden rose of that name; a large flower, ground colour pink streaked with white.

C. *compàcta* is a new double white, petals and flower not so large as the common, but more compact, and is considered a very fine variety.

C. *gloriòsa*, is said to be a fine dark double red.

C. *Róssii*, is said to be a fine rich double scarlet.

Callicòma serratifòlia, the only species and remarkable for tufted yellow heads of flowers, which come out at the axils, and continue from May to July. The foliage is ovate lanceolate, deeply serrated, and opposite.

Carmichælia austràlis, the only species, has very curious foliage, which the lilac leguminose flowers come out off, and continue from April to June.

Cunònia capénsis, the only species, and a handsome shrub, with large pinnated shining leaves, beautifully contrasted by numerous dense elongated branches of small white flowers, and twigs of a red colour, having the habit of a tropical more than a Cape of Good Hope plant.

Cléthra arbórea, and *C. arbórea variagàta*, are both fine shrubs; the latter is preferable; leaves are oblong, accuminate, and serrated with a gold edge; flowers white, downy, in large branching racemose spikes, and sweet-scented; grows freely.

Cotoneásters. Two of this genus are deserving a situation in the Green-house, *C. denticulàta*, and *C. microphylla*; the last is a native of the mountainous districts of Nepaul, and may prove hardy; the flowers are white, small, and solitary, but in the fall it is covered with pretty red berries, and then looks beautiful; culture very easy; will grow in any situation.

Cròwea solígna, is amongst one of the finest and easiest cultivated plants of New South Wales. It flowers at the axils of the leaves, colour pink, with five petals, connected by entangled hairs; in flower from April to December, and frequently through the winter; foliage lanceolate, and a fine green. The plant grows neat, and requires an airy situation; drain the pots well.

Chorizèmas, about six species, foliage very like some varieties of the *Holly*; flowers small and papilionaceous; colour red and yellow; though small, they are very neat. C. *nàna* and C. *ilicifòlia* are amongst the best; if grown from seed, they will flower freely the second year; drain the pots well.

Cineràrias, Cape aster, about twelve belong to the Green-house. They are herbaceous, or half shrubby, soft wooded plants. C. *speciòsa*, C. *amelloídes*, (now called *Agathæa cœléstus*,) C. *purpùrea*, and C. *lanàta*, are among the finest; flowers blue or yellow; the latter is considered the handsomest of the genus. The exterior petals are bright purple and the interior ones white, and with *A. cœléstus*, flowers most of the year; flowers syngenesious and star-like. The herbaceous species must be treated as previously mentioned for that kind of plants.

Cístus, or Rock rose. There are above thirty species, principally natives of Europe, consequently hardy there, and form a great ornament to their gardens, being very abundant and various in flower; but with us they will not stand the rigour of winter. We have no doubt, however, but, through time, some kinds may be grown that will withstand the greatest cold of the middle states; they are low shrubby plants of easy cultivation. C. *ladaníferus*, C. *monspeliénsis*, C. *sálignus*, C. *popolifòlius*, and C. *undulàtus*, are perhaps the best; the flowers are of short duration, frequently only for one day; but the quantity makes up this deficiency, being constantly in flower in May and June, and sometimes flower again in autumn. C. *crèticus* is most productive of the Gum laudanum, which is secreted about its leaves and branches. The flowers are generally five-petaled, and some of them large; centre full of stamens; the foundation of the natural order *Cistinea*.

Clématis, Virgin's Bower. There are only six of these belonging to this, all climbing plants. C. *aristàta* and C. *brachiàta* are the best, flowers in racemose clusters, pure white; foliage small; and natives of the Cape of Good Hope. The foliage of C. *aristàta* is cordate and blotched.

Cobæa scándens, the only species. It is a climber of very rapid growth, has been known to grow above two hundred feet in one summer; large bell-shaped flowers; when they are newly expanded, they are of a pale green colour, and change to dark purple; will grow in the garden during summer, bearing a continual profusion of flowers, but will not stand frost. When this plant becomes too large in the house, do not cut it close to the root, except there is a young shoot arising to carry off the superabundant sap, for the old wood will not push, which will soon cause a mortification.

The best method to adopt in such case is to turn back a shoot, and lay it in the ground to root, when it will become a young plant; which should always be done as soon as it appears unsightly. It does best to be planted in the ground, but will not give any satisfaction as to flowering in a pot. It will flower as an annual if sown in pots this month, and placed in a warm room or hot-bed, and planted into the garden about the end of May.

Coroníllas, a very few are fine species in the Green-house. C. *glaúca* is a celebrated plant amongst us, as a free and early flowering shrub. C. *valentíana* and C. *viminális* are equally so, flower from April to June, colour yellow; papilionaceous flowers in clusters; agree best with shade. In summer they ought to be kept behind a fence, or under a tree, as the sun would destroy them in a few weeks. Drain the pots well.

Corréas, five species, all very pretty dwarf shrubs, and flower profusely; foliage ovate, cordate, and either rusty or downy beneath. C. *álba* and C. *rúfa* have both white flowers a little tubular. C. *pulchélla* is a very handsome erect growing plant, flowers large and tubular, of a deep pink colour, and grows freely: it is thought the finest of the genus. C. *speciòsa* has been long admired as a splendid free flowering plant; flowers same shape as C. *pulchélla*, but not so large; colour red and yellowish green. C. *virèns* is a very free grower, flowers same shape as the two last, colour entirely green. These three last mentioned are abundant flowerers, having a continued succession from November to June, possessing the valuable requisite of flowering through the winter, and ought to be in every collection. They require an airy situation, and the pots to be well drained. The plants in summer must not be fully exposed to the sun.

Cratàgus. There are none of these belonging to the Green-house; but there is a plant in the collections, known as C. *glabra*, which is *Photínia serrulàta*, a native of China, and is a very handsome plant, has long foliage, deeply serrated, very shining. *P. arbutifòlia*, a native of California, and is the finest of the genus; flowers in large dense panicles, foliage larger than the former, and not so deeply serrated;

they are both comparatively hardy, and we soon expect to see them acclimated.

Cupréssus may be desired in collections, as erect and handsome growing evergreen shrubs. C. *lusitánica*, the famed cedar of Goa; C. *péndula* and C. *juniperoídes* are the most desirable; flowers are insignificant, and yellowish; we have no doubt they may prove hardy. C. *lusitánica* is the handsomest tree of the genus. Its abundant, very long dichotomous branchlets, distinguish it from all the evergreens of the conoferious tribe.

Calámpelis scábra, once *Eccremocárpus scáber*, is a very fine climber, where there is a convenience to plant it in the ground. It will flower profusely from March to November; foliage pinnate, with tendrils; flowers from the axils on young shoots in a kind of racemose, and of a golden colour; grows freely.

Celástris, staff-tree, about twenty-five species; of no particular beauty. Some of them have numerous small white flowers, in cymes and panicles; foliage generally ovate, acute, and serrated. C. *pyracántha*, C. *cymósa*, C. *multiflòrus*, and C. *lúcidus*, are the most conspicuous, and all the genera are of easy culture.

Coòkia púnctata, Wampee-tree of China, named in honour of the celebrated Capt. Cook. The fruit is much esteemed in China, where it grows to about the size of a walnut, in bunches; leaves pinnate, ovate, lanceolate, accuminate; when rubbed, have a strong odour; flower small white in racemose spikes, of slow growth.

C. *allistàchys*. There are two of them very handsome large growing shrubs. C. *lanceolàta* and C. *ovàta*, foliage silky-like, and light coloured; flowers yellow, papilionaceous, and very abundant.

Davièsias, above ten species, principally natives of New South Wales, all yellow papilionaceous flowers. *D. ulicìna*, *D. latifòlia*, *D. aciculàris*, and *D. inricssàta*, are very fine species, flower and grow freely, and require to be well drained; bloom from April to August.

Diósmas. This genus is now very much divided, and only contains about thirteen species: the generas that they have been given to, are *Adenándra*, *Barosma*, *Acmadènia*, and *Agathósma*. We will enumerate a few of the finest species of each. *D. capitála*, *D. oppositifólia*, *D. longifòlia*, *D. rùbra*, and *D. teretifòlia*, are the most conspicuous, all small white flowers except *D. rùbra*; foliage small, and all handsome growing evergreens.

Adenándras, eight species. This genus is the most select of those that have been subdivided. *A. speciòsa*, *A. umbellàta*, *A. álba*, *A. fragràns*, and *A. uniflòra*, are all splendid flowers: and all white except *A. fragràns*, which is red. Pots must be well drained.

Barósmas, above ten species. *B. serratifòlia*, *B. pulchèlla*, purple, *B. fœtidíssima*, blush, *B. odoràta*, white, and *B. dioíca*, pink, are the finest.

Acmadènias, five species. *A. lavigàta*, *A. púngens*, and *A. tetragònia*, blush, are good species.

Agathósmas, above twenty-five species, many of them very celebrated free flowering shrubby plants. *A. accuminàta*, *A. hybrida*, *A. Thunbergiàna*, *A. imbricàta*, *A. prolífera*, *A. pátula*, and *A. pulchélla*, which is the finest of the genus, the dried leaves of which the Hottentots use as powder to mix with the grease with which they anoint their bodies. Some travellers assert that it gives them so rank an odour, that they sometimes could not bear the smell of those who were their guides. In fact the foliage of all the five last mentioned generas, if rubbed by the hand while on the plant, has a very strong smell, some of them very agreeable, others disagreeable. They are all heath-like and evergreen small neat growing shrubs. They require while growing luxuriantly to have their young shoots topped to make them bushy; drain all the pots well, and keep them in airy situations, and not crowded with other plants, or they will become slender and unsightly.

Dryándras. This genus is closely allied in character and habits to *Bánksia*, and contains above sixteen species. D. *nívea*, has a most beautiful foliage, very long and deeply indented. D.*formòsa*, has a scent like the fruit of an Apricot. D. *nervòsa*, D. *floribúnda*, D. *armàta*, D. *plumòsa*, D. *Baxtèri*, D. *nervòsa*, and D. *falcàta*, are the most conspicuous, and all highly desirable plants in collections. They are very delicate of importation; flowers are straw and orange coloured and thistlelike. Seeds in small cones. Treat them the same as directed for *Bánksias*.

Dillwynias, above twelve species, and plants very little known. D. *floribúnda*, D. *teretifòlia*, and D. *phylicoides*, are desirable plants; flowers small, papilionaceous, and colour yellow. They are very liable to suffer from too much wet; while dormant, therefore, the pots must be effectually drained.

Dampièras, four species. The genus is named in honour of Captain W. Dampier, a famous voyager, has Lobelia-like flowers, either blue or purple. C. *purpùrea*, C. *undulàta*, and C. *strícta*, are the finest; the two former are shrubby; the latter is herbaceous; they all flower freely.

Edwárdsias, about four species, very beautiful foliaged plants and have very curious yellow flowers, but do not flower until the plant becomes large. *E. grandiflòra*, *E. chrysòphylla*, and *E. meirophylla*, are the best, and are tolerably hardy, though doubtful of ever being acclimated. The flowers are leguminose, foliage ovate, pinnate, from eight to forty on one footstalk, and appears to be covered with gold dust. The hardier they are grown, the more visible it will appear.

Elichrysums. This genus is now extinct, and two splendid species of it given to others. *E. proliferum* is now *Phænàcoma prolífera*, and has beautiful purple everlasting rayed flowers, and highly esteemed: the foliage round, ovate, smooth, and closely imbricated. *E. spectábile* is now *Aphélexis hùmilis*, has pine-like foliage, and large light purple flowers and everlasting; care must be taken that they are not over watered; drain the pots well.

Enkiánthus, only two species, both very fine. *E. quinqueflòrus* has large ovate accuminate foliage, flowers pink, and pendulous; very handsome. *E. reticulátus*, the foliage is netted, and the flowers blush; they are liable when dormant to suffer from wet. Be sure to drain the pots well, and sparing in water while in that state.

Epácris, above twelve species, and all very ornamental. *E. grandiflòra* has been celebrated ever since it was known; the foliage is small, flat, and accuminate; flowers tubular and pendulous, bright crimson, with a tinge of white, and very abundant, in flower from January to June. *E. pulchélla* is likewise a most beautiful plant; foliage very small and closely set, flowers pure white, and in long spikes, sweet-scented. *E. impréssa*, foliage impressed, and flowers rose-coloured. *E. paludòsa*, flowers white, and grows very handsomely. *E. purpuráscens rùbra* is a good variety, with bright red flowers. They are mostly erect growing plants; flower from

March till June, and a rough, turfy, sandy soil is found most congenial. They are natives of the mountainous districts of New South Wales. The pots must be well drained; the roots will run with avidity amongst the potshreds.

Erìcas, heath. There are in cultivation in Europe above five hundred and fifty species and varieties of this magnificent genus. About sixty, years ago it consisted only of a few humble British plants, with the heath of Spain, *E. Mediterrànea,* which is at present most common in our collections, though in a few years we may expect to see it supplanted by others more splendid.

In their native countries, they are adapted to a great many useful purposes. In the north of Britain, the poorer inhabitants cover their cabins or huts with heath, and build the walls with alternate layers of it and a kind of cement made with straw and clay. They likewise brew ale, and distil a hot spirit from the tender shoots; and it has been known to be used in dyeing, tanning, and many other useful domestic purposes. Encomium on their beauty is not requisite; they are almost as diversified in colour as colour itself. Many are graceful, and most elegant; hundreds are pretty; a few noble and splendid; others grotesque, curious, and odoriferous. To cultivate and propagate them is one of the most delicate branches of horticulture. Nevertheless, it has been said by a scientific writer, that "those who complain of the difficulty of growing the heath are ignorant people who have never had a heath to grow." The most splendid collection in Europe is under the care of Mr. M'Nab, of the Royal Botanic Garden, Edinburgh, where there are two large houses devoted to their culture; and through the whole year a continued profusion of bloom is kept up. Some of the plants are six feet in diameter, and twelve feet high. The soil used is a coarse sandy peat. Pots drained with potshreds, and pieces of freestone, are put down the sides of the large pots and tubs: where these can be had they are essential to the culture of mountainous plants, preventing them from being saturated with moisture, or from becoming dry, they being retentive of moisture, thus keeping the roots in a medium state; for if once the roots are allowed to get thoroughly dried, no art of the gardener can recover them. This may be the true reason why they are said to be difficult of cultivation.

In the summer season the pots must be kept out of the sun, for in a few hours the pot would become heated, dry the roots, and cause death, or a brownness of foliage which would never again become natural. Too much fire heat will hurt them. They only require to be kept free from frost, need a great deal of air and plenty of light; consequently, should be placed near the glass, that they may have the benefit of all the air that is admitted. Their flowers are as varied in shape as variety or colour, but they all partake of a wax-like nature, and are very persistent. For the finest and most select varieties, see the catalogue at the end of this work.

Eròdiums, Heron's bill. There are about thirty species, all of a Geranium character, and there are among them some very pretty flowering, soft wooded, shrubby, herbaceous, and annual plants. Only a few of them belong to the Green-house, of which *E. incarnàtum*, *E. crassifòlium*, and *E. laciniàtum*, are the finest; culture similar to *Geranium*. The flowers of these are scarlet, pentapetalous, and veiny.

Eucalyptus, above fifty species of them, and the tallest growing trees of New Holland; foliage very diversified, generally of a hard glaucous texture. From their rapid growth, they soon grow higher than the loftiest house. The most conspicuous are *E. cordàta*, *E. rostràta*, *E. radiàta*, *E. pulvigéra*, *E. glòbifera*, *E. pulverulénta*, and *E. resínefera*. In Van Dieman's Land, a manufactory has been established, where a tannin is extracted from many of the species. The last mentioned produces gum, like that which the druggists call *Kino*. They ought not to be too much fostered, as it would in some degree retard their growth. They are of a very hardy nature. When large, the plants will flower freely, and are similar in flower to *Myrtle*; many stamina proceeding from a hard nut-like capsule.

Eupatòrium. There is only one species deserving of cultivation in the Green-house; flowers syngenesious, white, and in large flattened panicles; very sweet-scented. The plant, when growing freely, in the beginning of summer, should be topped, which would make it more bushy; if not, it is apt to grow straggling. Known as *E. elegáns*, in our collections.

Eutáxia's, two species. *E. myrtifòlia* is a most beautiful free-flowering evergreen shrub; foliage small, but very neat; flowers leguminose, small, and very many; colour yellow and red; grows freely. The young plants should be frequently topped, or they will grow naked and unsightly. *E. pùngens*, similar to the other except in foliage. They flower from March to June, and ought to have a place in every Green-house. Culture very easy.

Euchìlus obcordàtus is the only species: Flowers similar to *Eutàxia*; foliage almost unique, being inverse, cordate; time of flowering from March to June.

Fúchsias, Ladies' ear drop. About twelve species. Several of them elegant and handsome shrubs. *F. virgáta* and *F. cònica* are the most splendid of deciduous Green-house shrubs; the nerves of the leaves and young wood of the former are tinged with purplish red; the large pendant flowers which are produced from the axils of the leaves of the young wood continue during the growing season. *F. cònica* grows strong, foliage green, flowers pendant, corolla more spreading than the other, and when in flower is a complete mass of scarlet blossoms. It flowers all summer. *F. coccínea* is a common and celebrated plant, and deservedly so. *F. microphylla* is a neat glowing, small flowering species. *F. arbórea*, has very large foliage, and rose coloured flowers; a scarce species, but very desirable. *F. gràcilis* and *F. thymifòlia*, are both fine; most of the flowers are a bright scarlet, the stamens are encircled with a petal of bright purple, and are of very curious construction; they bear a dark purple berry, and are of the easiest cultivation, but during summer they must be carefully kept in the shade.

Gelsèmium nìtidum, Carolina jessamine, a most beautiful climbing evergreen, flowering shrub. In the months of April and May, it produces many large yellow trumpet-like blossoms of delicious fragrance. If much fostered in growth, it will not flower so freely.

Gnaphàlium, everlasting. This genus has got all the beautiful Cape species taken out of it, and given to *Astélma* and *Helichrysum*. Of *Astélma* there are above ten species, most of them very splendid, everlasting flowers. *A. exímia* has brilliant red flowers. *A. spiràlis*, *A. speciosíssima*, *A. frùticans*, and *A. imbricàtum*, are all very fine; pots must be well drained.

Helychrysums, above forty species, chiefly belonging to the Green-house, all everlasting flowers. *H. grandiflòrum*, *H. arbòreum*, *H. orientàle*, *H.*

fràgrans, *H. adoratìssimum*, *H. frùticans*, and *H. fúlgidum*, are all very esteemed species, mostly soft white foliage. The pots should be well drained, and the plants kept in an airy situation, as they suffer from the least damp. If the flowers are cut off before they fade, they will retain for many years all the splendour of their beauty; but if allowed to decay on the plant, they will soon become musty, and all their colour fade.

Gompholòbiums, a genus of very pretty delicate plants, all papilionaceous; flowers generally yellow with a little red; foliage very variable. G. *barbígerum*, G. *polimórfum*, G. *latifòlium*, G. *grandiflòrum*, and G. *venústum*, are fine, the pots must be well drained, and care taken that they are not over watered; they grow freely.

Genístas: a few of these are very pretty free flowering shrubs. G. *canariénsis*, G. *tricuspidáta*, G. *cuspidòsa*, and G. *umbellàta*, are the finest Green-house species. All of them have yellow leguminose flowers in great abundance; leaves small, lanceolate.

Gnídias, about ten species of pretty Green-house shrubs. G. *símplex*, G. *serícea*, G. *imbérbis*, and G. *pinifòlia*, flower the most freely; flowers straw colour, tubular, and corymbose. G. *símplex* is sweet-scented, leaves small; the pots must be well drained, and care taken that they do not get either too wet or too dry, for the roots are very delicate. The plants must be kept near the glass, or they will be drawn weak.

Goodènia, a genus of about twelve species, with cordate, serate, alternate foliage. G. *stellígera*, and G. *suáveolens* are sweet-scented; G. *ovàta* and G. *grandiflòra* are the best. They are principally small shrubs, with terminale or axillary flowers, and flower during summer.

Gortèria personàta is the only species that belongs to this genus, and is an annual. There are several plants in our collections known as *Gortèrias*, but which properly are *Gazània*, of which there are five species. G. *rìngens*, when the flowers are fully expanded, (which will only be while exposed to the sun, closing at night, and opening again with the influence of the sun's rays,) is a great beauty. The rays of the flowers are bright orange, and the centre dark purple. *G. pavónia* has handsome foliage; flower similar to *G. rìngens*, except the centre of the flower being spotted, and is thought to be the finest, but does not flower so freely. *G. heterophylla* is of the same character, except the foliage, which is variable, the colour orange and vermilion. They are half shrubby dwarf growing plants, and during the months of July, August, and September, are liable to damp off at the surface of the earth, from the action of heat, and too much water. Pots must be well drained, and the plants kept partially in the shade. Their flowers are syngenesious, and about two inches in diameter.

Grevílleas, about thirty species. A few of them very handsome in flower and foliage, among which are *G. punícea*; *G. acanthifòlia*, (beautiful foliage); *G. concínna*, very pretty straw and rose-coloured flowers; *G. juniperìna*, green and straw-coloured; *G. lineàris*, white flowers. The flowers of the whole are curious, though not very attractive. Some carry their flowers in racemose spikes, others on flowering branches, which are recurved; the petals are very small and rugged; the stile longer than the appendage. They grow freely, flower and ripen seeds; all evergreen dwarf shrubs.

Hàkeas, about forty species, not generally so interesting or attractive as the last genus; flowers all white; construction similar to *Grevíllea*, but the foliage more varied. *H. gibbòsa*, *H. nítida*, *H. salígna*, *H. suavèolens*, sweet-scented, *H. conculàta*, and *H. lambérti*, are the best, and afford a curious variety of foliage; flower in June. Drain the pots well.

Hemerocállis, Day Lily. Only *H. speciòsa* of this genus belongs to the Green-house; the flower is spacious, and of copper colour. A native of Jamaica. It has not found its way into our collections. It is herbaceous, and while growing requires much water. The plant known with us as *H. japónica* is now *Fúnkia álba*, (and justly, for the most superficial observer could have distinguished it as not belonging to *Hemerocállis*.) It requires to be much fostered to flower well, and plenty of water. If properly treated, it is a magnificent flower, and continues flowering from July to September. We doubt not it may prove a hardy herbaceous plant, (the same as *F. cærùlea*,) if protected during the first winter.

Hermánnias, a genus of about forty species, all natives of the Cape of Good Hope, and not worth cultivating. They have yellow cup-like flowers, and are of the easiest cultivation. Several species are in our collections.

Hibbértias, about ten species. Three of them are very fine climbing evergreen shrubs, viz. *H. glossulariæfòlia*; *H. dentàta*; *H. volùbilis*, if closely approached has a disagreeable smell; *H. fasciculàta*, *H. salígna*, and H. *pedunculàta*, are evergreen shrubs; they have pure yellow flowers of five petals, blooming from May to September.

Habránthus, about ten species of small South American bulbs, nearly allied to *Amaryllis*. H. *Andersónii*, H. *versícolor*, and H. *robústa* are the finest; they are in colour yellow, blue, and lilac. We have very little doubt but these bulbs will do to plant out in the garden in April, and be lifted in October. Keep them from frost. Thus treated, they are very desirable bulbs.

Hòveas, about eight species, pretty plants of New South Wales, blue pea-flowering evergreen shrubs; the finest are H. *lineàris*, H. *rosmarinifòlia*, H. *longifòlia*, and H. *Célsii*, which is the most superb, and flowers in abundance. They grow and flower freely; the pots should be drained.

Hydrángea horténsis is a well known plant, and much esteemed for its great profusion of very elegant, though monstrous, flowers. They are naturally of a rose colour, but under certain circumstances of culture they become blue. If grown in brown loam with a little sand, they will preserve their original colour; but if grown in swamp earth with a little mould of decayed leaves, they will become blue. The swamp earth and vegetable mould being more combined with aluminous salt than brown loam, is the cause of the change; and, when first found out, (which was merely by chance,) was thought a great wonder. It must have a very plentiful supply of water when in flower, which is produced on the shoots of the previous year. They will neither grow nor flower well if they are not kept constantly in the shade. When kept in the sun, the foliage is very brown; and by being neglected in watering, we have seen the flowers completely scourged. Being tolerably hardy, when the winters are mild, by a little protection in the open air, they will flower profusely; the flowers will be very large, and in bloom from June to October. They are deciduous, soft wooded shrubs.

Hypéricums, St. John's wort, about twenty species. A few of them are very showy, and with few exceptions have yellow flowers. *H.*

monógynum, H. *balearicum*, H. *floribúndum*, H. *canariénse*, H. *ægyptìacum*, and H. *cochinchinense*, which has scarlet flowers, are amongst the best, and all of them flower freely; five petals, filaments many in three or five parcels. They are all of very easy cultivation, and bloom generally from April to September.

Ilex, Holly, of *I. aquifòlium*. There are above one hundred species of them in cultivation in Europe, differing in variegation, margin, shape, and size of the leaves; some are only prickly on the margin of the foliage, others prickly over all the surface. In Europe they are all hardy, but with us few or none of the varieties are so. If they become acclimated, they will be a great ornament to our gardens, being all low evergreen shrubs. The most common and conspicuous varieties are the *hedgehog*, *striped hedgehog*, *white edged*, *gold edged*, and *painted*; the flowers are white and small, berries yellow or red; they do not agree with exposure to the sun. *J. Cassíne* and *J. vomitòria* have very bitter leaves, and, though natives of Carolina, we have to give them the protection of a Green-house. It is said that at certain seasons of the year the Indians make a strong decoction of the leaves, which makes them vomit freely, and after drinking and vomiting for a few days, they consider themselves sufficiently purified.

Illíciums, Aniseed-tree, three species. *I. floridànum*, has very sweet-scented, double purple flowers, and the plant grows freely and systematically if properly treated, and deserves the attention of the admirers of flowers. *I. parviflòrum* has small yellow flowers; *I. anisàtum* is so very like *I. parviflòrum* in every respect, as to make us conclude they are the same, were *I. anisátum* not a native of China, and the other two natives of Florida. When the leaves and capsules of either of them are rubbed, they have a very strong smell of anise;—they grow very freely.

Indigófera; Indigo-tree, about twenty species, belong to the Green-house, and are chiefly pretty free flowering shrubs. *I. denudàta*, *I. amæna*, *I. austràlis*, *I. angulàta*, *I. càndicans*, and *I. filifòlia*, are very fine; flowers papilionaceous, in long panicles; colour various, red, blue, yellow, and pink.

Isopògons, about ten species of *Pròtea*-like plants, all natives of New Holland. They are very stiff shrubs, with leaves very much divided, and cone-like flowers at the extremity of the shoots. *I. formòsus*, *I.*

anemonifòlius, *I. attenuàtis*, and *I. polycéphalis*, are the finest; flowers are straw, lilac, white, and yellow coloured; the pots must be well drained, and the plants not over-crowded.

Justícias. Only a few of these belong to the Green-house, and are very simple looking flowers. The most beautiful of them belong to the Hot-house. *J. nìgricans*, small striped flower; *J. orchioídes* and *J. Adhátoda*, Malanut, are the only ones that are worth observation, and are very easily cultivated. *J. Adhátoda* has good looking foliage, but does not flower until the plant becomes large; colour white and light purple.

Jacksònias. A genus consisting of five species. The foliage is varied, and all natives of New South Wales. *J. scopària* is similar to a plant in our collections, called *Vimenària denudata*. *J. hórrida*, and *J. reticulàta*, are the finest; the small flowers come out of the young shoots, are yellow and papilionaceous; the pots should be well drained.

Kennèdias, about nine species, all evergreen climbers, of the easiest culture, and flower abundantly. *K. monophylla*, blue flowered, and *K. rubicúnda*, crimson flowered, are common in our collections. *K. prostràta*, (once *Glycine coccínea*) one-flowered scarlet, and *K. coccínea*, many flowered scarlet, are very pretty. *K. Comptoniàna* has splendid purple flowers, and *K. inophylla* is thought the most superb. It is very rare, and we have not seen it flower. They are large purple. The pots should be well drained; and if the plants are much fostered, they will not flower so well; flowers are either in racemose spikes, or solitary, which is rather too much distinction for the same genus.

Lambértias, four species of very fine plants, natives of New Holland. L. *formòsa* is the finest of the genus that we have seen; flowers large and of a splendid rose colour. L. *echinàta* is said to be finer, but has not flowered in cultivation. L. *uniflòra* has single red flowers, and L. *inérmis* orange coloured. They are rare plants in the collections on this side of the Atlantic. Drain the pots well; the foliage is narrow, and of a hard dry nature.

Lasiopètalums, only two species. There were a few more, but they are now *Thomàsias*, plants of no merit whatever, in regard to flower; foliage three lobed, small, rough, and rusty-like. *Thomàsia solanàcea* and

T. quereifòlia, are the best species; foliage of the former is large, cordate, and deep indented; they are all of the easiest culture.

Lavándulas, Lavender, about seven species belong to the Green-house, and a few of them very pretty soft-wooded, half shrubby plants, and if touched, are highly scented. L. *dentàta* has narrow serrated foliage, very neat. *L. formòsa* and *L. pinnàta* are desirable; blue flowers on a long spike; should be kept near the glass; they are of the easiest culture.

Laúrus. A few species are Green-house plants. This genus has been divided to *Cinnamòmum*; still there are a few celebrated plants in the original. L. *nòbilis*, sweet bay, though hardy, is kept under protection. It will bear the winter with a little straw covering, notwithstanding there should be a plant kept in the house in case of accident by frost or otherwise; there is a variegated variety of it. *L. índica*, royal bay, *L. fœtens*, *L. aggregàta*, and *L. glúaca*, are favourites. There is a species known in our collections as *L. scábra*. The Camphire tree, known as *L. camphòra*, is *Cinnamòmum camphòra*; the wood, leaves, and roots of this tree have a very strong odour of camphire. It is obtained by distillation from the roots and small branches, which are cut into chips, and put into a net suspended within an iron pot, the bottom of which is covered with water, having an earthen head fitted in it; heat is then applied, and the steam of the boiling water acting upon the contents of the net, elevates the camphire into the capital, where it concretes on the straws, with which this part of the apparatus is lined. They are all fine evergreens, (which the name denotes,) and easily cultivated,

Lìnums, Flax, two or three species are very fine, and flower freely. *L. trigynum* has large yellow flowers in clusters, and *L. ascyrifòlium*, whose flowers are large, blue, and white, and in long spikes. The shape of them is very like the flower vulgarly called Morning-glory.

Lobèlias. Several of them when well treated, form most magnificent flowering plants; they are principally herbaceous. L. *Tùpa* has the largest foliage, and fine scarlet flowers. L. *speciòsa*, flowers light purple; L. *fúlgens*, crimson flowers; L. *spléndens*, scarlet flowers. The three last are of the same habit; the colours brilliant; and to grow them well, they should be divided, (if there are several shoots arising,) when they begin to grow, putting them first into four inch pots, and shifting them frequently, having them to flower in those of nine or ten inches, which will be about the end of June, or first of July, and they will continue until October. The pots must be always kept in pans or saucers filled with water; likewise give plenty to the surface of the earth, which is to be done during their time of growth and flowering. If this is attended to, they will produce flower stalks from four to six feet in height, and covered with branches and spikes of flowers from bottom to top. The corolla is pentapetalous, three down and two up; they require a little shade. The genus consists of about eighty species; seventy of them are exotics; many of them natives of the Cape of Good Hope, with little flowers of brilliant colours. L. *cærùlea*, L. *Thunbérgii*, L. *corymbôsa*, L. *pyramidàlis*, and L. *ilicifòlia*, are very fine species, of weak growth, but flower freely.

Lomàtias, about six species; flowers are white or straw colour, and similar to *Grevíllea*, but the foliage more handsome.

Lophospérmum scándens. This is a magnificent new climbing soft wooded shrub, with purple, campanulate flowers, which are produced from the axils on the young wood; they bloom from May to September; leaves large, cordate, and tomentose; grows rapidly, and flowers abundantly.

Lachnæas, about five species, remarkable for their downy heads of white flowers; leaves small, ovate, lanceolate. L. *glaùca*, L. *conglomeràta*, and L. *eriocéphala*, are the best species. The pots must be well drained, and in summer the plants protected from the sun.

Leonòtis, Lion's-ear, four species. They have very fine scarlet tubular flowers, orifice-toothed. They come out in large whorls, and look elegant; but neither plant nor foliage has an agreeable appearance. They are of the easiest culture. L. *intermédia*, and L. *Leonùrus*, are the best flowering species.

Leucospérmums, about eighteen species, of Proteacious plants, chiefly low growing, and are mostly downy or hairy; flowers yellow, in terminale heads. L. *formósum*, L. *grandiflòrum*, L. *tomentósum*, and L. *candicans*, rose-scented. These are fine species. For treatment, see *Pròteas*.

Lipàrias, about five species, much esteemed for their beauty of foliage; leaves ovate, lanceolate, downy or woolly; flowers yellow, leguminose, and capitate. L. *sphærica*, L. *tomentósa*, L. *villósa*, and L. *serícea*, are the finest. L. *vistìta* and L. *villósa* are the same, although put in many catalogues as different species. None of them ought to be much watered over the foliage, as it adheres to the down, and causes the young shoots to damp off. Drain the pots well, and keep the plants in an airy situation.

Lysinèmas, four species, closely allied to *Epácris*. In every respect treatment the same. L. *pentapítalum*, L. *conspicum*, and L. *ròseum*, are the best; the flowers of the two former are white. L. *silaifòlia* has leaves bipinnatifid and smooth, segments wedge-shaped and cut. L. *dentàta* and L. *ilicifòlia* are the finest; the pots should be drained.

Lonícera japónica. There is a plant in our collections known by that name, which is now *Nintooa longiflàra*; flowers of a straw colour, but come out white. It has been known to withstand the winter, but does not flower, and is frequently killed entirely.

Lychnis coroàta, is an esteemed Chinese plant; flowers-in abundance, pentapetalous, large, and a little indented at the edges; colour a red-like orange; flowers terminale and axillary. The roots must be divided every spring, or they will dwindle away to nothing. Perhaps a good method of treatment would be to divide the roots, and plant them in the garden; they would flower well, and could be lifted in the fall, and put under protection. We have no doubt that it may become acclimated. If not done so, plant them in four inch pots, and repot them into those of six inch in May. Do not expose them while in flower to the mid-day sun, for it will deteriorate the fine colour.

Leptospérmums, about thirty species, all pretty New Holland evergreen dwarf shrubs, with small white flowers. L. *baccàtum*, L. *péndulum*, L. *juníperinum*, L. *ovátum*, L. *stellàtum*, L. *grandiflórum*, and L. *scopàrium*, are the best of the species. The latter was used as tea by Capt. Cook's ship's crew. It is an agreeable bitter, with a pleasant flavour, when fresh. When young plants are growing, they ought to be frequently topped to make them bushy, and kept in an airy situation, or they will be drawn and unsightly. They are of very easy culture.

Leucadéndrons, Silver tree, above forty species, all natives of Cape of Good Hope. They are evergreens with handsome, silvery-like foliage.

L. *argentéum* (once *Pròtea argentéa*) is a great beauty; foliage white, lanceolate, and silky. It is a plant that has been long in cultivation, greatly admired, and much sought for, and is the finest of the genus. L. *squarròsum*, L. *stellàtum*, (once *Pròtea stellaris*) L. *tórtum*, L. *seríceum*, L. *margìnàtum*, and L. *plumôsum* (once *P. parviflòra*) are all fine species. The pots must be well drained, and the plants never over-watered. They are very desirable in collections for their beauty of foliage; flowers similar to *Pròtea*.

Magnòlias. There are four species that require the protection of our Green-houses; all the others are hardy. M. *fuscàta*, and M. *annonæfòlia*, are very similar in foliage and flower: the young branches and leaves of M. *fuscàta* is covered with a brown, rusty-like down; the other by some is considered merely a variety; flowers small, brown, and very sweet-scented. M. *pùmila* is very dwarf growing; leaves large and netted; flowers semi-double, white, pendant, and fragrant. They are natives of China. We have several others from the east, but being deciduous are perfectly hardy. M. *odoratíssima*, now *Talàuma Candólii*, a native of the Island of Java, and said to be very odoriferous, but is very rare even in Europe; said to have a straw coloured flower. M. *conspícua* is desirable to have in the Green-house, if enarched on a stock of M. *purpùrea*, which will always keep it dwarf, and it will flower magnificently in February and March.

Melalèucas, above thirty species, and a beautiful genus of New Holland plants, of easy culture; flowers come out of the wood like fringes. M. *elíptica*, M. *fúlgens*, scarlet, M. *decussàta*, M. *hypericifòlia*, M. *squarròsa*, M. *linarifòlia*, M. *incana*, M. *tetragònia*, M. *thymifòlia*, are all very fine species, and flower freely if they have been grown from cuttings; the singularity of flower and diversity of foliage make them generally thought of.

Maurándias, three species, of very pretty climbing Green-house plants, flowering from March to October. M. *Barclàyana* has splendid flowers, large, light blue, campanulate, and very abundant. M. *semperflòrens* has rose coloured flowers, of the same character. They will flower best if planted in the ground.

Myrsínes, Cape Myrtle, dwarf cape evergreen shrubs covered with small flowers from March to May. M. *retùsa* has green and purple flowers; M. *rotundifòlia*, flowers white and purple. They will grow in any situation, and are of easy culture.

Méspilus japónica. The plant, known under that name, is now *Eriabòtrya japónica*, Loquat, is a fine plant with large lanceolate, distantly serrated leaves, white underneath; small white flowers on a racemose spike, and produces a fruit about the size of a walnut, of a fine yellow blush colour, and of delicious flavour. If it flowers in the fall, it will require the heat of a Hot-house to ripen the fruit. It is of very easy culture, and its noble aspect is never passed unobserved.

Metrosidèros, about five species. Many have been added to *Callistèmon*. M. *flòrida*, M. *umbellata*, and M. *angustifòlia*, are the best species. C. *salígnum*, C. *lanceolàtum*, variety *semperiflòrens*, C. *glaùcum*, once M. *speciòsa*, has splendid scarlet flowers and C. *formòsum*; these are all beautiful plants, with scarlet flowers. Other two beautiful species with white flowers have been given to *Angóphora*. A. *cordifòlia*, once M. *híspida*, and A. *lanceolàta*, once M. *costàta*; these genera are very easily distinguished from any other Australasian shrubs, by the peculiar character of having both sides of the leaves alike. The flowers consist of stamens, stiles, and anthers, coming in hundreds out of the young wood for the length of three or four inches, forming a dense cone crowned with a small twig; leaving capsules in the wood, which will keep their seeds perfect for a great number of years. They grow freely, and the pots should be well drained.

Myrtus, Myrtle, is a well known and popular shrub, especially the common varieties; and was a great favourite, (even to adoration,) among the ancients. It was the mark of authority for Athenian rulers, and is amongst the moderns an emblem of pre-eminence. They are elegant evergreen shrubs, with an agreeable odour. M. *commùnis multipléx*, double flowering, is a very neat shrub, and flowers abundantly. M. *commùnis leucocárpa*, White-fruited Myrtle, is quite unique, when the berries are on it. M. *itálica variagáta*, striped leaved; M. *itálica maculàta*, blotch leaved, are very fine shrubs; and M. *tomentòsa*, Chinese Myrtle, is a magnificent erect growing shrub, with a white down over the foliage; the flowers are the largest of the genus. When they first expand, they are white, and afterwards change to purple, so that there are beautiful flowers of several shades of colour on the plant. We have not the smallest doubt but this species will become in many instances as plentiful as the common myrtle. It is more easily grown, but cannot stand much exposure to the sun in summer. M. *tenuifòlia* is a very fine plant, and a native of New South Wales. Myrtles in general should be sprinkled with water in the evenings, to keep off mildew and red spider.

Nandìna doméstica, the only species, and a popular shrub in the gardens of Japan, where it is called *Nandin*. It has supra-decompound leaves, with entire lanceolate leaflets, a kind of foliage that is very rare; the flowers are small, whitish green, in panicles, succeeded by berries of the size of a pea; drain the pots well.

Nèrium, (Oleander,) is a genus of beautiful erect growing evergreen shrubs, of the easiest culture, and abundant in flower. *N. oleánder* is the common rose coloured single flowering species, from which six varieties have originated. At present the most popular is *N. oleánder splèndens*, which has a double rose coloured flower. There is one that has got in our collections as double white which is only semi-double. We have seen a white, variety as double as *N. o. splèndens*, and have no doubt but in a few years it will be plentiful. *N. oleánder elegantíssimum*, a most beautiful plant, with deep silver-edged foliage; and the young wood is striped white and green. We are not positive in respect to the beauty of its flowers, but it has a high character. We have heard of a double-yellow variety, but the reports are not properly authenticated; and we doubt it very much. There are likewise single yellow, single white, and single blotched varieties of *N. oleánder*. They are subject to the small white scaly insect, and should be frequently washed, as has been directed, to keep it off.

Oleas, Olive, about twelve species and varieties. *O. Europæa longifòlia*, is the species that is cultivated to such an extent in the south of France, and Italy. *O. Europæa latifòlia* is chiefly cultivated in Spain. The fruit is larger than that of Italy, but the oil is not so pleasant, which is obtained by crushing the fruit to a paste, and pressing it through a woollen bag, adding hot water as long as any oil is yielded. The oil is then skimmed off the water, and put into barrels, bottles, &c. for use. The tree seldom exceeds thirty feet, and is a branchy glaucous evergreen, and said to be of great longevity. Some plantations at Turin in Italy are supposed to have existed from the time of Pliny. It frequently flowers in our collections, but seldom carries fruit; flowers white, in small racemose axillary spikes. O. *cupénsis* has a thick large oblong foliage; flowers white, in large terminale panicles. O. *verrucòsa*, foliage flat, lanceolate, and white beneath, branches curiously warted. O. *fragráns*, foliage and blossoms are both highly odoriferous; the plant is much esteemed in China, and is said to be used to adulterate and flavour teas. Leaves are elliptic, lanceolate, and a little serrated; flowers white in lateral bunches. It is subject to the small, white scaly insect, and ought to be carefully kept from them by washing. O. *paniculata* is a fine species. They are all very easily cultivated.

Oxylòbiums, seven species, plants very similar to *Callistachys*, with ovate, cordate, light coloured, pubescent foliage, with papilionaceous flowers. O. *obtusifòlium* has scarlet flowers; O. *retùsum*, orange flowers; and O. *ellípticum*, yellow flowers. They grow freely, and should be well drained; flower from May to August.

Pelargòniums, Stork's Bill. This genus, so universally known amongst us as *Geràníum*, from which it was separated many years ago, is a family of great extent and variety, for which we are principally indebted to the Cape of Good Hope. By cultivation from seed many hundred beautiful species and well marked varieties have been obtained. There are about five hundred species, with upwards of two hundred varieties. They are of every character, colour and shade, of the most vivid description. The easy cultivation of the *Pelargònium* tribe, or *Geràniums*, as they are commonly called, has rendered them very popular; also the agreeableness of scent and fragrance of which many of them are possessed, makes them favourites. If their flowering season was of longer duration, the varieties and species would be quite indispensable in collections; but there is every appearance that in a few years the aspect of them will be changed. The present prevailing colour of the flower, (which has five petals, three hanging and two erect, the erect petals being always of the darkest shade,) is a white or pink ground, with lilac, purple, or pink stripes, flakes, or spots, and blooms from April to June; though they bloom profusely in large bunches, the time is limited. The species and varieties that have a red ground, with black or dark crimson stripes or spots, generally bloom during the whole summer. These, though scarce in the collections of the country, will in a few years root out those whose flowers are of such short duration, and by their blooms charm us half of the year.

The tuberous and fleshy stemmed species are far more interesting to the discriminating inquirer than the common kinds. Their habit and constitution are so peculiar, that we have frequently wondered that they have not been separated into distinct genera. The cultivation of them is more difficult, water being very prejudicial to them when they are inactive. When they are well managed, they flower beautifully, and the colours are very superior and peculiar, having frequently bright green and purple in the same flower. If some of the colours of these could be compounded with the large flowering kinds, those hybridised would be magnificent.

The best method to adopt in impregnating these, is to choose the female, one that has large flowers, of easy cultivation, and as nearly allied in character and other habits as possible. When a flower of the intended female is newly expanded, take a pair of very fine pointed scissors, and cut off the anthers before the pollen expands; then as soon as the summit of the stile divides, apply the pollen taken from the anthers of the intended male plant on a very fine camel hair pencil, or cut out the stigma entirely, and place the anther on the summit of the stile, which, if correctly done, will have the desired effect. As soon as the seed is ripe, sow it in light sandy soil; and when it has come up, take care not to over-water the soil, which would cause them to damp off. When they are about one inch high, put them into small pots, and treat as the other varieties. Have them all distinctly marked until they flower, which will be in the second year from the time of sowing.

Phórmium tènax, New Zealand flax lily, the only species; foliage resembling an *Iris*, and very thready. In New Zealand and Norfolk Island, the natives manufacture from this plant a kind of stuff like coarse linen, cordage, &c.; the plant is very hardy, and we would be no way surprised to see it stand the severity of our winters. It bears exposure to the open air in Europe in the 56th degree of north latitude. The flowers are said to be yellow and lily-like; of the easiest culture.

Phylicas, above twenty-five species. Several of them are very pretty growing evergreen shrubs, and of easy culture. P. *horizontàlis*, P. *squarròsa*, P. *imbricàta*, P. *myrtifòlia*, P. *callòsa*, P. *bícolor*, and P. *ericoídes*, are all neat growing; flowers small, white, in heads; drain the pots well, and keep them in an airy situation. The foliage of several of the species is downy.

Pimèleas, about fourteen species. Most of them are highly esteemed, and are not often seen in our collections. P. *decussàta* is the finest of the genus, both in foliage and flowers, which are red, and in large terminale clusters; P. *rôsea*, P. *linifòlia*, white, P. *spicàta*, and P. *drupàcea*, are all fine species. The latter has the largest foliage, which is ovate and accuminate; berry-bearing. They should be well drained. They are very small evergreen shrubs, with white or red flowers.

Pittósporums, about nine species, with handsome foliage, and small white flowers in clusters, which are fragrant. P. *Tobìra* is a native of China, and nearly hardy; leaves lucid, obovate, obtuse, and smooth. P. *undulàtum*, P. *coriàceum*, P. *revolùtum*, P. *fúlvum*, and P. *ferrugíneum*, are very ornamental evergreens, and will grow with the most simple treatment.

Platylòbiums, Flat Pea, four species of fine free flowering plants; flowers leguminose; colour yellow. P. *formòsum*, P. *oràtum*, and P. *triangulàre*, are the best; the foliage of the two former is cordate, ovate; the latter hastate, with spiny angles.

Pistàcias, seven species of trees, principally of the south of Europe. There is nothing particular in their appearance, except their productions in their native country. P. *terebínthus* is deciduous, and produces the Cyprus turpentine. P. *lentíscus* is the true mastich tree, which is obtained by cutting transverse incisions in the bark. P. *vèra* and P. *reticulàta* are good species; leaves pinnated; leaflets ovate, lanceolate; easily cultivated.

Plumbàgos, Lead-wort. There are only two species of any consequence belonging to the Green-house, P. *trístis* and P. *capénsis*. The former is a shy flowerer, but the latter flowers freely; colour beautiful light blue, and flowers in spikes; foliage oblong, entire, and a little glaucous; of very easy culture, and continues in bloom a considerable time.

Psoràleas, above forty species. A few of them are worthy of cultivation, P. *odoratíssima*, P. *spicàta*, P. *aculeàta*, P. *argéntea*, and P. *tomentòsa*. They have all blue flowers, and leguminose. They are chiefly low shrubs; and will flower and grow freely; the pots require draining.

Podalyrias, about fourteen species of pretty Cape shrubs; foliage oblong, obovate, and silky-like; the flowers leguminose; colour blue or pink. P. *serícea*, P. *styracifòlia*, P. *corúscans*, P. *argéntea*, P. *liparioídes*, and P. *subbiflòra*, are the finest and most distinct species, and flower abundantly.

Petsoónias, about sixteen species of dwarf evergreen shrubs; leaves oblong, or lanceolate, hairy, or downy; flowers axillary and solitary; the pots should be well drained, and the plants in summer protected from the sun. P. *hirsùta*, P. *móllis*, P. *teretifòlia*, and P. *lùcida*, are the most distinct, and grow freely.

Pròteas, about forty-four species. The foliage of this genus is very diversified; flowers very large, terminale; stamens protected by an involucrum; many-leaved and imbricated; which is very persistent. P. *cynaroídes* has the largest flower, which is purple, green, and red. P. *speciòsa*, P. *umbonàlis*, once P. *longifòlia*, P. *melaleùca*, P. *grandiflòra*, P. *coccínea*, P. *cenocárpa*, P. *pállens*, P. *formòsa*, P. *magnífica*, P. *speciòsa rúbra*, and P. *mellífera*, will afford a very good variety. It is almost impossible to describe their true colour, it being so various; red, white, straw, brown, green, and purple, are most predominant, and frequently to be seen in the same flower; the plants must be well drained; and during warm weather be careful that they are not neglected in water, for if they are suffered to droop, they seldom recover. For this reason the pots ought not to stand in the strong sun; the plants can bear it, but to the roots it is injurious.

Pultenæas, about forty species, pretty little dwarf growing shrubs of New South Wales; flowers small, leguminose, all yellow, with a little red outside of the petals. P. *villòsa*, P. *obcordàta*, P. *argéntea*, P. *plumòsa*, P. *fléxilis*, shining leaved, fragrant; P. *cándida*, and P. *strìcta*, are all fine species, and esteemed in collections. The leaves are all small; they require an airy exposure, and the pots drained.

Rhododéndrons (Rose tree), a magnificent genus, and contains some of the most superb and gigantic plants that adorn the Green-house. All the *Azàleas* (except A. *procúmbens*) both Chinese and American, have been arranged under this genus. At present the most admired is *R. arbòreum*, with varieties. *R. arbòreum* has deep scarlet flowers, with dark spots and flakes campanulated, and in large clusters; leaves lanceolate, acute, rough, and silvery beneath. *R. arbòreum albúm* is very rare. *R. arbòreum supérbum*, flowers same shape as *arbòreum*, colour bright scarlet; foliage one third larger, but not silvery beneath; grows freely, and generally thought the finest variety. *R. arbòrea álte-Clàrance* is also very superb. There are several other varieties of minor note. A Green-house without some of the scarlet varieties of that plant, is deficient of a flower whose beauty and grandeur are beyond the highest imagination. It is a native of Nepaul in India, and when found by Dr. Wallach awakened the ambition of every cultivator and connoisseur in Europe. There are several other species brought from that country lately, but none of them has yet flowered. They are highly valued from the productions of the above; the species are *R. campanulàtum*, *R. anthopògon*, and *R. cinnamòmeum*. This is named from the colour of the leaves, which are very peculiar and very handsome; the flowers are said to be rose-coloured. These three last cannot be purchased under an immense price; the others have been rarely seen in our collections, but another year or two will make them more plentiful. Their beauty of flower is beyond description. The pots should be well drained, and if they are large, put several pieces of sandy stones or potshreds around the side, for the fine fibres delight to twine about such, being mountainous plants.

Roéllas, pretty leafy shrubs, with blue terminale funnel-shaped flowers, lip-spreading; *R. cilliàta*, *R. spicàta*, and *R. pedunculàta*, are the finest of the genus. The pots must be well drained, and care taken that they are not over-watered.

Sálvia (Sage), is an extensive genus of soft-wooded, shrubby, or herbaceous plants; very few of them do well in the Green-house, and many of them are very trifling, having no other attraction than the flower, and those of the tender species, when compared with *S. élegans*, *S. spléndens*, *S. cœrúlea*, and *S. coccìnea*, (which in artificial climates constitute the standard of the genus,) are not worth cultivation. These last mentioned, if kept in the Green-house, will merely keep in life, but a situation in the Hot-house would cause them to flower frequently. The best method to adopt with the summer flowering kinds, is to plant them in the garden in May; they will grow strong and flower abundantly, and in the fall they can be lifted, and preserved during winter in pots. They neither grow nor flower so well as when planted out, and even a slip planted in the ground in moist weather will root in a few days, grow, and flower in a few weeks. *S. spléndens* is the best to select for the purpose. *S. aùrea*, *S. paniculàta*, and *S. índica*, are fine species. The latter is white and blue, with large leaves; flowers monopetalous, and irregular; colour generally red or blue in spiked whorls. All will grow easily with encouragement.

Senècios. Some species of this genus are pestiferous weeds all over the world. They are found near the limits of perpetual snow, where neither tree nor shrub is able to rear its head. Yet there are three species that are neat little plants, and are worthy of a situation, viz. *S. grandiflòrus*, *S. venústus*, and *S. cineráscens*, with the double white and red variety of *S. élegans*. The two last varieties are free flowering, but if allowed to grow several years, they become unsightly. Being very easily propagated, a few cuttings of them should be put in, in September, and in two weeks they will strike root, when they may be put in pots to keep through the winter, and then planted in the garden, continuing to renew them. The other mentioned species should be frequently done the same way. Do not keep them damp during winter, or they will rot off. Keep them in an airy exposure.

Schótias, a beautiful genus of six species, which will require the warmest part of the Green-house to keep them. The foliage is handsome; leaves compound: leaflets oval-lanceolate, and in pairs from six to ten; *S. speciòsa*, crimson, flowers nearly papilionaceous, and in bunches, the most superb of the genus. *S. alàta*, *S. latifòlia*, once *Omphalòbium Schótia*, and *S. tamarindifólia*, are the finest; the flowers of the others are red. The pots require to be drained, and the plants protected from the hot sun.

Swainsònas, four species of free flowering, soft wooded shrubs, natives of New South Wales. *S. galigifòlia*, *S. coronillæfòlia*, and *S.*

astragalifòlia, are red, purple, and white; leguminose flowers in spikes from the axils, are of easy culture, and deserving of a situation; the foliage is pinnate; leaflets ovate, acute.

Scòttias, three species of valuable plants; *S. dentàta*, with scarlet leguminose blossoms; leaves opposite, ovate, accuminate, serrate; *S. angustifòlia* has brown flowers; *S. trapezifòrmus*, leaves ovate, acute, serrulate. We do not know the colour of its flowers; the pots must be well drained, and the plants kept in the warmest part of the Green-house, and near the light.

Sparrmánnias, are strong growing Green-house shrubs. *S. africàna*, is a plant very common in our collections, with large three lobed cordate leaves, hairs on both sides; flowers from March to July. *S. rugósa.* The leaves are rugged; flowers of both are white, in a kind of corymb, supported by a long footstalk; buds drooping, flowers erect. There is a plant known in our collections, as the free-flowering *Sparrmánnia*, (which is *Entèlia arboréscens*,) and is easily distinguished from *Sparrmánnia* by the leaves being cordate, accuminate, and otherwise, by all its filaments being fertile, and the flowers more branching, and blooming from November to June, profusely; very easily cultivated, and desirable.

Sphærolòbiums, only two species of leafless plants, with yellow and red leguminose flowers, which proceed from the young shoots. *S. vimíneum* and *S. médium*. They flower freely, and are easily cultivated. The old wood should be frequently cut out where it is practicable. Drain the pots.

Sprengélia incarnàta,, the only species, a very pretty plant, allied to *Epàcris*; small foliage, long, accuminate; flowers small, pink, bearded, and in close spikes; grows freely, delighting in shade. The pots must be well drained, and the plants, when dormant, watered sparingly, for if they get sodden about the roots, they very seldom recover.

Stylidíums, six species of pretty litte plants, with small linear leaves, and remarkable for the singular elasticity of the style or column, which, when the flower is newly expanded, lays to one side, and on being touched with a pin starts with violence to the opposite side. S. *graminifòlium*, S. *fruticòsum*, S. *laricifòlium*, and S. *adnàtum*, are all free flowering; flowers in spikes, very small; colour light and dark pink; blooms from April to July. S. *adnàtum* is half herbaceous, and should, when growing, be kept nigh the glass, or it will be drawn, and the flowers become of a pale colour. They are all of easy cultivation.

Styphèlias, seven species of very showy flowers, with mucronate leaves; corolla in a long tubular form, having several bundles of hairs in it; segments reflex and bearded. *S. tubiflòra*, crimson, *S. triflòra*, crimson and green; *S. adscéndens*, and *S. longifòlia*, are beautiful species. They grow freely, and should be well drained, as too much water is very hurtful to them. In summer they ought not to be much exposed to the hot sun, or the foliage will become brown.

Salpiglóssis, four species of fine herbaceous Green-house plants, natives of Chili. The flowers are tubular and campanulate. *S. pícta*, flowers white and blue painted; *S. atropurpùrea*, flowers dark purple, and *S. isnuàta*, flowers crimson, are superb, and if planted in the garden during summer will flower profusely. They must be lifted in October, and taken under protection.

Tagètes lùcida is found in many of our collections. The leaves are simple, oblong, and finely serrated. When rubbed by the hand, they have an agreeable fragrance; the flowers are syngenesious, small, and in terminale bunches. It is herbaceous; and when about an inch grown should be divided and potted into five inch pots. Repot it again about the first of June. It keeps in flower from July to November.

Testudinària, Elephant's foot, or Hottentot's bread, two species remarkable for their appearance. The root or bulb, if it may be so called, is of a conical shape, and divided into transverse sections. Those of one foot diameter are computed to be 150 years of age. It is a climbing herbaceous plant, with entire reniforme leaves of no beauty; flowers small; colour green. The pots must be well drained, for when the plant is inactive it is in danger of suffering from moisture, and ought not to get any water. *T. Elephántiphes* and *T. montána* are the species, natives of the Cape of Good Hope, and require the warmest part of the house.

Táxus nucífera, is the only species that requires protection, and bears a small acorn; flowers are trifling; an evergreen, with ovate, lanceolate foliage, thickly set on the wood; will grow in any situation. There is a plant in our collections known as *T. chinénsis* or *T. elongáta*, which is *Podocárpus elongàtus*. It has lanceolate leaves, erect growing, and very hardy; flowers mœonacious, and of no estimation except to the curious.

Telopèa speciosíssimus, is the only species, and was once called *Embóthrium speciosíssimus*. It is now called *Telopèa* in allusion to the brilliant crimson flowers, which from their great size are seen at a large distance, and which render it one of the most conspicuous productions of New South Wales. The leaves are oblong, deeply toothed, veiny, and smooth; wood strong; flower ovate, connate, and terminale, and of considerable duration. There ought to be a specimen of it in every collection. The pots must be well drained, and the plant in the extreme heat of summer not too much exposed to the sun.

Templetònia, a very pretty genus, containing only two species. *T. retùsa* is an erect growing shrub, with wedge-shaped green leaves. *T. gláuca*, leaves glacuous, blunt, and a little apiculate; flowers of both scarlet. They are leguminose plants of free growth, and should be well drained; blooming from April to June.

Tristànias, seven species of evergreen shrubs. Several of them require to be very large before they flower. *T. neriifòlia* is a very neat little plant, and flowers abundantly; colour yellow; shape star-like, and in clusters; leaves lanceolate and opposite. *T. conférta*, white flowers in spikes, leaves alternate. *T. suavèolens*, sweet-scented; flowers yellow. They are all of very easy culture.

Verbénas. A few of these are showy, herbaceous, Green-house plants. *V. chamædryfòlia*, lately known as *V. Melíndres*, is a beautiful plant of a procumbent habit; flowers brilliant scarlet, in glomerated heads from the axils of the young shoots; blooming from April to October. A large plant will appear as a solid mass of scarlet. *V. lambértii* and *V. pulchélla* are also very pretty; colour, rose and lilac. A very good method of treating these plants, is, to plant them in the garden in April; and give them copious waterings in dry weather, and they will flower profusely, lifting some of the plants before frost, to preserve them during winter. They ought to be allowed to run according to their nature; for if tied up, they will not do so well, being in that way too much exposed. There is a plant known in our collections as *Verbéna triphylla*, which is *Aloysia citriodòra*. The flowers are in long spikes, very small, and pale purple. The celebrity of the plant is in the foliage, which is linear, lanceolate, ternate, and it has the most agreeable fragrance in the vegetable world. It is of very easy culture, and has been known to survive the winter, in open air, in Philadelphia. It is deciduous, and would do to plant in the garden during summer, lifting it again before frost, and putting it under protection through winter. When large before it begins to grow, in spring cut it into a neat shape or form.

Vibúrnums. A few of these are very ornamental evergreen shrubs, and almost hardy. *V. tìnus* is the well known Laurestine, (or what is commonly called Laurestinus,) is of the easiest culture; flowers small white, and in large flattened panicles; blooming from February to May, and universally esteemed. It will stand the winter by a little protection, but the flower buds being formed in the fall, the intense frost destroys them; consequently, it will not flower except by the buds, which sometimes form early in summer. *V. lùcidum* is a good species, and superior in flower and foliage to the former, but does not flower so freely, when the plants are small. When they grow large, they flower profusely. There is a desirable variegated variety. *V. odoratíssimum* has smooth evergreen, oblong, elliptic, distantly toothed, leaves, and frequently a stripe in them, is sweet-scented, and a free flowerer. *V. hirsútum* has flowers similar to the above; foliage ovate, with rough brown hairs on both sides, and very characteristic. *V. stríctum variagàtum* is a very fine variety, and upright growing. These plants are all very desirable, blooming early in spring, and continuing for several months; all easily cultivated.

Viminària denudàta, the only species. This plant is remarkable for its twiggy appearance, but it has no foliage, except when growing from seed. It has at the extremity of the twigs or shoots, an ovate, lanceolate, leaf, disappearing when the plant grows old; the flowers are small, yellow, coming out of the young shoots, to the astonishment of the beholder. It grows freely.

Virgília capènsis is a beautiful cape shrub, with a compound leaf of twenty-five leaflets, ovate, lanceolate, edges hairy; flowers in spikes at the axils; colour blue and leguminose. The pots require to be well drained, and the plants protected from the sun.

Volkamèria japónica. There is a plant known in our collections under that name, which is *Clerodéndron fràgrans múltiplex.* It keeps in a good Green-house, and flowers well, frequently blooming during winter, and if planted in the garden during summer, will flower superbly. The flowers have a delicious fragrance; but if the foliage is rubbed with the hand, the smell is not so pleasant. The leaves are large, round, ovate, and tomentose; flowers corymbose, compact, and terminale. There are several fine plants in *Clerodéndron* belonging to the Hot-house. This plant will not bear much fumigation.

Witsènias, four species. *W. corymbòsa* is a plant that has stood in high estimation ever since it was known, but unfortunately there is a very inferior plant, *Aristèa cyànea*, got into our collections under that name. The panicles of *W. corymbòsa* is quite smooth; those of *Aristèa* are hairy, which is itself sufficient to detect them; but otherwise the appearance of *W. corymbòsa* is much stronger, and more erect growing, not inclining to push at the roots so much as *Aristèa*. The foliage is lanceolate and amplexicaule, the leaves having much the nature and appearance of *Iris*. The plant is of easy culture, and blooms from November to April; colour fine blue. The true one has come into the country lately. *W. ramòsa* is a very fine species, similar to the above; flowers yellow and blue; plant branching.

Westríngias, a genus of four species, very like the common *Rosemary*. *W. rosmariniífórmis*, leaves lanceolate, and silvery beneath; *W. longifòlia* is similar; both have small white silvery flowers, and are easily cultivated.

Zàmias, about twenty species, eight of which belong to this compartment. The foliage is greatly admired, and is in large fronds, with oblique, lanceolate leaflets. Several of them glaucous. It bears heads of flowers of a brown colour in the centre of the plant, very like large pine cones. *Z. hórrida*, the finest, *Z. púngens*, *Z. spíralis*, and *Z. latifòlia*, are the most conspicuous. They must be kept in the warmest part of the Green-house; and give them large well drained pots. They are imported from the Cape of Good Hope. All the plants herein named requiring to be drained. In preparing the pots, place first a piece of broken pot, or any similar substitute, with the convex side on the hole of the pot, and then put in a few, or a handful, (according to the size of the pot,) of shivers of broken pots, or round gravel, about the size of garden pease. Those that we have mentioned in this *Repotting*, as to be done in this, or beginning of next month, is not intended to apply to plants in general, large and small, but to those that are young, and require encouragement, or to those that were not shifted last autumn. The roots must not be disturbed, but the ball turned out entire; and put as much earth as will raise the ball within about an inch of the rim of the pot. Press the earth down around it with a thin-narrow piece of wood, frequently shaking it that no vacancy may be left. If the roots are rotten, or otherwise injured, take all such off. If this be the case, the plant will be sickly. Give it a new pot of a smaller size, administering water moderately until there are visible signs of fresh growth. The plants must not be disturbed while flowering; let the repotting be done afterwards. Plants are, at certain stages of growth, if in good health, in such a state that no one can err in shifting them when desirous to hasten their growth. Those plants that make two or more growths during the summer may be repotted in the interim of any of these growths, and all others just before they begin to push in the spring; that is, when the wood buds are perceptibly swelled. Never saturate with water fresh potted plants. There are many kinds that, without injury, could be repotted when growing; but it requires an experienced operator to decide. It would be of no material service to enumerate them here. When done potting, tie all up neatly with stakes rather higher than the plant, that the new shoots may be tied thereto during their stage of growth, to prevent them from being destroyed by the wind. There may be many that do not require repotting, but would be benefited by a top-dressing. This should be done by probing off all the surface earth down to the roots, replacing it with fresh compost, suitable to the nature of the plant.

When the above is done, arrange all the plants in proper order, and syringe them clean; but if there are any of the Green-fly, they must be fumigated previous to syringing. Take an opportunity, on the first fine day, to wash out all the pavement of the house, which should be made dry before the evening if the nights are cold. Thus every part of the house will be in order before the hurry of the garden commences.

OF ENARCHING OR GRAFTING BY APPROACH, *also termed* ABLACTATION.

In this method of grafting, the scion is not separated from the parent plant until it is firmly united with the stock; consequently, they must stand contiguously. We intend the following method to apply directly to *Caméllias*, as they are the principal plants in the Green-house that are thus worked. The criterion for the operation is, just as the plants begin to grow, either in spring or mid-summer. Place the stock contiguous to the plant where the graft or enarch is to be taken from. If the branches, where the intended union is to take place, do not grow at equal heights, a slight stage may be erected to elevate the pot that holds the lower. Take the branch that is to be enarched, (the wood of last or previous year is the most proper,) and bring it in contact with the stock; mark the parts where they are to unite, so as to form a pointed arch. In that part of the branch which is to rest against the stock, pare off the bark and part of the wood to about two or three inches in length, and in the side of the stock which is to receive the graft, do the same, that the inside rind of each may be exactly opposite, which is the first part where a union will take place. Bind them firmly and neatly together with strands of Russia matting, and protect the joint from the air by a coat of close composition; clay of the consistency of thick paint, turpentine, or wax, will equally answer. Finish by fastening the grafted branch to the head of the stock or a rod. Many practitioners make a slit or tongue into the enarch and stock, but we find it unnecessary, more tedious, and likewise more danger in breaking. *Caméllias* are also grafted, and budded, but these two operations require great experience and continued attention, and seldom prove so successful as enarching. When they have perfectly taken, which will be after the first growth is over, begin to separate them by cutting the scion a little at three different periods, about a week apart, separating it at the third time. If the head is intended to be taken off the stock, do it in like manner after the second growth is over. By the above method, many kinds can be grown on the same stock. The same plan applies to all evergreens.

Flower Garden.

MARCH.

It is expected that all the pruning is finished. If not get all expeditiously done, according to directions given in the preceding months, likewise all digging, and that which was dug in the autumn, point over, or half dig, that all may have a neat appearance. This must not be done when the ground is too much imbibed with moisture, as that would harden the soil. Break it well with the spade, leaving it one or two days before the surface is raked smooth, that all may be ready to receive the seeds or plants that are intended to be sown or planted. As soon as the frost is entirely gone, uncover all plants or shrubs that have been protected; preserving carefully such articles as will answer the same purpose next year. The frost disappears generally from the middle to the end of this month. Cut off all decayed shoots, or such as have been hurt by the frost. The *Lagerstræmias* will flower in greater perfection if they are cut closely; that is, where the wood of last year is cut to within a few eyes of the wood of the previous year, at the same time having regard to the shape that the plant is required to take. Cut off the injured part of any of the evergreens that have had their foliage much injured by the severity of winter, leaving the part that is green, which is essential to the support of these kinds of plants.

Such work as can be done in this month, should not be delayed, such as hoeing, digging, raking, and clearing away all decayed leaves, and litter of every description that have been brought or blown in the garden, during autumn or winter.

BOX EDGINGS

May be planted any time this month, or beginning of next, which in most seasons will be preferable. We will give a few simple directions how to accomplish the work. In the first place, dig over the ground deeply where the edging is intended to be planted, breaking the soil fine, and keeping it to a proper height, viz. about one inch higher than the side of the walk; but the taste of the operator will best decide according to the situation. Rake the surface even, and tread it down with the feet, or beat it with the spade. Where it gives most continue to add, keeping the surface at the desired height. If the edging is to be in a direct line, either on a level or inclined plane, you may be correctly and simply regulated by making the desired level at each end of the line. Take three rods about four feet long each, having a piece of one foot to cross at one end, two of these pieces painted black, the other white. Have a black one at each end of the line on the level, take the white one for the centre, going along the line, and about every twenty feet, level a spot to the exact height, which will be seen by looking over the top of the rods from one end. Having found the level, drive in a peg to it, so that no mistake may occur; beat and level between them, leaving a smooth surface. This being done, strain the line, and with the spade proceed to cut out the trench perpendicularly on the side next the walk, six, eight, ten, or twelve inches deep, according to the length of the plants. Afterwards take the plants, and cut the tops even, with the knife or shears, at the same time shortening the roots. Then with the left hand next the line, plant forward, keeping the tops of the plants level, and from one to two inches above ground, keeping the plants close according to the required thickness. Put in the earth as you proceed, and tread it firm, then rake the surface even, and with the spade beat it smooth. If the weather sets in very dry, the box will be the better of a few waterings. Sometimes boxwood is planted without roots, but it seldom gives satisfaction; not growing equally.

TENDER ANNUALS.

When it is wished to have any of these flower early, if they were not sown as directed last month, on a hotbed, let it be done early in this. Those that were sown and now growing freely, must have plenty of air. In fine days the sashes may be taken off a few hours about mid-day; and where the plants are too thick, thin them out a few inches apart, that the air may circulate amongst them. Have another bed ready to transplant them into about the end of this or beginning of next month. When transplanted, sprinkle them with water, and shade them with mats from the sun, one or two days. By this treatment they will be much stronger for planting into the borders, about the first of May. For the different kinds, see list.

HARDY ANNUALS

May be sown in the borders about the end of the month, when the ground is prepared, and the weather fine, but avoid it at all times if the earth will not pulverise properly. The neatest and most expeditious method is to take a rod about one foot long, and one inch in diameter, rounding at the end, with which end draw a circle of nine inches diameter, from one inch to one eighth of an inch deep, according to the size of the seeds. Many very small seeds will grow best if sown on the surface of fine mould. When sown, cover in with the back of the rake, placing a small twig, or a tally with the name, in the centre of the circle, to prevent mistakes, either in sowing, planting, or hoeing. When they come above ground, the first moist day should be taken to pull up such as are too crowded. Annuals are generally too delicate to bear transplanting, therefore they ought always to be sown where they are intended to remain. A few kinds do best with removing, such as Balsam, Mary-gold, China Aster, Stockgilly, and several others of a free growing, strong-wooded nature. Annuals are such plants as grow from seed, flower, and perfect their productions, and then die, within one year. For hardy sorts, see list. Sow in rows or fancy spots the varieties of sweet pea.

BIENNIALS

Are such as are of two years' duration. Being sown this year they flower, seed, or fruit next year, and soon after decay. The seeds should be sown about the end of this or beginning of next month, either in the spot where they are intended to remain, or in a compartment by themselves, regularly marked, and transplanted when convenient. When they appear above ground, thin them out distinctly, that when they are to be removed, a little earth may adhere to them; and if put where they are to stand, leave only three plants.

PERENNIALS.

In every Flower-garden there ought to be a good selection of these plants. They are lasting ornaments, and when judiciously selected, will give yearly gratification. In making a choice, a view should be had to have those that flower abundantly, are of free growth, beauty, and continuation of flower. It would go beyond our limits, to give an extensive description of any, but a few remarks on some of the finest, with their names, are indispensable.

Adònis vernális, is a fine border flower, and will grow in any common soil; flowers large, yellow rayed, having in the rays about twelve petals; leaves much divided, bloom in April and May.

Anemóne, Wind-flower. Several fine species, with flowers from one to three inches in diameter. *A. Hallèri*, blue; *A. pulsatìlla*, blue pasque flower; *A. alpìna*, large white. These are fine plants, and are now given to a genus called *Pulsatìlla*. *A. palmàta flòre-plèno*, yellow; *A. stellàta versícolor*, various coloured; *A. pavonìna flòre-plèno*, scarlet; *A. narcissiflòra*, white. Any of these are very desirable.

Antirrhìnums, Snap-dragon. All the varieties of *A. màjus* are esteemed in the flower borders; the pure white and bright red are very showy. A few of the species, *A. mólle* and *A. sículum*, where there is variety required, deserve a situation. The flowers are all large, and similar to the snout of an animal.

Asclèpias. The finest of this genus are native plants, and are highly esteemed in Europe, but frequently rejected with us, because "they are wild plants." *A. tuberòsa* has beautiful orange flowers, and delight in dry situations. *A. rùbra*, *A. nívea*, *A. purpuráscens*; and *A. incarnàta*, are the finest of the family. It is best to plant *A. tuberòsa* in October.

Aconítums, Wolfs'-bane, one hundred and twenty-eight distinct species, with several varieties. Many of them are of consequence and beauty; the flower stems rise from one and a half to six feet upright, and strong, furnished with many palmate and digitate leaves, terminated by spikes of blue, yellow, or white flowers, similar to a hood; hence the name of Monk's Hood is often applied to them. They are scarce in collections, but in a few years we have no doubt but many of them will be plentiful. The finest species are *A. speciòsum*, *A. anthòra*, *A. neúrbergensis*, *A. amœnum*, *A. napéllus*, *A. venústum*, *A. zoóctonum*, *A. pyramidàle*, *A. lycóctonum*, *A. albùm*, and *A. versícolor*. They flower from May to September, and will grow in any common garden soil. The roots of *A. napéllus* are like small turnips, and are said to be poisonous.

Cáltha palústris flòre-plèno is a good border plant, delights in moist situations, has large cordate, crenated leaves; flowers double yellow; blooming from April till June; and is a desirable plant.

Béllis perénnis horténsis, Daisy. We might almost say with another, "every one knows the Daisy." It is named from being pretty, and is perfectly hardy, though generally kept under cover. They delight to have a shaded situation during summer, to protect them from the sun, which, as it were, scorches the roots. There are many double varieties in the gardens, which flower early. The one called *Crown*, or *Carnation* Daisy, is twice the size of the common varieties, and has white and red petals alternately, and very double. Loamy soil, inclined to moisture, is best adapted to their growth.

Campánulas. This genus affords many very ornamental plants for the Flower-garden and Shrubbery, and they flower superbly during the summer, agreeing better with our climate than with that of Europe. Several have two successions of flowers, *C. persicifòlia álba plèna*; *C. persicifòlia cærùlea plèno*; *C. urticifòlia*, white. Of this last there is also a double variety. *C. speciòsa*; *C. glomerata*; *C. versícolor*; with several others, are worthy of a situation in every garden. Their roots are strong, fleshy, and fibrous. They are easy of culture, and will retain their situation in the severest of our winters. *C. grandiflòra* is now *Wahlenbérgia grandiflòra*. It has fine blue large flowers; the flower stems are slender, and should be supported as soon as they grow.

Cheiránthus Chéiri vulgàris is the common garden Wall-flower. There are about ten varieties of it, all admired for their various colours and agreeable odour. The common variety survives the mildest of our winters. The most esteemed variety is *Hæmánthus*, Double bloody. They should all be protected by a frame. *C. mutábilis* is a beautiful species; it has many shades of colour from lilac to dark purple. The flowers are on extending racemose spikes; blooming from April to June; it requires a light rich soil; is a half shrubby evergreen plant.

Chelònes. This genus belongs entirely to this continent, and possesses many fine species. It is a matter of astonishment that they are not more cultivated and sought for in our collections. *C. glábra*; *C. oblíqua*; *C. barbàta*; *C. atropurpùrea*; *C. pulchélla*; *C. venústa*; and *C. speciòsa*; are all handsome, and flower from May to September; corolla large, ringent; ventricose flowers in spikes or panicles.

Chrysánthemums. There are few of this genus of any consequence as herbaceous plants, except the varieties of *C. sinénse*, of which there are about fifty, all desirable; but in small gardens, where there is a deficiency in room, the following are select in colour and quality: *Tubulòsum álbum*, quilled white; *supérbum*, superb white; *díscolor*, large lilac; *fúlvum*, Spanish brown; *atropurpùreum*, early crimson; *involùtum*, curled lilac; *fasciculàtum*, superb cluster yellow; *serotìnum*, late pale purple; *papyràceum*, paper white; *Waratáh*, yellow Waratah; *versícolor*, two-coloured red; *stellàtum*, starry purple; *verecúndum*, early blush; and *mutábile*, changeable pale buff. To grow these in perfection, they require rich light soil; and about the end of this month the roots should be lifted, divided, and planted into fresh soil, either by giving them a new situation, or changing the earth they were in. Two or three stems together are quite sufficient. The flowers, by the above treatment, will be much larger, more double, and finer in colour; where they are wanted to grow low and bushy, top them in June, but not later than the first of July. Where the soil is rich, and the plant having only one stem, by topping it, makes a beautiful bush. They are in flower from the first of October until severe frost; thus beautifying our gardens at a season when they would be destitute of one single attraction. If the season is dry, to water them with liquid manure will add to their vigour. They are all natives of China, and greatly esteemed by the Chinese, who only allow a few blooms to come out on the top of each stem, thereby having the flowers much finer.

Clématis, Virgin's-bower. A few species are good herbaceous plants, of upright growth, and blue flowers, *C. integrifòlia*; *C. angustifòlia*; and *C. erécta*; they grow best in light soil.

Coreópsis, chiefly native plants, and free-flowering; colour principally yellow; flowers rayed. *C. tenuifòlia*, *C. verticilláta*, *C. díscolor*, and *C. trípteris*, are the finest of the genus, and will grow in any common garden soil.

Delphínums. There are some showy border flowers of these, of strong growth. The leaves are much divided; the flowers in terminale spikes; colour blue, purple, red, white and yellow, with various shades. *D. grandiflòrum*, with its varieties, are the best of the genus. *D. intermèdium*, and its varieties, *D. elátum*, Bee Larkspur, from the ringent part of the flower being very like a bee, and *D. montánum*, are good varieties, and easily cultivated. When the plants become large, they ought to be divided, and planted in fresh soil. They are in bloom from May to September.

Diánthus. Some of the species of this genus are the most prominent of the Flower-garden, not only for their beauty, but also their fragrance, which is peculiarly grateful, especially in the well known and celebrated pink and carnation, with the Sweet-william, which was esteemed, in the days of old, "for its beauty to deck up the bosoms of the beautiful, and garlands and crowns for pleasure." The finest species are *D. barbàtus*, and *D. barbàtus plèno*, Sweet-william; *D. discolor D. chinènsis*; *D. alpínus*, *D. supérbus*; *D. caryophyllus*, from which have originated the Picotee and the Carnation; *D. plumàrius*, from which originated the Double Pink; *D. fràgrans* and *D. supérbus*. Several of these, although they will stand the severest cold, have to be protected in frames during winter, to have them in the perfection of beauty. For the character of a Pink and Carnation, see *May*.

Dictámnus. Two species of this genus, *D. fraxinélla* and *D. álbus*, have been cultivated and esteemed upwards of two hundred and forty years. A plant of the first of these species, when gently rubbed, emits an odour like that of lemon-peel; and when bruised emits a balsamic scent, which is strongest in the pedicles of the flowers. They have glands of a rusty colour, that exude a viscid juice, or resin, which exhales in vapour, and in a dark place may be seen to take fire. Its flowers are red, those of the other white, in loose terminale spikes; the flower has five petals, clawed and unequal, with glandular dots; in bloom from May to July; delights in sandy loam.

Dodecàtheon. This is a native genus, and commonly called American cowslip. The generic term, a name of the Romans, signifying twelve gods or divinities, is applied with great absurdity to a plant, a native of a world the Romans never saw nor had any idea of, neither resembling, in any particular, the poetical fancy of their writers. The most admired species is *D. mèdia*; the flowers are in umbels, on a pedicle, from six to twelve inches high; the corolla is rotata reflexa, colour light purple, bottom of petals lake and yellow; blooming in May. The white variety is very much esteemed, and surpasses the preceding. The ground is pure white, the bottom of the petals the same as the other. There is also a spotted variety found on the banks of the Missouri. They delight in brown loam, a half shady situation, inclining to moisture. The foliage soon decays after flowering.

Digitàlis, Fox-glove, about forty species of annuals and herbaceous plants. A few are cultivated in the flower borders, and are very showy. These are D. *leucophæa*, D. *ferrugínea*, D. *ochroleùca*, large yellow; and D. *purpuráscens*; and are good species. D. *purpúrea* and D. *álba*, are very conspicuous biennials; the flowers are solitary, and in long spikes; the corolla of D. *purpúrea* is campanulate, ventricose, and ringent; the interior is spotted, and is considered the finest of the genus. Delights in poor soil, with a little shade.

Eupatóriums. These generally are native plants, not worthy of notice here, except for two species. *E. cœlestínum* has syngenesious flowers in flattened panicles, colour fine light blue, blooming from September to November, desirable for its beauty at that season. *E. aromàticum* may be cultivated for its spicy odour; flowers white, in loose terminale panicles; blooming from August to October. Either of them will grow in common soil.

Gentiánas, a genus of very showy plants, and flower in great abundance. The flowers are tubular and inflated; colour generally blue. A few species are yellow, and some white; flowers in whorls, terminale, or solitary. They grow best in a light rich soil. *G. lútea*, *G. purpúrea*, *G. septémfida*. *G. acaúlis* is a pretty dwarf growing species, and often used as edgings in flower compartments; the flower dark and light blue; interior of the corolla spotted; has a succession of flower from April to June. We have no doubt of it succeeding in our gardens, but not being plentiful, it has not been perfectly tried. A few years will exhibit it in abundance. *G. imbricàta* and *G. conférta*. They are all fine exotics, but many of them may give place to our native species, such as *G. Catesbæí*; *G. ochroleúca*; *G. incarnàta*; with several others, and *G. crinàta*, which is a biennial, and finely fringed; colour light blue.

Gèum. There are only two species that are worth cultivation, viz. *G. quéllyon*, once *G. coccíneum*; and *G. hybridum*. *G. urbànum* is sometimes cultivated for its roots, which, when chewed, sweeten the breath. They are all of easy culture. *G. quéllyon* flowers from May to October, and is a very desirable small plant for the borders, and much esteemed in Europe.

Hemerocállis, Day Lily; two species, *H. fúlva* and *H. graminea*, flower well, and are remarkable among the border flowers for their large yellow or copper coloured corollas, some of them about six inches diameter; bloom from May to July, and will grow in almost any soil. There is a plant known in our gardens as *H. cærùlea*, which is *Fúnkia cærùlea*, and has a campanulate corolla, with a cylindrical tube; flowers in spikes; leaves ovate, accuminate.

Hibíscus. There are several herbaceous species very showy and handsome, *H. palústris*; *H. ròseus*; *H. militàris*; *H. speciòsus*; *H. grandiflòrus*; and *H. púngens*. They grow best in moist situations, and where these are not to be had, give them plenty of water, and plant in sandy soil enriched with decayed leaves. The flowers are about six inches in diameter, flowering up the stem, either solitary or in small bunches. *H. speciòsus* is the most splendid, and deserves a situation in every garden. The roots in winter ought to be covered by litter, tan, or saw dust; but a better method is to lift them, and put them in the cellar, covered with dry earth, and kept from the frost. All the above mentioned species are improved by being protected during winter.

Iris, Flower-de-luce, has many fine species of various shades and colours, *I. subiflòra*, *I. nepalénsis*, *I. Pallàsii*, *I. pállida*, *I. cristàta*, *I. arenària*, *I. furcàta*, *I. germánica*, *I. florentìna*, *I. vérna*, and *I. susiàna*. The last is the finest of the herbaceous species; the flowers are striped, blue, brown, and spotted; but we are not certain if it will stand the severity of our winters. The roots of *I. florentìna* is the orrice root of the druggists. They are all of easy culture in any loamy soil inclining to moisture. The bulbous species will be treated of in *September* or *October*. Corolla six-petaled, three erect, and three reclined alternately; proceeding from spathes or sheaths with flowers in succession.

Lìatris is a genus of native plants, containing several fine species, *L. squarròsa*, large purple heads of beautiful flowers; *L. élegans*; *L. paniculàta*. *L. macróstachya*, now *L. spicàta*, is a fine large growing species. They have syngenesious purple flowers in long close spikes, differing from other spiked flowering genera by blooming first at the extremity. They grow best in strong heavy soil.

Lychnis. Three species are very desirable in the flower borders. *L. chalcedónica* has bright scarlet crowned flowers; the double scarlet variety is splendid. There is also a double white variety, *L. fúlgens* and *L. flós-jòvis.* They ought to be frequently lifted, and planted afresh, or they will dwindle to nothing. The best time is when they begin to grow. There is a plant known in our collections as *Lychnis flós-cucùla*, which is now *Agrostéma flós-cucùla*; it is a fine and showy border plant with double red flowers. They delight in a light sandy rich soil.

Lythrums. A few species flower well, and have small pink blossoms in great profusion, *L. alàtum*, *L. virgàtum*, *L. diffùsum*, and *L. lanceolàtum.* They will grow in any common garden soil if not too much shaded; and flower from June to September.

Mimùlus, Monkey-flower. A few species may be cultivated. They will grow in any soil or situation. *M. lùteus* and *M. rivulàris* are the best. *M. moschàtus* has a very strong musk scent, to many agreeable. We think it will prove hardy. The two former have large gaping flowers, of a gold yellow, and beautifully spotted with purple in the interior.

Monárdas, a fine native genus and showy. The foliage of several of the species is aromatic, and resembles mint. *M. dídyma* has long scarlet ringent flowers, in headed whorls; *M. kalmiana*, flowers very long, and a beautiful crimson, with fragrant leaves. *M. Russelliana* has red and white flowers; curious and handsome. *M. punctata* has yellow and red flowers; they grow in any common soil.

Mathíola, is the generic of the Stock-gilly. None of them will survive severe winters; yet many of them are indispensable in the Flower-garden. *M. simplicicáulis*, Brompton-stock, and its varieties; with *M. incàna*, Queen-stock, and its varieties, require the protection of a good frame in winter, and about the end of this month, or beginning of next, plant them in good light rich soil to flower, which they will do all summer, if attended to with frequent supplies of water. *M. ánnua* has about sixteen varieties, valuable for flowering the first year from seed, and are all annuals. They ought to be sown on a gentle hot-bed about the first of this month, and carefully pricked out so as they may be ready to transplant about the end of April or the first of May. Plant them in light rich soil, and they will flower profusely through the season; if it is very dry, they must be watered to keep them growing. The scarlet, white, and purple varieties are the finest; but there are many intermediate sorts all handsome. *M. glàbra* is the Wall-flower leaved stock, and requires the same treatment as the two former. There are about eight varieties of this, all various in colour. In planting any of these into the open ground, choose cloudy weather, except they have been in pots; in such case, plant at any time in beds, keeping each kind separate.

Œnothèras. The most of them are indigenous, and in Europe they afford a continual ornament to the Flower-garden from April to November, but in our gardens they are entirely neglected. By rejecting these and many others, our Flower-gardens are deprived both of much beauty and interest they might easily possess. These plants delight in light rich soil. *Œ. odoràta*, sweet scented; *Œ. macrocárpa*; *Œ. mèdia*; *Œ. latiflòra*; *Œ. Frazèri*; *Œ. speciòsa*; and *Œ. pállida*; are all fine native herbaceous plants, mostly with large yellow four-petaled corollas; in bloom from April to September. There are several of them beautiful annual and biennial plants. For the finest, see list.

Phlóx, another American genus, and one of the most handsome in cultivation. It consists of elegant border flowers, valuable for flowering early, and more so for blossoming late in autumn. While the majority of plants blooming late in the season are generally syngenesious, with yellow flowers, these delight us with their lively colours of purple, red, and white. A collection of them properly attended to, would of themselves constitute a beautiful flower garden. It will be difficult to state which are the finest, but the following are select varieties: P. *paniculàta*; P. *acuminàta*; P. *intermèdia*; P. *odoràta*; P. *pyramidàlis*; with *pyramidàlis álba*, which is splendid; P. *suavèolens*; P. *refléxa*; P. *stolonífera*; P. *pilòsa*; P. *divaricàta*; P. *nivàlis*; and P. *subulàta*. In the spring of 1831, an eminent British collector[A] exclaimed, on seeing a patch of P. *subulàta* in one of the pine barrens of New Jersey, "The beauty of that alone is worth coming to America to see, it is so splendid." Most of the species delight in a rich light sandy loam. When the plants become large, they ought to be divided, and planted in fresh ground.

[A] Mr. Drummond.

Prímulas, Primrose. To this genus belong the celebrated *Cowslip*, *Oxlip*, *Primrose*, and the esteemed *Auricula*. The double varieties of Primrose have originated from *P. vulgàris*. These are such as carry their flowers on separate pedicles, rising from the root on a small stem. The double varieties are desirable for their beauty, but require the protection of a frame during winter. They are in colour red, white, yellow, lilac, purple, and crimson. P. *elàtior* is the Oxlip, from which all the *Polyánthuses* have been grown. They are in variety innumerable, and are those whose flowers are in umbels, on a scape or flower-stalk, rising from three to nine inches. The rules for judging of their merits are wholly artificial, agreed on from time to time by Florists. The one that is the leading beauty this year would in a few years be far in the rear. The principal character is that the corolla is not notched or fringed; the colours pure and distinct, not running into one another; the tube small; the eye round, and a little prominent. Being surrounded with white, and the ground purple, is a fine character. P. *auricula*. From this the highly esteemed varieties have originated. The cultivated *auricula* has many admirers, both for its exquisite beauty and fragrance. For the criterion of a fine flower see *May*. There are several other species worthy of a situation, such as P. *cortusoídes*, P. *dentiflòra*, P. *suavèolens*, P. *decòra*, with P. *scótica* and P. *farinòsa*, both small neat species. A shady situation agrees best with them; and they require loamy soil, free from any kind of manure, except it be fully decomposed. The leaves of P. *vèris* are recommended for feeding silk worms.

Potentíllas. We mention this genus here as affording several free flowering dwarf plants; not as being certain that any of the most desired species will withstand our winters, being natives of Nepaul; but, from the character of the plant, we think that they are adapted to bear severe cold. They are similar to the strawberry in habit and appearance. P. *nepalénsis*, or *formòsa*, has rose-coloured flowers; P. *atropurpùrea*; P. *Russelliàna*, scarlet; P. *Hopwoodiàna*, rose and scarlet; and P. *spléndens*, yellow, with superb leaves. These are the finest of the genus, and flower from May to September. It will be well to protect them in a frame with the Carnations; they delight in light soil.

Saponària officinàlis, and *S. O. plèna*, are fine free-flowering dwarf plants; the colour is pink in both double and single varieties. The roots run under ground, and care should be taken to keep them within bounds: they flower from June till October. *S. cæspitòsa* is a neat growing species of a rose colour. They will grow in any soil.

Silène. Several of this genus are popular annuals, but the herbaceous species are very indifferent. *S. viscósa* and S. *viscósa flòre plèna*, are frequently cultivated for their beauty; they will grow well if not too much shaded.

Saxífraga, above one hundred species. Many of them are beautiful plants for rock-work. They are regardless of cold, but will not generally withstand much moisture. A few of them are highly deserving a situation in any garden. *S. hirsùtum*, and *S. crassifòlia*, are used in some countries for tanning. *S. granulàta multipléx* has fine double-white flowers, and is desirable. *S. umbròsa*, London-pride, makes a beautiful edging for a flower border; the flowers are small, but on close examination its colours are unrivalled. It is vulgarly called, "none so pretty." *S. sarmentòsa* is kept in the Green-house, but is perfectly hardy, and makes a fine plant in a shaded situation. We have no doubt but it would make a good fancy edging. *S. pulchélla*, straw coloured, and *S. pyramidàlis*; these are all easily cultivated; and flower in spikes from May to July.

Spiræas. A few species are showy plants, and continue flowering from May to September. *S. ulmària múltiplex*, Meadow-sweet, has sweet scented white flowers, in long dense spikes. *S. Filipéndula múltiplex*, Drop-wort, double white. *S. lobàta* is a native, and has fine rose coloured flowers, in June and July; these are the finest of the herbaceous species, and will grow in any common garden soil.

Státice, Thrift. A genus containing many fine herbaceous plants, only a few of them are common in collections. The finest of them are scarce, and said to be "bad to cultivate." *S. vulgàris*, once *Armèria vulgàris*, is the most valuable plant for an edging, next to box, that the Flower-garden is possessed of, and does extremely well in our climate, flowering in great profusion from May to July. When done flowering, the stems should be cut off. The foliage is an agreeable evergreen; the plant increases rapidly, and in a few years may be planted to a great extent. *S. speciòsa* has red flowers, crowded in spreading panicles. *S. tatàrica* has also very showy flowers, and is now given to the genus *Taxànthema*. *S. latifòlia* and *S. maritìma* are the finest. *T. latifòlia* and *T. conspícua* deserve attention. They should be lifted every alternate year, and sunk deeper into the soil, because they incline to grow out, and are sometimes during summer killed by the drought. Hence they are said to be "bad to cultivate."

Tróllius europæus, and *T. asiàticus*, are fine border plants, with large yellow semi-double flowers; the petals are much cupped, which causes the flowers to have a globular appearance. They are easily grown in any loamy soil, and flower from May to July. Few flowers have the curious globular character which these have.

Verónica, Speed-well. This genus consists of about one hundred and twenty species of herbaceous plants, besides several varieties. The flowers are in long close spikes, either white, flesh coloured, or blue; they are generally of the latter colour. Above sixty species are equally fine, and being generally of the same character, the Catalogue at the end of this work will contain the best selection that we can make. Very few of them are in the collections of the country, although they are very showy, and flower from June to August. They will grow in any soil, but will not flourish where they are much shaded. *V. officinàlis* has been used in Germany and Sweden as a substitute for tea. Some prefer *V. chamædrys* for the same purpose.

Valerìanas. Several species are showy border plants, with small flowers in large close flattened panicles. *V. dioíca* is remarkable for having the stamens and pistils in separate flowers, situated on different plants; the flowers are of a blush colour, and the roots when planted must be protected from the cats, for they are delighted with them, and scrape them up. *V. phù*, a large growing species with white flowers; and *V. rùbra*, with its varieties, are the finest of the genus. They are now given to *Centrànthus*. They are all of easy culture in common garden earth, but preferring moist shady situations. In flower from May to September.

Vìola, a genus consisting of upwards of eighty species, of low pretty plants, of great diversity of colour and foliage. Many of them are natives, and well worth a situation in our gardens. They mostly delight in sandy loam, and a little shade. A few of the species grow in moist situations. The most esteemed varieties for fragrance are, *V. odoràta purpúrea plèna*, double purple, with *V. odoràta àlba plèna*, double white. They flower very early, and make good edgings where they are kept in order; flowering profusely from April to June, and flowering again in autumn.

Yúcca, Adam's-needle. This is a very showy and ornamental genus; their character forming a picturesque contrast in the Flower-garden; foliage long, narrow, lanceolate, and stiff; with white companulate flowers, about two inches in diameter, in conical spikes from two to four feet long, arising from the centre of the plant, containing frequently from two to four hundred florets. They are principally native plants. *Y. strícta* is the freest flowerer. *Y. supérba*; *Y. aloifòlia*; *Y. angustifòlia*, *Y. acuminàta*, *Y. serrulàta*, and *Y. filamentòsa*, are all fine species, and will grow in any common soil. When in flower, if protected from the sun by an awning, they will be of considerable duration. There are variegated varieties of *Strícta*, *Aloifòlia*, and *Serrulàta*, which look very handsome in foliage, but are at present very rare, and it will be a number of years before they are plentiful. There ought at least to be one specimen of some of the free-flowering species in every garden.

Having given the names and characters of a few herbaceous plants, all or most of them easily obtained, many of them extremely handsome, and such as agree best with transplanting at this season of the year; for several others, such as *Pæònias*, or any other strong fibrous or bulbous sorts, see *September* and *October*. Where they are in pots, they can be planted at any time, the weather permitting, provided the ball of earth is not broken. But where they are only to be removed, the best time is just as vegetation commences. That herbaceous plants may look to the best advantage, and flower well, they must not be allowed to get into large stools; but as soon as they are above one foot in diameter, they should be divided.

Very frequently those who perform this operation, take the spade, and cut a piece off all round, which to a degree improves the look of the plant; but this is only half justice. It should be lifted entirely, fresh soil given, or removed a few feet, and planted a little deeper than it was before, as the plant tends apparently to grow out of the soil when allowed to stand long. If the weather becomes dry shortly after transplanting, give them a few waterings, until they have taken fresh roots, which will be within two weeks. Colour should be diversified through the garden as much as practicable, and the highest growing sorts planted farthest from the walk, so as all may appear in view. At all times avoid crowding the plants together.

BULBOUS ROOTS.

About the middle of this month, let the covering of tan, saw-dust, or decayed leaves, be cleared from the beds of such as were directed to be covered in November; afterwards carefully stirring the surface among them with a kind of wooden spatula, or wedge, breaking the surface fine; then dress all the alleys smooth and neat with the hoe and rake, clearing away every particle of litter. When the leaves of Tulips are expanding, they frequently become entangled so much, that the force of growth breaks the foliage: if there are any appearance of this at any time, they should be set right with the hand. In early seasons these roots will be far advanced, and perhaps one night of frost unexpectedly might materially injure them. When there is any suspicion of cold weather, hoops should be spanned across the beds, so that the necessary mats or canvass could in a few minutes be placed over them, to ward off danger. Protect the finest sorts from heavy drenching rains, and give them small neat rods for support, as they grow up. If the rods and tyings are painted green, the effect will be improved. These directions equally apply to *Narcissus*, *Jonquils*, *Iris*, and all Holland bulbs.

CARNATIONS, PINKS, PRIMROSES, &c.

Which have been protected by frames through the winter, must have at all favourable opportunities plenty of air admitted to them by lifting the sashes, and in fine mild days and nights, the sashes may be taken entirely off. Divest them of all decayed leaves, and stir up the earth on the surface of the pots; those that are intended to be planted in the garden may be set to one side, while those that are to be kept in pots must be more strictly attended to. Of these the Pinks and Carnations should be repotted about the first of the month. Those that have been kept in four inch pots, should be put into pots of seven inches, and those that are in five inch pots may be put into eight inch. Give a gentle watering after repotting. Pinks do not require the pots so large, but the same treatment in every other respect. Where the extremity of the leaves are decayed, cut them off, with any other decayed leaves: the pots must be well drained with shivers or fine gravel. Give them plenty of air, otherwise they will be weak in growth.

Primroses require only a little fresh earth on the top of the pots. *Daisies* may be planted out in shady situations; the sun destroys them during summer if exposed.

AURICULAS.

These beautiful and highly interesting plants are, to a great degree, neglected in our collections. It cannot be from want of beauty or fragrance that they have not attracted our attention, for they are exquisite in both. We are rather inclined to think that those who have them do not give them the treatment they require yearly to perfect their bloom. They should now have the surface earth taken off about half an inch down, and fresh soil added, which will cause them to put out fresh fibres about the upper part of the roots, and greatly increase their growth. The frame in which they are placed should now face the east, as the sun will be too strong for them; and about the end of the month turn it to the north. The glass of the frame may be white-washed, which will partially shade them from the sun, that being their delight. Give them water sparingly until they begin to grow, and never water them over the foliage previous to flowering, as water injures that fine mealy-like substance found on many of the sorts, and which so greatly improves their beauty. Defend them, therefore, from rain and high winds. To have them flower strongly, only one flower stem should be allowed to grow. The first one that shows is generally the best. At all events leave the strongest, and cut off all the others, or only nip off the flower pips, which answers the same end. Never keep the sash off during night, lest it should rain before morning.

RANUNCULUS AND ANEMONE.

The frames must have plenty of air, and give frequent sprinklings of water. The sashes or boards should be taken entirely off every mild day, and in fine nights leave them exposed to the dew; stir up the earth amongst them, breaking it fine, making all neat. They require liberal supplies of water after they begin to grow.

ROSES.

This is the most favourable month for planting all kinds of garden roses, which must be done as soon as the weather opens, and the ground in a proper state. The earlier in the month they flower the more perfect they will be. Never delay planting when there is an opportunity; for if delayed until the leaves are expanding, the bloom will be much weakened, and the probability is there will be no flowers, and the plants meet with a premature death. It has been said, "there is a particular advantage in planting some every ten days, even to the middle of May; for the flowering of them may be retarded in this way, and the bloom of these delightful shrubs continue for a much longer period." One moment's reflection will convince us, that nature, while in her own element, will not be retarded, suppose there was no danger of instantaneous death to the plants. The artificial means that might be judiciously adopted, with which we are acquainted, to keep back the blooming of hardy plants, is to lift them as soon in spring as is practicable, put them in boxes of earth, and then place them in the driest part of an icehouse until the desired time of planting, which may be delayed as long as the required time of flowering. This will be found a true method of retarding the flowering of roses especially, and not going counter to the rules and principles of nature. There are many beautiful varieties of the garden rose in cultivation, the names of the finest of which we will give in the Catalogue, but perhaps it may be proper to mention here a few of the most particular sorts. The finest unquestionably when in bloom, is the *Moss* and its varieties, but the flowering is of so limited duration, that it is in a great degree surpassed by others. There is said to be a striped variety of the *Moss Rose*, but we do not credit it. The *Blush Moss*, *Clinton White Moss*, and *Mottled Moss*, at present certainly are the most superb of that kind. *Lee's Crimson Perpetual* is a magnificent rose, and flowers in profusion from June to October. This is considered, and justly too, the finest of all the garden roses; its fragrance is exquisite, and the plant highly valued. There is a striped *Unique Rose*, and a *Rosa tricolor*, which are much thought of. We have mentioned these as the finest we have seen, but amongst two thousand cultivated varieties of the garden rose, there must be many of equal beauty. Of *Rósa spinosíssima* there are above three hundred varieties; *R. gàllica*; two hundred; *R. centifòlia*, one hundred and fifty; R. *damascène*, above one hundred; R. *álba*, fifty; R. *rubiginósa*, thirty; and of various sorts above eleven hundred. In several individual collections of Europe, there are cultivated above fifteen hundred species, sub-species, and varieties.

When planted, they are too frequently crowded indiscriminately amongst other shrubs, which prevents them having the effect they would have if planted singly or grouped. They vary in size in different sorts from one to ten feet. When planted in the latter method, they should be assimilated in size of leaves and manner of growth, with the greatest variation of flower; or if planted in many small patches, giving each a distinct colour, which has a picturesque effect. An other desirable and fanciful method, is to plant them in figures, giving them edgings of wire, willow, or any other substitute, in imitation of basket work, which is called "baskets of roses;" the ground enclosed in the basket margin to be made convex, which will present a greater surface to the eye; the strong shoots to be layered, or kept down by pegs into the ground, having the points of the shoots only to appear above the soil, which should be covered with moss. With this treatment, in a few years the whole surface of the basket will be covered with rose buds and leaves, of one or various sorts. If two or three of the larger growing sorts are taken, such as *Moss* or *Provins*, they may be trained so as to cover a surface of several square yards. One of these covered with *Lee's Crimson Perpetual Rose*, would be one of the greatest ornaments of the Flower-garden.

A modern invention in the cultivation of the rose is, to grow them in shape of trees, by budding on strong growing kinds at different heights from the ground, according to taste, and the purposes intended. They will form in a few years handsome round heads, which will flower more freely than by layers, or trained on their own stalk. They are particularly desirable amongst low shrubs. When planted, they should be well supported by strong rods, to prevent the wind from destroying them. If any of the roots have been bruised in lifting, cut off the bruised part with the knife, and likewise shorten the young shoots; breaking the earth well about their roots when planting. This has been an esteemed shrub among all civilized nations. The flowers are double, semi-double, and single; the colours are pink, red, purple, white, yellow, and striped, with almost every shade and mixture; the odour universally grateful. This plant is cultivated in every garden, from the humblest cottager to the loftiest prince, and by commercial gardeners in Europe extensively, for distilling rose water, and making the essential oil of roses. They delight in a rich loamy soil, and require plenty of moisture while in a growing state. Those sorts which throw up numerous suckers should be lifted every three or four years, reduced, and then transplanted. When thus removing them, avoid as much as possible exposing their roots; and when newly planted, mulching is of considerable advantage; that is, putting half rotten stable-manure on the surface of the ground round their roots, which prevents evaporation, and keeps up a constant moisture. If this was done in general to our roses in dry seasons, it would greatly improve their flowering. For China roses see next month.

CLIMBING ROSES.

This is the best time to prune ever-blooming climbing roses, such as *Champney*, *Scarlet Cluster*, *Duchesse de Dino*, *Notsette*, *Burgenville*, &c. Many of these, when allowed to grow year after year without pruning, become unsightly; they never bear flowers on the old wood, that is, wood of three or four years. Having a tendency to throw out young shoots from the bottom of the stem, the old wood should be cut out, thus encouraging the young wood, which the second year bears the most and finest flowers. In severe winters, the extremities of the shoots are frequently killed, and we have often seen all the wood black or brown, and apparently dead. When that is the case it is best to leave it until they begin to grow, which will show what is dead or alive, when they can be pruned to better advantage.

DECIDUOUS ORNAMENTAL FLOWERING SHRUBS.

The earlier the planting of these shrubs is attended to in this month, the more will their growth and flowering be promoted, having all finished before the buds begin to expand. (For kinds recommended see List, end of the volume.) They should never be planted too thick, but leave space for them to grow as they respectively require, and according as they are designed for open or close shrubberies, clumps, or thickets. Have all in readiness, that it may be done with as much expedition as possible, to prevent their roots from being dried by the sun and wind in time of planting. Make the holes intended for their reception round, capacious, and deep enough to hold their roots, without confining them in the least, and loosen the bottom well, putting new and fresh soil under their roots, breaking and pulverizing it during the operation, and frequently shaking the plant as you progress in filling up. When done, make all firm with the foot, leaving a circular cavity to hold the water they will require during dry weather. Give rods, and tie with bands all that need that support before they are left, lest they should be neglected. Cut off any of the bruised roots or irregular growths of the branches.

GRASS PLATS AND WALKS.

Rake and sweep off from these all litter and worm cast earth, and give an occasional rolling to settle the ground, and render the surface smooth, where the scythe is to be used. The grass will likewise grow better by rolling it where the frost has partially thrown it out, and add greatly to the beauty of the whole. Cut the edgings with an edging iron or spade, so that the whole will have a finished appearance. If any new turf is required to be laid down, this is a very good time to do it, before vegetation is strong; as the turf that is now laid will have taken root before the dry season commences. Where a great extent is to be done, sowing might be adopted; but it will not have the effect of turf under three years, and during that time must be carefully cut, after the first season, every three weeks, while growing, nor must it be walked upon. White clover and true perennial rye-grass are the seeds most proper for sowing. The ground must in the first place be all equally made up, and levelled with the spade and rake; not "cart loads of soil laid down and leveled," which would finally become very uneven, and would need to be lifted and relaid next year. The best turf is that of a close growing pasture or common, free from all kinds of weeds or strong roots, and the grass short. To cut it expeditiously, be provided with a turfing-iron; but if that cannot be conveniently had, a spade may do very well. Strain a line tight, cutting the turf lengthways, at equal distances, from twelve to eighteen inches. Next draw the line across, cutting from one and a half to two feet; then cut them up with the spade, about one and a half inch thick. In laying, join them close and alternately; when done, beat them firm with a level wooden beater, and roll with a heavy roller.

Grass walks, in the last century, were very popular; but time having put them to the test, they are found unfit for walking upon or using in any manner, almost for one half of the year; therefore not answering the purposes intended. They require great attention to keep them in order; and if not always neat and clean, they are a disagreeable object in a garden; but when they are well dressed, their effect is very enlivening. Where they are desired, prepare the ground as above directed; making the walk a little higher than the adjoining borders, to prevent the earth from being washed on it by the rain. Allowing the walks to be six feet wide, make the centre five inches higher than the sides, or about seven-eighths of an inch to the foot whatever the breadth may be, which will form a gentle declivity to throw off the rain. When laid, beat and roll it well; cutting the edge neat and even. Water frequently if the weather sets in dry. To keep grass walks or plats in order, they should be mown once every three or four weeks from May to September, and the grass each time swept clean off. When the grass is allowed to get long before being cut, the roots become tender; and die when exposed to the sun; at last the grass is all in spots, and in another year requires to be relaid.

GRAVEL WALKS.

A practice once existed of turning these into heaps or ridges during winter to destroy weeds, &c. But this has almost been given up as unnecessary, unsightly, inconvenient, and not doing any material service.

Where the surface of these has become foul, irregular, or mossy, they had better be turned over four or five inches deep where the gravel will admit of it; but if not, hoe and rake them perfectly clean, give a new coat of gravel, and pick up any stones that you think too large; then give them a good rolling, applying it frequently after showers of rain. When they are well attended to just now, they will look well all the season; but if neglected, they take more labour, and are never in such good condition.

Fancy edgings of *Thyme*, *Thrift*, *Gentiana*, *Lavender*, and *Violets*—(*Daisies* may be used if the situation is shaded.) The whole of these may be planted by the line with the dibber except *Thyme*, which lay as directed for *Box*. See this month, under that head. Any time in this or beginning of next month will answer to make edgings of these; and if dry weather occurs before they begin to grow after planting, they must have frequent waterings until they have taken fresh root. Thyme requires to be dressed twice during the season to keep it in order.

OF GRAFTING.

There are four methods of grafting. The one we will describe is *whip* or *tongue grafting*, which is the preferable and most expeditious plan with all deciduous shrubs or trees. The stock upon which it is performed must be slender, from two-thirds of an inch to any diameter suitable to the thickness of the graft. Having headed the stock at a clear smooth part, slope it on one side with a sharp knife at a very acute angle, make a slit on the lower side of the slope about an inch downwards, to receive the tongue or wedge of the graft or scion. Secondly, having the prepared scions cut into lengths of 3, 4, or 5 eyes, take one which matches the stock in size, and slope the bottom of it so as to fit the stock, that the rinds of both may correspond exactly, especially on one side and at bottom; make also a slit upward in the graft, like that in the slope of the stock, so as the one may be inserted in the other as evenly and completely as possible. Let the graft be carefully held in its due position, while a bandage is applied. Take strands of Russian mat, and bind them in a neat manner several times round the stock and graft. Lastly, cover the joint with well worked clay, coat from half an inch below the bottom of the graft to an inch above the top of the stock, and to the thickness of half an inch all round, finish it in an oblong globular form, taking care to work it close, that no air may penetrate. If the clay is covered with moss, it will partially prevent it from cracking.

The grafts will have taken when they begin to grow freely; then the clay may be taken off, and the bandage loosened, and put on again, but not so tight; give the grafts a stake for support, tying them thereto to prevent accidents from the wind. Allow no shoots to arise from the stock.

Any of the rare deciduous trees may, by the above method, be grafted on one of its own family, that is more common, and in that respect is the finest species of propagation that is resorted to.

MARCH.

If the plants in these situations have been properly attended to by admitting air at all favourable times, and when the apartment was below 36° a little fire heat applied to counteract the cold, keeping the heat above that degree; your attention will be rewarded by the healthy appearance of your plants. The weather by this time has generally become milder, so that air may be more freely admitted, especially from ten to three o'clock. Where the leaves are grown to one side, turn the plant with the dark side to the light. They will require a more liberal supply of water, but always avoid keeping them wet. Pick off all decayed leaves, and tie up any straggling shoots; stir up the earth on the top of the pots, breaking it fine where it is hardened by the frequent waterings. This will allow the fresh air to act upon the roots, which is one of the principal assistants in vegetation. For those that require shifting or repotting, see *Green-house, March*; the plants enumerated there equally apply here, if they are in the collection, with this difference, that well kept rooms are about two weeks earlier than the Green-house. After the end of this month, where there is a convenience, plants will do better in windows that look to the east, in which the direct rays of a hot sun are prevented from falling upon them, and the morning sun is more congenial for plants in this country than the afternoon sun. Where there is any dust on the leaves of any of them, take a sponge and water, and make the whole clean, likewise divest them of all insects. The green-fly is perhaps on the roses; if there are no conveniences for fumigating, wash them off as previously directed. Where there are only a few plants, these pests could be very easily kept off by examining the plants every day. For the scaly insect, see *January*. If they have not been cleared off, get it done directly; for by the heat of the weather they will increase tenfold.

FLOWERING PLANTS.

Hyacinths, *Tulips*, *Narcissus*, *Jonquils*, and *Crocus*, will be generally in flower. The former requires plenty of water, and the saucers under the pots should be constantly full until they are done blooming. The others need only be liberally supplied at the surface of the pot. Give them neat green-painted rods to support their flower stems, and keep them all near the light. The spring flowering *Oxalis* will not open except it is exposed to the full rays of the sun. The *Lachenàlia* is greatly improved in colour with exposure to the sun, though when in flower its beauties are preserved by keeping it a little in the shade.

Prímulas, or Primrose, both Chinese and European, delight in an airy exposure; but the sun destroys the beauty of their flowers by making the colours fade.

Camélias. Many of them will be in perfection. See Green-house this month for a description of the finest varieties. Do not let the sun shine upon the blooms. Those that are done flowering, will, in small pots, require to be repotted. The *Cálla* or Æthopian water-lily, when in flower, ought to stand in saucers with water.

The Hyacinths that are in glasses must be regularly supplied with water. The roots will be very much reduced by this method; therefore, when the bloom is over, if possible plant them in the garden, or bury them in pots of earth, to ripen and strengthen the bulbs. They will take two years with good encouragement, before they can satisfactorily be again flowered in glasses, and properly they ought not be allowed to bloom next year. Those that are done flowering in pots, can be set aside, and the usual waterings gradually withdrawn. Treat all other Dutch bulbs in a similar manner.

Hot-House.

APRIL.

Where the Hot-house has been properly conducted, the plants generally will have a vigorous and healthful aspect. An error frequently arises in the conducting of these departments, by inexperienced operators being ambitious of outstripping their competitors. They keep the house in a very high temperature, and admit little or no air. Where such mode has been pursued, the plants will have got over their first growth, and the foliage look yellow and decaying, thus throwing the plants into a state of inactivity, when nature herself commences her most active movements. The temperature should not be under 60° nor much above 75°, without admitting a little air by the top lights. It will not do yet to give air by the front sashes, the wind being cool, and a current in the house would be hurtful. The sun is not so powerful but the heat can be kept down by the air given from above. In very cold cutting winds, though the effects of sun heat be great, admitting of much air may be injurious. Whatever error may arise, let it be on the side of caution. However, when high winds prevail, there is little danger of the house becoming overheated by the effect of the sun. Hot-house or tropical plants will not be hurt with 110°, if they are not touching the glass. And if the plants are near the glass generally, the glass should have a coat of very thin white-wash (not lime), where the glass is thin and light in colour; but if it is thick and green, there need be no white-washing.

The plants will need a liberal supply of water every day. We have so constantly cautioned the operator on administering this element, that a repetition here is unnecessary. Sprinkle them well with the syringe or engine in the evenings about sundown, four or five times a week, and strictly observe that none of them are omitted; for where there are such, it is probable they are attacked by the red spider. If any of these are detected, syringe them powerfully morning and evening. Water is most effectual in their destruction, and most congenial to the plants. Give regular fumigations to destroy the green-fly. Wherever there is dust or foulness contracted on the foliage, wash all clean with sponge and water; for on these insects are harboured in such quantities that they, in a short time, would overrun all the plants in the house. Keeping the house constantly clean, the plants clear of decayed leaves and every thing of a corroding nature, and duly syringing them, is the surest method of not being much troubled with insects.

For repotting plants, see next month; except those that you are fostering to a great extent, such as *Alstrœmèrias*, *Calceolàrias*, or any herbaceous plants that require great encouragement to make them flower well. These should always be repotted, as soon as the roots come to be round the outside of the ball.

APRIL.

Regarding the shifting or repotting of plants, the directions given last month may be followed. If the plants are not shifted that require it, get them done as soon as possible, for they will soon get into a luxuriant state of growth, and then it would not be advisable to shift them. Those that were repotted last month will have taken fresh root in the new soil, and the advantage will soon be perceptible. In order to strengthen the plants, and keep them from becoming drawn and spindly, admit large portions of air every mild day. Indeed there will be very few days in this month, that a little air may not be given, always observing to divide the quantity regularly over the house, in cool nights closing in time. About the end of the month an abundance of air is indispensable, leaving the sashes and doors open every mild night, that the plants may be inured to the open exposure they will have in a few weeks.

WATERING.

As the season advances and vegetation increases, the waterings will require to be more copious and more frequent. Look over all plants minutely every day, and with judicious care supply their wants. Those that are of a soft shrubby nature, and in a free-growing state, will require a larger portion at one time than those of a hard texture, which may only want it every two or three days. The weather and situation in some instances may require a modification of these directions. Plants in general will not suffer so soon from being a little dry as from being over-watered. The health and beauty of the foliage of the plants may be much improved by syringing them freely three evenings in the week, except in moist weather, when it ought not to be done. The ravages of many insects also will be retarded, especially mildew and red spider, which will be entirely destroyed. If the red spider is on any of the plants, particularly take them aside evening and morning, and give them a good dashing with water through the syringe. Where there is mildew, after syringing the plant, dust it on the affected parts with flowers of sulphur, and set them for a few days where they will be sheltered from the wind, after which wash off the sulphur. If the cure is not complete, renew the dose. Always sweep out and dry up the water in the house when any is spilt. The succulent plants will be in want of a little water about once a week, but do not overwater them, as there is not heat enough to absorb much moisture. If the soil is damp, it is quite sufficient.

ORANGES, LEMONS, &c.

Will in many instances about the end of this month be showing flowers or flower buds. They must under these circumstances have plenty of air to prevent them from falling off when entirely exposed. The reason that we see so much fine blossom falling to the ground where the trees are brought out of the house in May, is from the confinement they have had. Where there is a convenience of giving air from the back of the Green-house, it should always be given in mild days, especially in those houses that have a recess back from the top of the sashes, for even if the sashes are let down every day, still the house will not be properly ventilated. Any plants that are sickly and intended to be planted in the garden next month to renovate their growth, may be cut back, (if not already done,) as far as is required to give the tree a handsome form, taking care not to cut below the graft or inoculation. Let the operation be done with a fine saw and sharp knife, smoothing the amputations that are made by the saw; and if they are large, put a little well made clay over the wound, to prevent the air from mortifying the shoot. Turpentine is preferable to clay, not being subject to crack or fall off by the weather.

If there are any *Lagerstrœmias*, *Pomegranate*, or *Hydràngeas* in the cellar, they should be brought out about the first of the month, and planted in their respective situations. Give the *Hydràngea* a very shady spot. It does not require one ray of the sun, providing it has plenty of air, and do not plant it into soil that has been lately manured. A large plant must have great supplies of water in dry weather. If the plant is very thick, the oldest branches may be thinned out, but do not cut out any of the young shoots, as they contain the embryo of the flower. *Lagerstrœmias* will flower abundantly without pruning, but to have fine large spikes of flowers, cut in the wood of last year to about three eyes from the wood of the preceding year; by this they will be much finer.

Pomegranates will only require a little of the superfluous wood cut out. Perhaps some of them may be desired to flower in pots or tubs during summer: the balls will admit of being much reduced, and by this a pot or tub very little larger will do for them. Do not give much water until they begin to grow.

MYRTLES AND OLEANDERS.

If any of these have grown irregularly, and are not headed down or otherwise pruned, as directed last month, they should now be done. Oleanders are very subject to the white scaly insect, and before the heat of summer begins, they should be completely cleansed. This insect is likewise found on *Myrtles*, which are worse to clean, and ought to be minutely examined twice every year. We have observed mildew on these shrubs, which makes the foliage brown and unsightly. If it is detected in time, syringing is an effectual remedy.

GERANIUMS.

Some of the earliest blooming kinds of these will now begin to flower, and the sun will greatly deteriorate their rich colours where they are near the glass with a south aspect. The glass should be white-washed, which will cast a thin shade over them, and prolong the duration of the bloom, but if they are above five feet from the glass, white-washing is not requisite. The strong kinds will be growing very luxuriantly, and require liberal supplies of water. When syringing, do not sprinkle the flowers, as it would make the colours intermingle with each other, and cause them to decay prematurely. If they have been properly attended to in that respect, it may be dispensed with after they have generally come in flower, which will not be until about the first of May.

HERBACEOUS PLANTS AND BULBOUS ROOTS.

If any of the herbaceous plants were neglected to be divided last month, do not omit it now. They will not flower so well if potted entire, and their growth by this time will be much hurt, if not carefully shaded from the sun. After dividing, sprinkle gently with water three times a day, until they have taken fresh root, when they can be put amongst the other plants.

Cape Bulbs. Those that flowered late in autumn, as soon as the foliage begins to decay, may be set aside, and the water withheld by degrees. When the foliage is entirely gone, and the roots dry, clear them from the earth, and after laying exposed in the shade for a few days to dry, pack them up in dry moss, with their respective names attached, until August, when they may be again potted. Treat those that are in flower the same as directed in last month.

Dutch Roots. All the species and varieties of these that have been kept in the Green-house during winter, will now be done flowering; the water should be withdrawn gradually from them; and then the pots turned on their sides to ripen the bulbs. Or, a superior method is, where there is the convenience of a garden, to select a bed not much exposed. Turn the balls out of the pots and plant them; the roots will ripen better this way than any other. Have them correctly marked, that no error may take place. They can be lifted with the other garden bulbs.

FLOWERING PLANTS.

The best situation for most plants while in flower, is where they are shaded from the sun, and fully exposed to the air. *Primroses*, both European and Chinese, flower best, and the colours are finest when the plants are in the front of the house, and entirely shaded from the sun. The Chinese *Azàleas* and *Rhododéndrons* require, while in flower, a similar situation. Have all the shoots tied naturally to neat rods, and keep them clear from others by elevating them on empty pots, or any other substitute. See that there are no insect upon them; for they make a miserable contrast with flowers. The *Cálla æthiopica* should stand in water when in flower, and even before flowering they will be much strengthened by it.

INSECTS.

Insects will on some plants be very perplexing. The weather may admit of those that are infected to be taken out of doors, and put into a frame in any way that is most convenient. Fumigating them about half an hour, if the day is calm, will be sufficient; but if windy, they will take an hour. When done, syringe them well, and put them in their respective situations. By the above method, the house will not be made disagreeable with the fumes of tobacco.

Tie up neatly all the climbing plants. Keep those that are running up the rafters of the house close to the longitudinal wires. As previously observed, running plants should not be taken across the house, except in some instances where it can be done over the pathway, otherwise it shades the house too much. Clear off all decayed leaves, and all contracted foulness, that the house and plants may in this month have an enlivening aspect, as it is undoubtedly one of the most interesting seasons of the year in the Green-house.

FLOWERING STOCKS.

Those that have been kept in the Green-house, or in frames, should be planted into beds or the borders, where they will seed better than if kept in the pots. The method generally adopted is to select the plants that are intended for seed; plant the different kinds distinctly and separately; then take a few double flowering plants of each kind, which plant round their respective single varieties that are to be kept for seed. Whenever any of the colours sport, that is, become spotted or striped with other colours, pull these up, and destroy them, for they will soon degenerate the whole, and ought never to be seen in collections that have any pretensions to purity. Many have been the plans recommended as the best for saving, and growing from seed the double varieties of German stock. In every method we have tried we have been successful and unsuccessful; although we generally practise planting the double kinds beside the single, where they are intended for seed. We have no scientific reason for it; not seeing what influence these monsters of flowers can have over a flower where the male and female organs are perfect; which in these are wanting. Some say that the semi-double sorts are best: we have likewise found them both abortive and fruitful in the desired results.

Flower Garden.

APRIL.

The ambition of every attentive gardener, during this month, is to be at the head of every department, and over every spot. The operator's activity in this month regulates the whole season. Every weed ought to be cut down as soon as it appears, and the proverbial saying will be realized, "a garden that is well kept is easily kept." A wet day need cause no loss of time. Prepare rods, bands, and tallies, to be in readiness when required. Damp weather should always be taken to prick out or transplant annuals, or stocks, but by no means go on the borders while they are wet. If it cannot be done by keeping on the walks, defer it until they are in a proper state. One day of laborious attention just now will save two in the heat of summer. Many in the height of bustle never finish properly as they proceed, which is the worst of practices. Every operation ought to be completely and properly finished before another is taken in hand, which will ultimately prove the quickest and best method to work upon.

Let digging, pruning, hoeing, raking, &c. be done as expeditiously as strength will allow; that the time may be devoted for a few weeks to the beautifying of the garden by sowing and planting.

ANNUALS.

Those that are tender and were sown last month, according to directions, will be ready to prick out into another light hot-bed, about two feet high, prepared as directed in February. Keep them a few inches apart to let the air circulate. Give them frequent sprinklings with water, and shade them with a mat for a few days until they have taken fresh root; then give them plenty of air, and by the first of next month expose them night and day to harden the plants for the open ground. A few of the annual seeds of every description, and of every country and climate, may be sown any time after the middle of the month. If the season prove favourable they will do well; but reserving a part to sow about the 15th of May, will guard against every extreme.

Those that have come above ground should be thinned out, the dwarf-growing kinds to two or three inches, and the large sorts to four or five inches apart; or they may be only separated about an inch, going over them again in a few weeks; when a few might be taken of those that will bear removing, and plant them in vacant spaces that require filling up. All the varieties of French and African Marygold answer best when transplanted, likewise the species of *Coreopsis* that were sown in autumn. The varieties of *Ten-week Stock*, *Balsams*, *Coxcombs*, and other strong growing sorts, generally flower stronger when replanted.

BIENNIALS AND PERENNIALS.

Any biennials that are intended to be removed, and not done last month, must not be delayed longer. The roots of many of them will be very strong, and if possible a cloudy day should be chosen for the operation. Give copious waterings in the evenings until they begin to grow. When the sun is strong, they must be shaded by a piece of board, shingle, or any similar substitute, for some days. When the seeds of these are sown, they should be distinctly marked. The initial B. is the most appropriate.

Perennials. For a limited description of several genera and species, see last month. Those that have not been divided and replanted, where large, they should be done directly, if the weather is dry. They must be carefully watered, and shaded as above directed for *Biennials*.

DAHLIAS.

Dáhlia supérflua, or what is now called *Georgìana variábilis*, is one of the most fashionable and popular hardy herbaceous plants of the present day. The varieties of the present species are almost endless. The double kinds only are cultivated, the single varieties having been thrown aside. Several collections in Europe contain upwards of three hundred double varieties, of every colour and taste, occupying more than two acres of ground. It will be difficult to specify the finest; but in this country the dwarf-growing sorts are preferred. To make them flower freely, they should be planted in poor heavy soil. From the end of this month to the middle of May, take the roots from their winter quarters to the garden, and with a spade make a hole sufficiently wide and deep to receive the crowns of the roots one inch deeper than the surface of the ground, cutting off with a sharp knife the old stumps close to the eyes. They have the finest effect in rows; plant them four feet apart in the row, and the rows six feet asunder. Individual plants of a dwarf nature look extremely well. The best one for this is the *Dwarf Globe Crimson*, and is perhaps the finest that is known, being prolific, compact, beautiful, and very dwarf, never exceeding three feet: if properly grown, *Púlla elècta*, *Famæa*, and *Zenò*, are also fine dwarf sorts; as tall growing kinds *Etna*; *Imperiòsa*; *Ciceró*; *Cocàde*; *Cambridge Surprise*; *Dutchess of Wellington*; *Countess of Liverpool*; *Barret's William Fourth*; *True Mountain of Snow*; *Diàna*; *Crimson Bonnet*; and *Exímia*, are all superb, and at present the highest in estimation. For the names of more of the finest varieties, with their colour, see Catalogue at the end of the work.

When the roots become very large, they ought to be divided, and in dry seasons they require to be liberally supplied with water to keep them growing. If their growth is obstructed, the flowering will be imperfect. Where they are grown to any extent, it would be advisable to put up a large hot-bed about the end of March, and plant them close together therein, about the beginning of April, which would immediately cause them to grow. Give plenty of air, and about the middle of May plant them in the borders, beds, or rows, which will in cool seasons cause them to flower earlier.

The flowers are from three to eight inches in diameter. There ought to be a few of the most distinct and superb varieties, in every garden. Some individuals consider the *Anemoné-flowered* varieties the finest; but those who never saw a *Dáhlia* flower of any character, would, in our opinion, chose the large petaled flowers. The *Anemoné-flowered* sorts likewise are not so large in flower as the other varieties.

The foliage has no particular attraction about it; the stems look strong, but are soft in substance. If seeds are sown on a hot-bed in March, most of them will flower the same year, by transplanting in the garden about the end of May; but the fine double kinds seldom produce seeds.

CHINA ROSES.

From the first to the middle of this month is the best time to plant the varieties of Chinese roses. If they are to be removed out of the ground, the earlier in the month the better; but where they are in pots, the precise time is not so material. There are about seventy varieties, including the species of these in cultivation; all of them do extremely well in this country, growing freely, and flowering abundantly in the open air. A few of them require protection during winter. The List at the end of the work will contain all the finest varieties; but as they are not generally known, and the greater part of them highly deserving a situation in every garden, a few limited specific observations is obviously desirable to those who are not acquainted with their beauty and fragrance.

No. 1. *Ròsa índica*, common China or daily. From the last name an error has taken place, that it blooms every day. In one sense of the word it does. Plants that are young, and in good ground, will grow and flower constantly from the end of April until the buds are killed with frost; but they will never flower when not growing; the bloom being produced on the young wood. The flower is about three inches in diameter, of a dark blush or rose colour, petals large, and loose, between a semi-double and double, and perfectly hardy.

No. 2. *[B] *Rose Animated*, daily, is a very fine rose, and its merits are appreciated by those who have it in their collections. It is more double, and better formed than No. 1, and partakes of the fragrance of No. 8, is perfectly hardy, colour a fine blush, grows freely, and flowers abundantly; and is coming into great repute.

[B] Those marked thus * we have grown from seed.

No. 3. *Rosa Indìca mínor*, is the smallest of the China roses that we are familiar with; about the end of April or beginning of May it is completely covered with pretty little flowers, and much admired for its diminutiveness: colour same as No. 1.

No. 4. *Rosa Bengal elongáta*, named from the foliage being more elongate than the other common roses. It grows and flowers freely, petals large, colour light red, very distinguishable from any of the other sorts.

No. 5. *Rosa belle Chinese*, is a beautiful French rose, and blooms in great abundance; flowers large and double, colour when first expanded pink, and changes to crimson, making a striking appearance, and greatly admired.

No. 6. *Rosa la tendere japonica*, an erect growing rose, of a handsome purple colour, with large petals; much like the garden velvet rose.

No. 7. *Rosa belle vibert*, does not produce so large flowers as the three last mentioned; but they are very double, blooming abundantly in the latter part of summer; colour very dark, and by some called the Black China Rose.

No. 8. *Rosa odoràta*, or Tea-rose, celebrated in this country for its fragrance being similar to fine Hyson tea. It justly deserves the preference of all the China roses, for the delicacy of its flavour. The flowers are a cream coloured blush, the petals round and full, forming a very large rose; when full blown, it is pendulous. It will withstand the winter of the middle states with a little protection, such as straw, box, or barrel; requires very rich light soil.

No. 9. *Rosa Florence*, or Scarlet-tea. This rose partakes of the fragrance of No. 8, is perfectly hardy, grows freely, and flowers profusely. The flower is well formed, very double, and a distinct variety from any that we know. The flower is lightest when first expanded.

No. 10. *Rose, Purple-tea.* We have not found how this name has originated: but when the plant known in our collections under that name is compared, there is no difference between it and No. 9.

No. 11. *Rosa odoràta álba*, or White-tea, is not so odorous as No. 8, but blooms more profusely, and grows more freely. The beautiful and neat appearance of the buds, when half expanded, is not surpassed; and when full blown, they are a fine delicate white. The bush in that state is showy, much admired, and scarce; we are not positive of its being hardy.

No. 12. *Rosa Bengal*, or Yellow-tea, is a very free flowerer, the shape of the flower is more like No. 8. than any of the others; the petals are large and gracefully set, having a peculiar scent or flavour, and is of a sulphur colour. We cannot say as to its being hardy, but suppose it as much so as No. 8.

No. 13. *Rosa Venella*, or Venella Scented-tea, is undoubtedly a handsome rose, and has many admirers; colour a bloody velvet; flowers large and very double, rising in the centre more than any of the others; blooming freely, and of pleasant flavour; rendering it altogether a desirable rose.

No. 14. *Rosa belle de monza.* The flower of this rose is flatter than any of the other sorts; the petals are regularly laid over each other making it very compact; it is about four inches in diameter when well grown; the plant is of quick growth, free in flowering, darker in colour than No. 1, equally as hardy, and ought to have a situation in every garden where roses are grown.

No. 15. *Rosa amaránthe*, is a showy brilliant scarlet rose, flower compact, and of a moderate size.

No. 16. **Rosa Clintónia*, is a good rose, and in a favourable situation will produce abundantly large, round, and compact flowers, differing in shape from any of the others; colour similar to the provins rose.

No. 17. *Rosa semperflòrens plèno*, or sanguinea, is a celebrated rose, the foliage small, and of a reddish appearance. The flower is well shaped, and of a blood colour; wood of a slender growth, requires some protection in winter, or it will die to the surface of the ground; delights in sandy soil. This rose is frequently called anemone-flowered, though in no respects similar to the character of an anemone-flower. The *Otaheite* rose is of the same colour, but very inferior.

No. 18. **Rosa purple sanguinea*, is of a purple colour, same in shape as No. 17, but in size larger; is a good flowerer, making a fine variety. We do not know any similar to it.

No. 19. *Rosa grandvàl*, is a magnificent rose; flower full and large, petals closely set, colour dark crimson. The wood and leaves are like the *Hamilton* rose, but it grows and flowers more freely. It is scarce.

No. 20. *Rosa Indica álba plèno*, or white China, is a rose of free growth, abundant in flower, and pure white, which renders it very desirable; is larger than No. 1, is greatly admired, and rare; requires rich light soil.

No. 21. *Rosa Magnifier, magnificent*, or *magnìfica*. It is known under all these names. The general appearance of the plant resembles No. 19, but the flowers in shape and colour are similar to the garden Provins rose, and nearly as large.

No. 22. **Rosa florabùnda multiplèx*. This rose is very correctly named, although the plant is of a moderate stature. The whole is covered with immense clusters of various coloured flowers, changing from pink to dark crimson; the flowers very double, and greatly admired.

No. 23. **Rosa flamæa*, has a very striking appearance, is of a flame colour, and distinct from any other of the China roses; blooms freely, and is a little fragrant, which makes it desirable.

No. 24. **Rosa Hibbèrtia*, is a superb rose of a light red colour; flower of a common size, double and compact, very fragrant, and abundant in bloom. The buds are of a particular shape, being flat at the extremity where others are pointed. It is highly deserving of a situation, and universally admired.

No. 25. **Rosa Jacksónia*, is deep red, large, and very double, of luxuriant growth; is more spiny and elastic than any of the China roses that have come under our observation. The plant altogether is unique in its character, and flowers profusely.

No. 26. *R. Adamsônia*, is dwarf growing; has flowers of a beautiful purple velvet colour, inclining to black; and is much admired. When well grown, it will bloom freely.

No. 27. **Rosa Webestèria.*[C] None of the China roses approaches this, except *Hortensia*, and it is much inferior. The rose is very double, and particularly well formed; colour similar to No. 8, with a beautiful rich blush in the centre, flowing to the extremity of the petals. It blooms profusely, and grows freely in light rich soil.

[C] Named in honour of D. Webster, Esq. whose productions deserve a place in every library; and this plant a spot in every garden.

No. 28. *Rosa gigántea.* Without exception, this is the handsomest shaped China rose that has come under our observation, the colour dark crimson, with a few shades through it. The centre is full set; petals regular and large, the flower very double, plant strong, growing and free blooming—it is scarce.

No. 29. *Rosa Washington*,[D] is a very good and distinct variety; the foliage is pale green with red nerves; flower full and compact, the extremity of the petals dark red, the bottom white; showing, when the flower is full expanded, a white centre, and is frequently a little striped; grows well, and blooms freely, in light sandy soil.

[D] Originated on the substantial establishment of D. & C. Landreth, and called by them "Scarlet and White."

No. 30. **Rosa calyxifòlia*. The calyx of this rose has large leaflets attached to it. It blooms very early, and is of a deep crimson colour, with recurved petals, which give it a singular and beautiful appearance. The young shoots and leaves are of a purple hue. It grows and flowers freely, and is quite characteristic, and surpasses any we know for flowering early in the Green-house or Rooms.

No. 31. *Rosa Montezùma* (Mexican-rose.) This is an esteemed variety, with large double flowers of a red colour, and when the flowers begin to fade they become darker; it is of a strong growing and hardy nature, much admired, and scarce.

No. 32. *Rosa horténsia.* The buds of this rose are very beautiful before expansion, and when fully expanded, are of a fine colour, assimilated to No. 8; flowers large in proportion to the growth of the plant.

These roses are all of a shrubby nature, and the finest flowering varieties that have come under our observation and culture. The China roses generally are not completely double, though going under the name of double flowers, and having the appearance of such. Those that are mentioned above as *double* and *very double* are those that are more double than No. 1, which is a rose that is generally known. The whole of them are much admired, and being now of great variety in colour, shade and aspect, constitute a valuable addition to the Flower-garden. A bed of varieties planted therein in good light rich soil, and well dressed by hoeing deep, raking, &c. during the early stage of their growth every season, will form an ornament varied in colour, unrivalled, and as yet not found in our Flower-gardens. Their nature agrees so well with our summer seasons, that it will not surprise us to see, in a few years, selections of them planted in rows or hedges, dividing the compartments in our gardens.

They are all hardy, but of those that are not perfectly so, we have mentioned the required protection. Any of them that have not been proved hardy in your collections, it would be extremely injudicious to leave them exposed the first winter after planting out. Caution is necessary on every unknown point; therefore, we would recommend to give them slight protection, by a covering of straw, mats, boxes, &c. and if they appear to withstand the winter in perfect safety, they will not need again to be covered.

The best season of the year for pruning them is about the first of this month. In doing so it is not advisable to shorten any of the young shoots, except in cutting off the injured parts, that being the wood most productive of bloom; but where there is old stinted wood, it should be cut out as close to the surface of the ground as the other parts of the bush will permit, with any other of the oldest wood that is too crowded. If the plants have been long established, dig in amongst their roots a little well decomposed manure, and stir and hoe them frequently during the summer.

CLIMBING ROSES.

No. 1. *Rosa Champneyàna.* This celebrated rose has a situation in almost every garden in our city, and forms a great ornament, flowering very profusely in immense clusters from May to November. Many of these having more than thirty buds upon them of a light pink colour, it is sometimes called "Pink Cluster." It is of rapid growth, and does well for covering arbours, fences, or any unsightly object. The foliage is of a lucid green, and the wood very strong in growth. This rose is at present one of the most abundant in flower, the easiest of cultivation, (growing in any exposure,) and in every respect is highly deserving of attention.

No. 2. *Rosa blush Noisettià* is very similar to No. 1. in habit; the flowers are lighter in colour, and a little larger; but the plant does not flower so profusely during the heat of the season. There is a variety of *Noisettia* in our gardens, known from this by the bud being more rounded, and another under the name of *Charles 10th*, which has fine large flowers of a dark blush colour.

No. 3. *Rosa red Noisettià*, or what we consider more properly *Scarlet cluster.* It is very distinct from any other of the Noisettias in habit. It is an excellent variety, and blooms abundantly; of a scarlet colour; forming a fine contrast with the two last, which are light in colour, and though not generally known is very desirable.

No. 4. *Rosa moschàta*, musk-scented, or white cluster, is an esteemed rose both for profusion of flower and agreeableness in fragrance. It is not of so rapid growth as the three previous, and may be kept as a bush; though it will grow to a considerable height if protected by a wall or close fence, being tacked thereto. Where kept as a bush, in very severe winters, it is the better of a slight covering, and is the latest flowering rose in the garden. The flowers are frequently on the same bush single, semi-double, and double, but mostly semi-double.

No. 5. *Rosa moschàta supérba*, or superb white cluster. This in habit and appearance is the same as No. 4, only the roses are double, and never vary; which makes it a very superior rose. It is highly esteemed and scarce.

No. 6. *Rosa Aralie Noisettià.* This has been called by some *Purple Noisettià*, (which is a very different rose, and not generally known.) In growth it is similar to No. 4, and could be kept in the same manner. The flowers are of a dark pink colour, very prolific, but not so large as No. 2.

These are all what are termed with us ever-blooming roses, being in flower from May until the buds are destroyed by frost. They should be pruned about the first of this month. The young wood is most productive of bloom; where the branches are too crowded, cut out the oldest wood as close to the ground as is practicable, and any of the dead branches. The shoots when tied to the trellis, arbour, wall, or fence, should be about six inches clear. The branches when made fast to their support ought to be in direct lines, which must at all times be strictly observed. It is very unsightly to see shoots trained crooked, or over each other, and, unsightly or unscientifical as it may be, it is too prevalent in every garden.

No. 7. R. *Bourbòn* is a double rose of brilliant red colour, petals large, stiff, and neatly set; the flower about the size of a common Provins rose, and finely scented; grows freely. The wood is strong, and undoubtedly it is the finest climbing rose that has come under our observation, and is highly admired.

No. 8. R. *Boursault.* This rose is much thought of in Europe. It is of a purple colour (and once called *Purpurea*), has a little fragrance, flower nearly the size of No. 7; wood more slender, and of very rapid growth, and capable of covering a large space. When in flower it is very showy. The old wood is of a purple colour. There is a white variety of it.

No. 9. R. *Lisle*, is of a light pink colour, about the shape and size of No. 8, grows freely, and flowers abundantly. This and No. 8. are the hardiest climbing roses that we know.

No. 10. R. *microphylla.* This rose is unique in every character, resembling No. 21. more than any other. The foliage is very small and neat, and the calyx thick and bristly. The flowers are produced at the extremity of the young shoots in twos or threes, according to the strength of the plant; they are large and double; the exterior petals large and full; those of the interior are very short and thick set; the colour in the centre is dark, shading lighter towards the exterior; the spines are in pairs on each side of the compound leaves. It is perfectly hardy, and greatly esteemed, and not so subject to be attacked by insects as other roses.

No. 11. R. *Franklinia*, or Cluster-tea, generally flowers well in May and June, but during the remainder of the season the heat appears to be too strong for it, the buds dropping off before expansion. The flower bud is larger than that of the Tea-rose; the petals large but loose, colour light blush.

No. 12. R. *Bánksiæ*, or Lady Banks' rose, is a free growing kind, and has a lucid green foliage; flowers small white clusters with pink centre, very double, and sweet scented; in bloom during May. From what we have seen of it, the spring months appear too changeable for perfecting all its bloom, many falling off from the chilliness of the nights. The plant naturally is an evergreen, but in our city is deciduous; grows best in sandy soil, and should be protected by mats during winter.

No. 13. R. *Bánksiæ lùtea pléno.* The habit and foliage of this are the same as No. 12, and whether hardy or not we have not proved. In Europe it is considered more hardy than the preceding variety. The flowers are larger, of a fine gold yellow, very double, and neatly set. It is considered very pretty.

No. 14. R. *multiflòra*, was amongst the first climbing roses that was planted in this city, and was so highly admired, that twenty dollars were given for one plant. It bears its flowers in close clusters on the wood of last year; the colour is a deep blush; petals thickly set, making it a close and compact small rose; blooming in June. It is losing its celebrity, and giving place to *Champnèy*, *Noisèttia*, *Grevìllii*, &c.

No. 15. R. *white multiflòra.* In all respects same as No. 14, except in flower, which is much lighter, but not a pure white.

No. 16. R. *scarlet multiflòra*, is darker in colour than No. 14, but is not properly a scarlet flower.

No. 17. R. *purple multiflòra.* We suspect that there is some confusion in this plant being confounded either with *Scarlet multiflòra* or with *Grevìllii.* Plants imported as such have proved to be the latter.

No. 18. R. *Grevìllii*, is a very curious rose, flowered the first time with us in June 1830. It is of the variety of No. 14, and of China origin; growth free and luxuriant; leaves large and deeply nerved; flowers in large clusters, almost every eye of the wood of last year producing one cluster, having on it from eight to twenty roses, according to the state of the plant, each rose expanding differently in colour or shade. Many suppose that they expand all of the same colour, and change afterwards. This is not the case. We have seen them white, pink, red, purple, and various other shades when the bloom expanded; and on two clusters we have observed twenty-two distinct shades of colour. In fact, it is a complete nondescript, having roses, single, semi-double, and double, large and small, and every colour between white and purple, forming, in every garden where it is planted, a wonder of the vegetable world. It is very hardy; an eastern aspect will answer it best, preserving the flowers from the direct rays of the sun, which will keep the colours purer. We readily recommend it to every lover of *Flora*.

No. 19. R. *arvénsis scándens multiplèx*, or double Ayrshire. We imported this rose last year, as being a very double blush, sweet-scented variety. It is highly valued, and said to be more rapid in growth than any other variety, and likewise a profuse flowerer. As far as we know it remains to be proved how it will agree with our climate, and have its high characters substantiated; although we have no reason to doubt the authority we received it from.

No. 20. R. *sempervírens plenò*. This is a most handsome double white rose. The strong shoots of last year will produce a large cluster of flowers from almost every eye, and as a profuse flowering double white climbing rose we have seen none to surpass it. It grows freely, the foliage and wood pure green, leaves much nerved.

No. 21. R. *bracteàta plenò*, double Macartney, is a very fine large double white variety, with strongly marked red edged petals; blooming from May to July. It is very scarce, and grows best in sandy soil.

The best time for pruning those roses which only bloom once in the season, and are of a climbing habit, is immediately after flowering, cutting out all the old wood that has produced flowers, thereby invigorating the young wood that is to bear the flowers the ensuing year; and the stronger the wood of this year can be made to grow, the finer and more profuse will be the flowers. The plants of Nos. 12, 14, 18, and the intermediate varieties, have been pruned on a wrong system. In place of giving them a general dressing in spring, they ought to have it immediately after flowering; the old wood cut out, leaving only the young and such as is of a healthy nature. Avoid crowding them together, and tie them all straight and regular. Never top the shoots except where there is a supply of wood wanted. In spring the only dressing requisite is to cut off the injured shoots or branches, making good the tyings that have given way.

Trellises for these roses are generally made too wide; the shoots cannot be neatly kept to them. They ought never to exceed nine inches between each spar or rod.

There are several species and varieties of climbing roses of high standing in character, but not being perfectly known to us in regard to hardiness, &c. we forbear making any remarks upon them, knowing that much exaggeration exists.

CLIMBING PLANTS.

As shade is much required in this country, and plants suitable for covering arbours, &c. eagerly sought for, we will make a few remarks on those which are preferred for their beauty, growth, hardiness, &c.

Atragène alpìna, is a free growing deciduous shrub, with large blush-coloured flowers, which continue blooming from May to July; has small pinnated foliage.

Clématis viticélla pulchélla, or double purple virgin's bower, is an esteemed climbing plant; of rapid growth, with large flowers in great profusion from June to September. There are several varieties of the above, two of them single, and it is said that there is likewise a double red.

C. flámmula, sweet scented virgin's bower, is of very rapid growth. Established plants will grow from twenty to forty feet in one season, producing at the axils of the young shoots large panicles of small white flowers of exquisite fragrance; the leaves are compound pinnate; in bloom from June to November, but in June, July, September, and October, the flowers are in great profusion, perfuming the whole garden. This is one of the best climbing hardy plants that we know, and it ought to have a situation in every garden.

C. Virgiàna, is of rapid growth, and well adapted for arbours; flowers small white in axillary panicles, diœcious, leaves ternate, segments cordate, acute, coarsely toothed and lobed, in bloom from June to August. A native, and a little fragrant.

C. flòrida plenò, is a fine free flowering plant, though generally considered a shrub, is more herbaceous than shrubby; the flowers are large double white; in growth will not exceed ten feet in one season.

Glycine frutéscens, a beautiful native climbing shrub, known in our gardens under that name, but is properly *Wistèria frutéscens*. It has large pendulous branches of blue (leguminose) flowers, blooming from May to August; pinnated leaves with nine ovate downy leaflets; grows freely.

Glycine chinénsis, is given to Wistèria, and is the finest climbing shrub of the phaseolious tribe. The flowers are light blue, in long nodding many-flowered racemose spikes, blooming from May to August profusely; leaves pinnated, with eleven ovate lanceolate silky leaflets, and is of a very rapid growth. We are not certain if it will withstand our winters without protection.

Bignònia crucígera, is an evergreen which is very desirable in many situations, being likewise of luxuriant growth. It will cover in a few years an area of fifty feet; flowers of an orange scarlet colour, blooming from May to August.

B. grandiflòra, now given to *Tecôma*, has large orange coloured flowers, blooming from June to August, and grows very fast. We are not positive that it will stand our winters without protection.

B. rádicans, is likewise given to *Tecòma*, and is a native plant. When in flower it is highly ornamental, but it requires great attention to keep it in regular order, being of a strong rough nature; in bloom from June to August.

Periplàca græca, is a climber of extraordinary growth. Well established plants grow thirty or forty feet in one season; flowers in clusters from May to July, of a brownish yellow colour, and hairy inside; leaves smooth, ovate, lanceolate, wood slender, twining, and elastic.

Hedéra Hélix, Irish Ivy, is a valuable evergreen for covering naked walls, or any other unsightly object. The foliage is of a lively green, leaves from three to five angled. There are several varieties of it, all valuable for growing in confined shady situations where no other plant will thrive.

Ampelópsis hederàcea. This plant is commonly employed for covering walls, for which the rapidity of its growth, and the largeness of the leaves, render it extremely appropriate. There are several species of the genus, all resembling the *Vine* in habit and in flower.

It is called by some *Císsus hederàcea*, which is certainly improper, this belonging to *Tetandria*, and the former to *Pentandria*.

There are several other plants of a climbing habit, both curious and ornamental; but our limits will not admit of a detail.

DECIDUOUS SHRUBS.

Finish planting all deciduous shrubs in the early part of the month. These plants are generally delayed too long, the leaves in many instances are beginning to expand, thereby giving a check to the ascending sap, which we may safely assert causes the death of one third of the plants, when perhaps the operator or some individual more distantly concerned is blamed.

These shrubs, if properly removed and planted at the exact starting of vegetation, pressing the earth close to their roots when planting, (previously taking care that the small fibres have not become dry by exposure,) will not, by these simple attentions, one out of fifty fail. Those that are late planted should have frequent waterings, and if large, firmly supported, that the wind may have no effect in disturbing the young and tender fibrous roots.

OF PLANTING EVERGREEN SHRUBS.

Now is the season to plant all kinds of evergreen trees and shrubs. In most seasons the middle of the month is the most proper time, the weather then being mild and moist; or if a late season, defer it to the end of the month. When planted earlier, they will remain dormant until this time, and their tender fibrous roots in that case frequently perish from their liability to injury from frost or frosty winds, being more susceptible of such injury than fibres of deciduous plants. They now begin to vegetate, which is the *grand criterion* for transplanting any plant. The buds begin to swell, the roots to push, and if they can be quickly lifted and replanted, they will hardly receive a check. At all events care must be taken that they are not long out of the ground and exposed to the air, which greatly assists the success in planting. It may be observed that evergreens in general succeed the better the smaller they are, although we have seen plants, trees, and evergreens, successfully lifted upwards of thirteen feet high and fifteen in diameter, and carried several miles. By the second year there was no appearance that such operation had taken place. In preparing a hole for the reception of these plants, make it larger than the roots, breaking the bottom thereof fine, and putting in some fresh soil. Place the plant upright in the centre, putting in the earth and breaking it fine, and give the plant a few gentle shakes. When the roots are more than half covered, put in a pot or pail full of water, allowing it to subside, then cover all the roots, give a second or third pail full, and when subsided the earth will be close to all the roots. Cover with more earth, pressing all firm with the foot. Put more soil loosely on, which will give it a finished appearance, and prevent it from becoming dry, and not requiring mulching, which has an unsightly appearance. All that the wind will have any hurtful effect upon, must be firmly supported, especially large plants. If the weather sets in dry and hot, they should be watered as often as necessity shall direct.

Those that are established, it will be necessary to go over them (if not already done) to cut off all wood killed in winter, and also to thin them if too thick and crowded.

When the above is done, let every part of the shrubbery be dressed off as directed in *March*. Shrubs of all kinds will now begin to look gay and lively, which may be very much heightened or depreciated, according to the state in which the ground and contiguous walks are kept. Always keep in view that weeds are no objects of beauty.

CARE OF CHOICE BULBS.

Hyacinths of the earliest sorts will begin to expand and show their colours, of which we can boast of a few as fine sorts in the vicinity of Philadelphia, as in any garden of Europe; but even these very superior sorts, when in bloom, are too frequently neglected, being allowed to stand without rods, stakes, or any means of support, likewise equally exposed to drenching rains and scorching suns; and the finest collections may be seen after heavy rains prostrate on the ground, whereas a few hours' trouble would give them the requisite support, thereby preserving their beauty much longer, and giving more gratification. As soon as the stems advance to any height, they should be supported by wires, rods, &c. and tied slightly thereto with threads of matting, or any other substitute, repeat the tying as they advance, avoid tying amongst the florets, because they grow by extension, and are liable to be broken off by so doing. The sun deteriorates the colours very much, especially the red, blue, and yellow sorts; whereas if they were simply protected from the sun by an awning of thin canvass, the colours would be preserved and the beauty protracted. If there are stakes drove into the ground on each side of the beds, about three feet high, with others in the centre about eight feet, having laths or hoops from the side to the centre, formed similar to the roof of a house, so that people may walk or sit under it, the canvass or awning being thin to admit of the light freely, the effect in the time of sunshine from the brilliancy of the colours is peculiarly gratifying. Where an awning is thus erected, it requires to be kept on only from nine to three o'clock in sunshine days, and during nights or time of rain, allowing the awning on the most northern side to come close to the ground when necessary, to shelter them from cold cutting winds.

Tulips in every respect should have the same care and protection, never neglecting to have the beds with a smooth clean surface, and the stems neatly tied up, although they are not in so much danger as Hyacinths.

The properties of a good Hyacinth are, viz—the stem strong and erect, the florets or bells occupying one half of the stem, each floret suspended by a short strong footstalk, longest at the bottom, the uppermost floret quite erect, so that the whole may form a pyramid. Each floret well filled with petals rising towards the centre, that it may appear to the eye a little convex. Regarding colour, fancy does not agree, and the scrupulous cultivators differ materially. However the more pure and bright the finer, or a white with a pink centre, or the centre of the petals with a paler or deeper colour appearing striped, which is considered to have a good effect.

Those of a good *Tulip* are—the stem strong, elastic, and erect, about two feet high, the flower large and composed of six petals, proceeding a little horizontally at first, and then turning upwards, forming a flat-bottomed cup, rather widest at the top; the three exterior petals should be larger than the three interior ones, and broader at their base; the edges of the petals entire, free from notch or ruggedness; the top of each well rounded; the colour of the flower at the bottom of the cup ought to be pure, white, or yellow, and the rich coloured stripes which are the principal ornament should be pure, bold, regular, and distinct on the margin, and terminate in fine points elegantly pencilled. The centre of each petal should have one bold stripe, or blotch of rich colouring. The ground colours that are most esteemed are white, the purer the finer; or, on the other hand, the dark grounds, and of course the darker the better; but these vary in estimation, according to the prevailing taste of amateurs.

ANEMONES AND RANUNCULUS.

Moist weather and frequent showers are highly essential to the perfecting of these flowers, and if these should fail at this season of the year, artificial means must be used to supply the deficiency. Take a watering-pot without the rose, and run the water (river or rain water is best) gently between the rows, taking care not to make holes in the ground. When they have got a good watering at root, take the syringe and give them a gentle sprinkling in fine evenings, observing not to use force for fear of breaking the flower stems. In dry weather the result of a deficiency of water would be that the stems and flowers of the strongest roots will be weak, and make no progress, and many of them will not bloom; the foliage of a sickly, yellow appearance, from which they would not recover; and the roots when taken up of little use for farther transplanting.

A good plan in dry seasons is to cover the ground between the rows with cow manure, which will prevent the moisture from evaporating, and the rain or water passing through it greatly enriches the soil, and strengthens the roots.

AURICULAS.

Having under this head last month given ample directions for the treatment of these plants previous to flowering, we refer to that head to avoid repetition.

CARNATIONS, PINKS, &c.

If any of these were omitted to be shifted last month, or planted out according to directions therein given, let it be done forthwith. Where they are still protected with frames, give them plenty of air, keeping the sashes entirely off during the day, keep the pots perfectly free from weeds, and give the foliage frequent sprinklings with water.

Polyanthus and *primroses* will be exhibiting their beautiful flowers. They require the same treatment, and delight in moisture and a shaded situation. Do not sprinkle them while in flower, and keep them clear of weeds or decayed leaves, never exposing them to the sun. They are very hardy, and where required may be planted in very shady situations, for they will suffer more from the influence of the sun's rays than from frost. Those plants in pots in general that have been protected in frames, and are destined for the borders, should now as soon as possible be planted in their destined situations, having nothing to fear from chilling winds or frosts after the middle of this month, except in uncommon seasons. Those that are to be kept in pots, if not repotted, do it immediately, and give regular supplies of water.

POLIANTHUS TUBEROSA FLORE PLENO.

This very popular bulb, generally known as *Tuberose*, has been cultivated in England upwards of two centuries, whence we no doubt have received it, and now can return those of our production to supply their demand. The flowers are many and highly odoriferous, and of the purest white, and on a flower stem from three to five feet high. To have them in the greatest perfection, they should be planted in a lively hot-bed, about the first of this month in six inch pots filled with light rich earth, giving very little water until they begin to grow, when they ought to be liberally supplied with plenty of air, and about the end of next month they may be planted in the borders, providing a spot for them that is or has been well worked, and enriched with well decomposed manure. Secure their flower stems to proper rods. Previous to planting the roots, all the off-sets should be taken off and planted separately; keep the crown of the bulb level with the surface of the pot, and when they are replanted in the open ground, put them two inches deeper.

But when the convenience of a hot-bed cannot be obtained, they will succeed very well if planted about the end of this month or first of next in the garden, in a bed of earth prepared for their reception. Let it be dug deep, and make the soil light and rich, by giving it a good supply of manure two years old, well broken and incorporated with the earth, adding a little sand where the soil is heavy. The black earth from the woods produced from decayed leaves is equally as good without sand. Having the ground in proper order, draw drills about two and a half inches deep, and eighteen inches apart; plant the bulbs (after divesting them of their off-sets) nine inches apart in the row, covering the crown of the bulb about an inch and a half. When done, carefully rake and finish off the beds. When they shoot up their flower stems, give them neat rods for their support. Plant the off-sets in closer rows to produce flowering roots for next year, because they seldom flower the second time.

AMARYLLIS FORMOSISSIMA, OR JACOBEA LILY.

About the end of this or beginning of next month, is the most proper time for planting out these bulbs. This flower is of the most beautiful and rich crimson velvet colour. The bulb generally produces two stems, the one after the other, about the end of May or first of June. The stem is from nine inches to one foot high, surmounted by a single flower, composed of six petals, three hanging down, three erect and recurved; the stamens droop on the centre of the under petals. The flower thus appears nodding on one side of the stem, and has a most graceful and charming appearance. If planted in a bed, prepare the ground as before directed for *Tuberoses*. Keep the rows one foot asunder, and the bulbs six inches apart in the rows, covering them two inches over their crowns. This plant is now called *Spreikèlia formosíssima*, and we think properly too, for its habit differs from *Amaryllis*.

We have not the smallest doubt that in a few years, not only this superb South American bulb will adorn our flower gardens, but many of the rich bulbs of Brazil and South America generally will yearly exhibit to us the beauty of their colours and the beautiful construction of their flowers and foliage, of which we are now generally deprived, perhaps because we have not the conveniency of a proper hot-house for their protection during winter. But it will be found, in many instances, that these bulbs will do perfectly well to be kept dry in a warm room from October to May, when the heat of our summer is sufficient for the perfection of their flowers, and many species will ripen their seeds. The bulb that is known as *Amaryllis Belladónna*, now called *Belladónna purpuráscens*, is hardy.

TIGER FLOWER.

Tigrídia, a genus of Mexican bulbs belonging to *Monadelphia Triándria*, and produce the most beautiful flowers of the natural order of *Irideæ*. *T. pavònia* is of the brightest scarlet, tinged and spotted with pure yellow. *T. conchiiflòra*, colour rich yellow, tinged and spotted with bright crimson. The colours are very rich, and purely contrasted. The corolla is about four inches in diameter, composed of six petals; the outer are reflexed, the flower of the largest, though splendid in beauty, exists only one day; but to compensate for that, a plant will produce flowers for several weeks; and where a bed of them can be collected, they will bloom in profusion from July to September. They like a light rich free soil. Lift the bulbs in October, and preserve them as directed in that month for *Tuberoses*. Be sure that they be kept dry, and secure from frost. A bed of these should be in every garden. A writer says, "it is the most beautiful flower that is cultivated." Plant them about the end of this or first of next month; if in beds keep them one foot apart each way.

WALKS.

The walks in general should be put in the neatest order during this month. Little requires to be added to the observations of last month, but if these have not been executed, fail not to have it done the first opportunity, choosing dry weather for the operation of *turning* the old or adding new gravel to them, levelling, raking, and rolling neatly as you proceed. Always after rain give the whole of the gravel walks a good rolling. This being frequently done during the early part of the season, will be a saving of much labour and time through the summer. The walks having a firm surface, the growth of weeds will be retarded, and the heavy rains will not be so apt to injure them. Where there are any pretensions to keeping these in order, they ought to be picked of weeds and litter once a week, and gone over with the roller at least once every two weeks during the season.

Sweep and divest the grass walks of all worm casts, litter, &c. cutting the edgings neatly. Mow the grass every two weeks from this time to October, sweeping off the grass clean each time, and give frequent rollings to keep the surface smooth. If any require to be laid with turf, delay it no longer. For directions see last month. The above observations on walks in general, will apply through the season; therefore we will not repeat this subject until October.

EVERGREEN HEDGES.

We have previously observed, under the head of Evergreens, that this is the best season for their replanting. We cannot pass over the observations of this month, without having reference to evergreen hedges, so much neglected amongst us, and yet so important to the diversity of aspect, and especially to soften a little the gloomy appearance of our winters. There are three indigenous shrubs, and at least one exotic, that are well adapted for the purpose, viz, *Pìnus canadénsis*, Hemlock-spruce; *Thùja occidentàlis*, American arbor-vitæ; and *Junípers virginiána*, Red cedar. These are natives, and the two former are admirably adapted for the purpose. Where there is to be a hedge of any of these planted, select plants about two feet high; lift them carefully, preserving the roots as much as possible. Dig a trench from one and a half to two feet wide, and from one to one foot and a half deep. This will admit the soil about the roots to be well broken, which must be done in planting. Keep the plants in the centre of the trench, mixing the shortest and the tallest, that it may be of one height, putting the earth close about their roots as you proceed, and make it firm with the foot; fill up, and water as directed for evergreens in this month. If the season is very dry, give it frequent copious waterings.

None of them should be topped for a few seasons, except such as are much above the others in height, keeping the sides regular and even by clipping or shearing once a year, either in this month or at the end of August. It is better to keep the top (when they have got to the desired height) pointed, than broad. The latter method retains a heavy weight of snow, which frequently breaks down, or otherwise deforms, that which has cost much labour to put into shape.

BOX EDGINGS.

Where these have not been laid, this month is the proper time. Do not delay the planting of such any later. For ample directions see *March* under this head. Clipping of those should be done about the middle of this month. There will then be no danger of frosts to brown the cut leaves, and the young foliage will not be expanded. To keep these edgings in order, they must be cut once a year, and never be allowed to get above four inches high, and two inches wide. What we consider the neatest edging is three inches high, two inches wide at the bottom, tapering to a thin edge at the top. It is very unsightly to see large bushy edgings, especially to narrow walks.

The use of edgings is to keep the soil from the gravel, and the larger they are allowed to grow the more ineffectual they become; growing more open below as they advance in height. The operation may be done very expeditiously by clipping the tops level, going longitudinally along with shears for the purpose, called "box shears." Strain a line along the centre of the edgings, cutting perpendicularly from the line to the bottom on each side, leaving only the breadth of the line at top. Edgings, cut in this manner, every spring will always look well, and the trouble, comparatively, is a mere trifle.

GRASS PLATS, &c.

If these have not been laid down where wanted, delay it no longer, for which see directions in *March*; and where these are desired to be kept in order, they should be mown every two or three weeks at farthest; from this month to October when cut, the grass should be clean swept off, and the edgings, if out of order, adjusted. To mention this subject again will be only a repetition, therefore we will let this suffice.

GENERAL CARE OF PLANTS COMING INTO FLOWER.

Every part of the flower ground should be put into neat order, giving such plants about the borders as are shooting up their flower stems, and are tender, and in danger of being hurt or broken by the wind, proper sticks or rods for their support. In doing this, endeavour to conceal the rods, &c. as much as possible, by dressing the stems and leaves in a natural looking manner over them. Let the stakes be in proportion to the heighth and growth of the plants. It looks very unsightly to see strong stakes to short and weak growing plants. The tyings likewise should be proportionate.

Examine all the beds and patches of seedling flowers now coming up, and let them be refreshed with water as it may be necessary, and pick out the weeds as they appear.

We cannot leave this department at this season of the year, without enforcing the benefit and beauty that will result from keeping the weeds down during this and next month. Therefore strictly observe that there are none running to seed in any part of the garden; in fact, they ought not to be allowed to rear their heads above one day in sight.

APRIL.

We remarked last month, that about this season, where it is convenient, an eastern window is more congenial to plants than a southern. The sun becomes too powerful, and the morning sun is preferable to that of the afternoon. West is also preferable to south. Some keep their plants in excellent order at a north window. But the weather is so mild after this, that there is no difficulty in protecting and growing plants in rooms. They generally suffer most from want of air and water; the window must be up a few inches, or altogether, according to the mildness of the day. And as plants are more liable to get covered with dust in rooms than in any other department, and not so convenient to be syringed or otherwise cleaned, take the first opportunity of a mild day to carry them to a shady situation, and syringe such as are not in flower well with water; or for want of a syringe take a watering-pot with a rose upon it: allowing them to stand until they drip, when they may be put into their respective situations.

DIRECTIONS FOR PLANTS BROUGHT FROM THE GREEN-HOUSE.

Any plants that are brought from the Green-house during the spring months ought to be as little exposed to the direct rays of the sun as possible. Keep them in airy situations, with plenty of light, giving frequent and liberal supplies of water. Plants may be often observed through our city during this month fully exposed in the outside of a south window, with the blaze of a mid-day sun upon them, and these too just come from the temperate and damp atmosphere of a well regulated Green-house. Being thus placed in an arid situation, scorched between the glass and the sun whose heat is too powerful for them to withstand, the transition being so sudden, that, however great their beauties may have appeared, they in a few days become brown, the flowers tarnished or decayed, and the failure generally attributed to individuals not at all concerned. From this and similar causes many have drawn the unjust conclusion, viz. that "plants from Green-houses are of too delicate a nature to be exposed in rooms or windows at this early season." But every year gives more and more proof to the contrary. There are ladies in Philadelphia, and those not a few, whose rooms and windows at this period vie with the finest of our Green-houses, with respect to the health, beauty and order of their plants, and we might almost say in variety. Some of them have got above eight kinds of Camellias in their collections, which afford a continual beauty through the winter, with many other desirable and equally valuable plants. Exposure to the sun, and want of water, are the general cause of failures at this period. We have spoken so minutely and so frequently on these two subjects, that we think more repetition unnecessary. The plants generally are growing pretty freely by this time, and are not so liable to suffer from liberal supplies of water, observing never to give it until the soil in the pot is inclining to become dry, and administering it always in the evenings.

FLOWERING PLANTS.

Our directions last month under this head will equally apply now. The China *roses* that are now coming plentifully in flower should be kept near the light, and in airy exposures, to brighten their colours, otherwise they will be very pale and sickly. *Geraniums* too ought to have the like treatment.

BRINGING PLANTS OUT OF THE CELLAR, &c.

All or most of the plants that have been in the cellar during winter, such as *Pomegranates*, *Lagerstrœmias*, *Hydrángeas*, *Oleanders*, *Sweet-bay*, *&c.* may be brought out to the open air any time about the middle of the month. If any of them stand in need of larger pots or tubs, have them turned out, the balls reduced, and put them in others a little larger; or where convenient they may be planted in the ground, except *Oleanders*, which do best to be a little confined. Be sure to keep the *Hydrángeas* in shady situations. It will not be advisable to expose entirely the Orange and Lemon trees, until the end of this or first of next month. Where there are any scale or foulness of any kind collected on the foliage or wood, have them cleaned directly before the heat increases the one, and to get clear of the disagreeable appearance of the other.

Hot-House.

MAY.

Very few directions for this department remain to be given; except for shifting plants, and a few observations on those that are most desirable for the Hot-house; which we will do in this month, considering May and June the best months of the year for that operation.

The days and nights will be very mild by this time, and the sashes in every favourable day should be opened both in front and top, so that the plants may be enured to the open air, which they will be exposed to by the end of the month, Leave in the beginning of the month the top sashes a little open every mild night, and gradually as the heat increases leave the front sashes and doors open. Continue to syringe them at least every alternate night, and if possible every night; and give them all, according to their respective wants, liberal supplies of water every day. Absorption amongst Hot-house plants is as great during this month as in any period of the year.

OF REPOTTING PLANTS, &c.

It is our candid opinion that this and next month are the best periods for shifting or repotting all or most of Hot-house plants. The end of August being the time always adopted around Philadelphia for that operation (and then they are done indiscriminately,) we will assign a few reasons for our practice.

First, that it is not congenial to the nature of these plants to have their roots surrounded with fresh soil, when they are becoming inactive; *secondly*, that there is not a sufficiency of heat naturally to quicken them to an active state when they are encouraged; and *thirdly*, being thus in new soil while dormant, they have a yellow and sickly aspect until they begin to grow; and the foliage thus deprived of its natural vigour will not appear so healthful again. Whereas, if they are shifted or repotted in this or next month, at which season they are between two stages of growth, they immediately, on receiving fresh assistance, and by the increasing heat of the summer, make new growths, are perfectly ripened before the approach of winter, and never lose that verdureal appearance they have attained. These are our reasons acquired from a close practice and observation, and are not influenced by the doings of others which are so much aside. No practical operator especially, nor in fact any individual, ought to be governed by custom in regard to the treatment of plants, without having an idea as to why and wherefore, founded on the principles of nature, and governed by her unerring results.

As many are desirous of having a knowledge of plants, before they order them, and likewise which are the finest flowerers and their general character, especially those who are at a great distance, and seldom have the privilege of seeing what is most desirable, our descriptions will be limited, and simply such as are given for the Green-house in March.

Acàcias. Several of these are desirable in the Hot-house, for the grandeur of their foliage, beauty of flower, and a few of them as specimens of valuable medicinal plants. *A. Houstóni*, now *Anneslèia Houstóni*, is one of the most magnificent of the *Mimòsa* tribe, blooming from August to November in large terminale spikes, of a crimson colour, stamens very long, and beautiful; leaves bipinnated in pairs. *A. grandiflòra*, likewise given to *Anneslèia*, and similar to the former in colour; has very large compound bipinnate leaves, with from twenty to forty pairs. *A. Catèchu*, flowers yellow, wood spiny, leaves bipinnated, about ten pairs. The inner wood of this tree is of a brown colour, from which the *Catèchu* used in medicine is prepared. It is disputed whether *A. Véra*, or *A. Arábica* produces the gum Arabic. We are inclined to think it is the latter, which grows principally on the Atlas mountains. The gum exudes spontaneously from the bark of the tree in a soft half fluid state. There are many others of this genus belonging to the Hot-house, but being shy in flowering, are not generally esteemed. Most of the flowers have the appearance of yellow balls of down, and are hermaphrodite. The pots should all be well drained.

Aloe. These grotesque looking succulent plants are principally natives of the Cape of Good Hope, and consequently will do well in the warmest part of the Green-house, although when convenient, they frequently get a situation in the Hot-house. It is not requisite, except for *A. vulgàris*, known as *A. barbadénsis*; which has orange yellow flowers; *A. oblíqua*, now called *Gastèria oblíqua*; *A. dichótoma*; and *A. lineàta*, which is perhaps the finest of the genus. The leaves are beautifully striped, with red spines, flowers scarlet and green. These are the only ones that actually need heat during winter. They ought to have very little water, once a month is sufficient. They would grow without it, and several of them would also grow by being suspended in the house, without earth or any substitute about their roots, by being frequently sprinkled with water.

Few of them are admired for the beauty of their flowers, but the whole are considered curious. They flower from May to September.

Ardísias, about eighteen species. Plants highly esteemed for the beauty of their foliage, flowers, and berries. The most popular in our collections is *A. crenulàta*. It has rose coloured star-like flowers, in terminale panicles, and produces beautiful small red berries, which continue until other berries are produced the following year, and frequently there may be seen on one plant, the berries of three successive years, thus being a very ornamental plant and very desirable. It is vulgarly called the Dwarf ever-bearing cherry. It will keep in a good Green-house, but not grow freely. *A. solanàcea* has large oblong leaves, narrowed at each end, and bears purple berries; *A. élegans* has entire, oblong, shining leaves; *A. umbellàta*, once *A. littoràlis*, is the finest of the genus for abundance of flower and beauty of foliage. The flowers are pink, in large decompound panicles, the leaves the largest of all the species, oblong, wedge shaped, nearly sessile, entire, smooth, and reflexed. They are all evergreens, and the pots should be well drained. They are natives of the East Indies, and delight in a high temperature.

Aristolochias, Birth-wort. There are several of these belonging to the Hot-house, but none of them deserving particular observation, except *A. labiosa.* The leaves are reniform, roundish, cordate, and amplexicaule; the flower or corolla is of a curious construction, being incurved, and at the base swelled or saccate with a large lip, and all beautifully spotted; colour greenish brown. It is a climbing plant, and requires a strong heat.

Astrapœas, three species. *A. Wallichii* is a celebrated plant in Europe, and a few specimens of it are in this country. It has scarlet unbellated flowers, with an involucre, has twenty-five stamens united into a tube, bearing the corolla with five petals; leaves roundish, cordate, accuminate, very large with persistent, ovate wavy stipules. The plant is of easy culture, and grows freely, wood very strong.

Areca, Cabbage-tree, ten species. They are a kind of palms, with large pinnated leaves, or properly fronds. In their indigenous state they are from six to forty feet high, but in the Hot-house they seldom exceed twenty feet. *A. catechu* is used in medicine. *A. olerácea* is cultivated extensively in the West Indies, and the tender part of the top is eaten by the natives. *A. montana* is most frequent in collections. There is no particular beauty in the flowers. They are all easily grown, if plenty of heat be given.

Brunsvigias are all large bulbs from the Cape of Good Hope, and will keep in the Green-house during winter, but are better where they can obtain a situation in the Hot-house. It is a splendid genus, containing about ten species. Some of the bulbs grow to an enormous size, and all of them while growing require a liberal supply of water; but when dormant it must be wholly withheld, and they should have large pots to make them grow and flower in perfection. *B. multiflora*, flowers scarlet and green; the leaves lay on the surface of the pot. *B. laticoma*, flowers pale purple. *B. Josephinæ* has splendid rose coloured flowers, and is the most admired species of the genus: the foliage spreading, half erect, and glacous; flowers numerous, and in large umbels, on a stem two feet high, blooming successively; there is a variety that has striped flowers.

Several other species have been given to different genera. *B. falcata* is now *Ammocharis falcata*; *B. marginata*, now *Imhofia*; and *B. cilliaris*, is now *Buphone cilliaris*. They all flower in umbels, on stems from six inches to two feet; flowers lily-like with six petals.

Bambusa, Bamboo-cane, two species. Plants of very strong growth, and are used in the East Indies, where they are indigenous, for every purpose in the construction of huts, for furniture both domestic and rural, for fences, boats, boxes, paper, &c. It is frequently used as pipes to convey water. The species thus useful, is *B. arundinacea*, which grows to a great height. We do not mention it as interesting in beauty, but as a valuable plant, for the many useful purposes to which it is applied. It requires to be kept wet.

Banistèrias, a genus of about fourteen climbing evergreen plants. Three of them are esteemed. *B. fúlgens*, yellow flowers in racemose spikes, leaves subovate, and downy beneath. *B. Chrisophylla* has beautiful foliage, as if covered with a shining gold coloured dust; leaves large, oblong, acute. *B. splèndens*, flowers in spikes of a yellow colour; foliage large and silvery like; the pots should be well drained.

Barringtònias, two species. *B. speciòsa* has produced a great excitement amongst cultivators, and is one of the handsomest plants produced within the tropics. The leaves are large, oblong, acute, shining, with fleshy nerves, tinged with red; the flowers are large, full of stamens with four petals, opens in the evening and fades at sunrise; colour purple and white; grows freely in strong heat.

Brôwneas, five species of splendid plants, but scarce in collections. *B. coccínea* has scarlet flowers in pendulous bunches, corolla semi-double, foliage bipinnate, in three pairs. *B. ròsa*, mountain rose of Trinidad. *B. grandicéps* is the finest of the genus, leaves bipinnated; leaflets cordate, accuminate, downy and pendulous, flowers rose colour, in large close heads. Drain the pots well.

Calathèa zebrìna, frequently known as *Maránta zebrìna*, and now *Phrynum zebrìnum*, is a plant unique in its appearance. The large elongated ovate leaves are beautifully striped with green and dark purple, and called *Zebra plant*. It has light blue flowers in ovate spikes, about the size of large pine cones. It is a herbaceous plant; but in the warmest part of the Hot-house retains its splendid foliage; requires a very liberal supply of water, and ought to be in every collection.

Cánnas, about thirty species, several of them deserving cultivation both for flower and foliage; they are principally natives of the West Indies, and might all be easily obtained. The finest are *C. gigántea*, has large leaves and orange flowers; *C. limbàta*, flowers scarlet and yellow; *C. díscolor*, has large cordate, accuminate leaves of a crimson colour, the flowers are scarlet; *C. iridiflòra*, has large crimson nodding flowers, very different from any of the others, and the finest of the genus. They all, while in a growing state, require a liberal supply of water; and being herbaceous plants watering ought to be given up about the first of November, and renewed about the first of January, thus giving them a cessation which they require to flower freely; but when water is constantly given, which is the general plan in our collections, they continue to push weak shoots and few flowers.

Cáctus. This extensive genus is curious, grotesque, interesting, and varied in character and habit; is now divided into six distinct genera according to their natural appearance and habit. We will describe a few of each genus, none of which going under the name of *Cáctus*, we will give them the six following.

Mamillàrias, above twenty species, and are those which are covered with roundish bearded tubercles, and with small red and white flowers. *M. coccínea*; *M. simplex*; *M. pusílla*, and *M. cònica*, are good species, and will do well with water five or six times during summer.

Melocáctus, seven species, and are those that are roundish with deep and many angles, with spines in clusters on the top of the angle. *M. commùnis*, is the Turk's cap, named from having an ovate conate crown upon the top, from which proceed the small red flowers.

M. macránthus, has large spines; *M. pyramidàlis*, is a conical growing species. These require the same treatment as the last.

Echinocáctus, about twenty species; are those that have many deep angles, and have a remarkable swelling, with each parcel of spines; *E. gibbòsus*; *E. crispàtus*; *E. recúrvus*; are curious in appearance, with small white and purple flowers. These three genera in most collections are not well known specifically, but it is easy to discriminate which genus they are connected with.

Cèreus. This is the most magnificent genus with regard to the magnitude and beauty of the flowers, but not so closely allied. It takes in all those of a trailing or erect growing habit, having spines in clusters, solitary, or spineless. *C. peruviànus* and *C. heptagònus*, grow very erect, and to the height of thirty or forty feet in Peru and Mexico, where they plant them close together as fences, and they are in a few years impenetrable. *C. flagellifórmus* is a well known creeping free flowering species, has ten angles; will keep in a good Green-house, and produce in May and June a great number of blooms. The petals are of a fine pink and red colour; the tube of the flower is long, and will stand a few days in perfection, when others come out successively for the space of two months, and during their continuance make a brilliant appearance. *C. grandiflòrus* is the celebrated "Night-blooming Cereus." The flowers are very large, beautiful, and sweet-scented. They begin to open about sun-down, and are fully expanded about eleven o'clock. The corolla, or rather calyx, is from seven to ten inches in diameter, the outside of which is a brown, and the inside a fine straw yellow colour; the petals are of the purest white, with the stamens surrounding the stile in the centre of the flower, which add to its lustre, and make it appear like a bright star. Its scent is agreeable, and perfumes the air to a considerable distance; but these beauties are of momentary duration. By sunrise they fade, and hang down quite decayed, and never open again.[E] One of these ought to be in every collection, and if trained up a naked wall will not occupy much room, and grow and flower profusely. They need very little water. C. *speciosíssimus* has most beautiful large flowers, about six inches diameter; the outside petals are a bright scarlet, those of the inside a fine light purple. One flower lasts a few days, and a large plant will produce every year from ten to twenty flowers, blooming from May to August. It has flowered in some of our collections, and is highly esteemed. *C. triangulàris* has the largest flower of the *Cacteæ* family; the bloom is of a cream colour, and about one foot in diameter. In its indigenous state, it produces a fine fruit called "Strawberry Pear," and is much esteemed in the West Indies as being slightly acid, and at the same time sweet, pleasant, and cooling. It seldom flowers. C. *phyllanthoídes*, once *Cáctus speciósus*, is one of the most profuse in flowering; the branches are ensate, compressed, and obovate, without spines; flowers of a pink colour, about four inches in diameter; the stamens as long as the corolla, with white anthers. It will keep well in a Green-house or Room. If in either of the two latter, give water only a few times during winter. This is becoming a very popular plant. C. *Jenkinsòni* is a magnificent hybrid from C. *speciosíssimus*. The flowers are equally as large, and of a brilliant scarlet colour, with a profusion of pure white anthers; is greatly admired, and is only in a few collections. C. *Ackermánni* is very similar to C. *phyllanthoídes*, flowering equally as profusely, the colour a bright scarlet, and the scarcest species of the genus that is worthy of notice. C. *truncàtus*, branches truncated, flowers deep scarlet and tubular, from two to three inches in diameter; the stamens protrude from the corolla; the plant is of a dwarf growth and branched; when in flower it is quite a picture. It is said that there are free and shy flowering varieties of this species, but we doubt it; perhaps it is owing to the cultivation and soil.

[E] They may be preserved if cut off when in perfection, and put in spirits of wine, in a chrystal vase, made air tight. A plant flowered in our collection in May 1830, at 12 o'clock at noon—the only instance of the kind we ever heard of.

Opúntias, about forty species, and are those whose branches are in joints flatly oblong, or ovate, spines solitary, or in clusters. The plants are not so desirable for beauty of flower as the species of the former genus, but many of them are remarkable for their strong grotesque and spiny appearance; besides several of the species are extensively cultivated for the Cochineal insect. The one most valued for that purpose, is *O. cochiníllifera*, which has only small clusters of bristles upon the oblong ovate joints, and produces small red flowers; C. *ficus índica*, is also used, but is very spiny.

Peréskias. About four species, and those that are of a shrubby nature producing leaves; *P. aculeàta* bears a fruit called "Barbadoes-gooseberry." The flowers are very small and simple, spines about half an inch long, leaves fleshy and elliptical.

The whole of the plants in the family of *Cacteæ* require very little water, and delight in a dry warm situation. They do not agree with frequent repotting; once in two or three years to young plants, and in five or six to those that are established, with the exception of the large, free flowering species, which should be repotted once in two years.

Coffèa Arábica. It produces the celebrated coffee, and is a plant universally known in our collections, and of easy culture. The leaves are opposite, oblong, wavy and shining, the flowers white, of a grateful odour, but of short duration. There is a plant known as C.

occidentalis, which is now *Tetramèrium odoratíssimum*. It requires a great heat to grow well, therefore should be kept in the warmest part of the Hothouse. The flowers are white, in panicles, and larger than the common jasmine, and is very sweet-scented; leaves oblong, lanceolate, accuminate.

Callicárpas. About twelve species, and are generally admitted into collections, though of no particular interest or beauty, except in the bright purple berries they produce, which is rarely. The foliage is of a rugose, hoary appearance.

Carolíneas. About six species of tender plants, with large digitate leaves, and of handsome growth. The flowers have numerous filaments, and are large and singular. C. *insígnis* has the largest and compactest blossoms; C. *àlba* is the only one of the genus that has white flowers, all the others being red; C. *prínceps* and C. *robústa* are noble looking species, and are much esteemed. They require a good heat, with which they will grow freely.

Caryòtas. A genus of palms. C. *ùrens* is an admired species, produces flowers in long pendulous spikes, which are succeeded by strings of succulent globular berries. In its native state it produces a sweet liquor in large quantities, and no stronger than water.

Coccolòbas, Sea-side grape. This genus is admired for its beautiful large foliage, which is oblong ovate, and cordate ovate; C. *pubéscens* and C. *latifòlia* are the finest species. They bear berries in clusters like the grape, but never come to perfection in artificial cultivation.

Cùphea Melvílla, is the only species of the genus that is particularly deserving of a situation, has lanceolate scabrous leaves, narrowed at each end, flowers tubular in a terminale whorl, colour scarlet and green. The plant must be well drained. It will flower from May to September.

Cròtons. About twenty-eight species, few of them deserving cultivation; but the genus is celebrated for its beautiful C. *pìctus*, leaves oblong-lanceolate, variegated with yellow, and stained with red, flowers small green, on axillary spikes. C. *variagàtus*, variety *latifòlia*, is finer than the original *variagàtus*, the nerves in the leaves are yellow, and the leaves lanceolate, entire and smooth. To make them grow freely, give the warmest part of the Hot-house, and drain the pots well.

Cérberas. About twelve species of strong growing trees, full of poisonous juice. C. *thevètia* is an elegant plant, with accumulate leaves, and large, nodding, yellow, solitary, fragrant flowers, proceeding from the axil; C. *ahoùai* produces a nut which is deadly poison. C. *odàllam*, once C. *mànghas*, has large star-like flowers, white, shaded with red. They are principally East India plants, and require great heat.

Cycas, four species, generally called *Sago palm*, as an English name. The plant that *Sago* is extracted from, belongs to another genus, (see *Sàgus*.) C. *revolùta* is a well known palm, and will keep perfectly well in the Green-house. We have seen a beautiful specimen of it which is kept every winter in the cellar, but those that are kept so cool in winter only grow every alternate year, while those that are kept in the Hot-house grow every year, which shows that heat is their element. C. *circinàlis* is a large growing species; the fronds are much longer, but not so close and thick. C. *glaùca* is a fine species; the foliage is slightly glaucous. They require plenty of pot room, are much infested with the small white scaly insect, and ought to be frequently examined and carefully washed as prescribed in January.

Combrètums. Nine species of beautiful flowering climbing plants, standing in very high estimation. The leaves of the principal part of them are ovate, acute, flowers small but on large branches, the flowers all coming out on one side of the branch. They have a magnificent effect. *C. èlegans*, red; *C. formòsum*, red and yellow; *C. pulchéllum*, scarlet; *C. comòsum* has crimson flowers in tufts; *C. purpùreum* is the most splendid of the genus. It was first cultivated in 1818, and so much admired, that the whole of the species as soon as introduced, was extravagantly bought up, and none of them has retained their character, except *C. purpùreum*, which is now called *Poívrea coccínea.* The flowers are bright scarlet, in large branches, blooming profusely from April to September, and flower best in a pot. When planted in the ground it grows too much to wood, carrying few flowers. This plant ought to be in every Hot-house.

Cràssula. This genus has no plants in it attractive in beauty. Several beautiful plants in our collections belong to *Ròchea* and *Kalosánthus.*

There is a strong growing succulent plant, known in our collections as *C. falcàta*, which is *R. falcàta*. It seldom flowers; the minor variety blooms profusely every year from May to August, and has showy scarlet flowers in terminale panicles. The plants known as *C. coccínea* and *C. versícolor* are now given to the genus *Kalosánthus*. The flowers of the former are like scarlet wax, terminale and sessile; *K. odoratíssima* has yellow terminale sweet-scented flowers. They require very little water, only a few times in winter, and about twice a week in summer; they are all desirable plants.

Córyphas, (Large fan Palm,) five species of the most noble and magnificent of palms. *C. ambraculífera*, the fronds or leaves are palmate; in Ceylon, where the tree is indigenous, they are frequently found fifteen feet wide and twenty feet long. Knox says they will cover from fifteen to twenty men, and when dried will fold up in the shape of a rod, and can be easily carried about, and serve to protect them from the scorching sun. *C. talièra*, now *Talièra bengalénsis*, being stronger, is of great utility for covering houses. They do not grow to such immense extent in artificial cultivation, but require large houses to grow them.

Crìnums, about one hundred species, chiefly stove bulbs, many of them beautiful. Those that are of great celebrity are *C. cruéntum*, colour red; *C. scàbrum*, crimson and white; *C. amàbile*, purple and white; the neck of the bulb of the latter is long and easily distinguished from its purplish colour, and is considered the finest of the genus. Several specimens of it are in our collections. Their flowers are in umbels, on a stalk from one to three feet high; corolla funnel shaped; petals recurved. They require large pots to make them flower well, and when growing to be liberally supplied with water.

Cyrtànthus, a genus of Cape bulbs, containing nine species, and will do very well in the Green-house, but we find the assistance of the Hot-house a great advantage. They are closely allied to *Crìnum*. The tubes of the flowers are long and round, with various shades of orange, yellow, red, and green. *C. odòrus*, *C. striátus*, *C. oblíquus*, and *C. vittàtus*, are the finest. When the bulbs are dormant, which will be from October to January, they should not get any water; before they begin to grow, turn the bulb out of the old earth, repotting it immediately. At this time they should be potted with the balls of earth entire, which will cause them to flower stronger.

Caryophyllus aromáticus, is the only species, and the tree that produces cloves. The whole plant is aromatic, and closely allied to *Myrtus*; the flowers are in loose panicles, the leaves oblong, accuminate, entire. It is a fine evergreen. Pots must be well drained.

Dillènias, three species of fine plants, with beautiful foliage. *D. speciòsa* has produced considerable excitement in our collections. The leaves are elliptic, oblong, simply serrated, nerves deep; the flower is white, with five bold petals, centre filled with barren anthers; it has not been known to flower in America. *D. scándens* has ovate, simply serrated leaves, but is not known as to flower; it is a fine climber.

Dracænas, Dragon-tree, about twelve species of Asiatic plants, varied in character. *D. férrea* is plentiful in our collections, and will keep in the Green-house; but the foliage is not so well retained as when kept in the Hot-house; the leaves are lanceolate, acute, of a dark purple colour. *D. fràgrans*, when in bloom, will scent the air for a considerable distance, leaves green and lanceolate. *D. marginàta* is rare, yet it is to be seen in a few of our collections. *D. strícta* is now *Charlwòodia*[F] *strícta*, flowers blush and in loose panicles. *D. Dráco* is admired, and the most conspicuous of the genus.

[F] In honour of Mr. Charlwood, an extensive seedsman of London, who has made several botanical excursions on this continent.

Eránthemums, about ten species. *E. pulchéllum* and *E. bícolor* are the finest of the genus; the former is in our collections, but miserably treated. The soil in which it is grown is too stiff and loamy, and it seldom gets enough of heat. The latter is indispensable to make it flower in perfection; therefore it should have the warmest part of the house, and it will produce flowers of a fine blue colour from January to September. The flowers of the latter are white and dark purple, with a few brown spots in the white; blooms from April to August. Drain the pots well, and give the plants little sun during summer.

Eugènias, about thirty species, esteemed for their handsome evergreen foliage. This genus once contained a few celebrated species, which have been divided. (See *Jambòsa*.) The Allspice tree, known as

Myrtus Piménta, is now *E. Piménta*; the leaves are ovate, lanceolate, and when broken have an agreeable scent. There are several varieties all of the same spicy fragrance. The plant is in very few of our collections. *E. fràgrans* is sweet scented; the flowers are on axillary peduncles; leaves ovate, obtuse.

Euphórbia (spurg), a genus of plants disseminated over every quarter of the globe; a few are beautiful, many grotesque, and several the most worthless weeds on the earth. There are about two hundred species, and from all of them, when probed, a thick milky fluid exudes. Those of the tropics are the most curious, and very similar in appearance to *Cáctus*, but easily detected by the above perforation. There is a magnificent species in our collections, which was lately introduced from Mexico.[G] It goes under the name of *E. heterophylla*. The flowers of the whole genus are apetalous, and the beauty is in the bracteæ; of the species alluded to the bracteæ is bright crimson, very persistent, and above six inches in diameter, when well grown. The plant requires a strong heat, or the foliage will become yellow and fall off. We question whether this species is nondescript or as above. It is a brilliant ornament to the Hot-house three fourths of the year, and always during winter, and should have a situation in every tropical collection.

[G] By Poinsett the American Consul for Mexico in 1828.

Erythrìnas (Coral tree), a genus containing about thirty species of leguminose, scarlet-flowering plants. Several species are greatly esteemed for their beauty and profusion of flowers, which in well established plants are produced in long spikes at the end of the stems and branches. *E. Corallodéndrum* blooms magnificently in the West Indies, but in our collections has never flowered. Perhaps if it was kept dry during its dormant season, which is from November to January, and when growing greatly encouraged, it might produce flowers. *E. speciòsa* is a splendid flowerer, leaves large, ternated, and prickly beneath; stem prickly. *E. pubéscens* is valued for its large peculiar brown pubescent leaves.

In regard to *E. herbàcea*, which is a native of the Carolinas, and frequently treated as a Hot-house plant, it is our opinion that it would be more perfectly grown if planted about the first of this month in the garden; and when growing, if well supplied with water it would flower from July to September. About the first of November lift the roots and preserve them in half dry earth, in the same place with the *Dáhlias*. *E. laurifòlia* and *E. crísta-gálli* are likewise often treated as Hot-house plants, and in such situations they cast prematurely their first flowers, by the confined state of the air. They will keep in perfect preservation during winter in a dry cellar, half covered with earth, or entirely covered with half dry earth; consequently, the best and easiest method of treatment, is to plant them in the garden about the first of May, and when growing, if the ground becomes dry, give them frequent waterings. They will flower profusely three or four times in the course of summer.

We freely recommend the last species to all our patrons, confident that it will give ample satisfaction, both in profusion of flower and beauty of colour. The soil they are to be planted into should be according to that prescribed in the list; or if they are kept in pots, they must be enlarged three or four times, when they are in a growing state, to make them flower perfectly; otherwise they will be diminutive.

Fìcus, Fig-tree, a genus containing above fifty Hot-house species, besides several that belong to the Green-house; greatly admired for the beauty of their foliage. A few of them are deciduous, and all of the easiest culture. We have seen plants of *F. elástica* hung in the back of the Hot-house, without the smallest particle of earth, their only support being sprinklings of water every day. *F. Brássii* is the finest looking species that has come under our observation; the leaves are very large, shining, cordate, accuminate; nerves strong and white. As the beauty of these plants is entirely in the foliage and habit, we will select the best of them in the list to which we refer.

Gærtnèra racemòsa, is a large climbing woody shrub, with pinnated leaves, leaflets ovate, lanceolate, flowers white, five petaled, beautifully fringed; blooms in dense panicles. When the plants are allowed to climb, they do not flower freely; but if closely cut in, they will flower every year in great profusion, after the plants are well established. It is now called *Hiptàge Madablòta*.

Geissomèria longiflòra. This is a new genus, and closely allied to *Ruéllia*. The species alluded to, is a free flowerer, blooming from May to August, in close spikes of a scarlet colour; leaves opposite, ovate, elongate, and shining; the plants must be well drained, and in summer kept from the direct influence of the sun.

Gardènias, a genus containing about seventeen species, several of them very popular in our collections, going under the name of *Cape Jasmine*, which do well in the Green-house, (see *May*.) The species requiring this department, and deserving attention, are *G. campanulàta*, of a soft woody nature, with ovate, accuminate leaves; flowers of a straw colour, and solitary; *G. amœna*, the flowers are white, tinged with crimson, terminale and solitary; *G. costàta*, admired for its beautiful ribbed foliage, *G. lùcida* has a handsome, ovate, accuminate, shining foliage; flowers white and solitary. They require to have the pots well drained.

Heritièra littóralis, Looking-glass plant. This plant is unisexual, has beautiful large, ovate, veiny leaves; the flowers are small, red, with male and female on the same plant, but different flowers. It requires a strong heat, and plenty of pot room. How the English name becomes applicable to it, we are not acquainted.

Hibíscus. This genus affords many fine species and varieties of plants for the Hot-house, besides others for every department of the garden. The most popular in our collections for the Hot-house, is *H. Ròsa sinénsis*, with its varieties, which are magnificent, and flower profusely, from April to September. The single or original species is seldom seen in cultivation; the varieties are *H. Ròsa sinénsis rùbro plénus*, double red; *H. R. S. cárnea plènus*, double salmon; *H. R. S. variegàtus*, double striped; *H. R. S. flávo-plènus*, double buff; *H. R. S. lùtea plènus*, double yellow, or rather sulphur. The plants grow freely, and produce their flowers three or four inches of diameter, from the young wood; the leaves are ovate, accuminate, smooth, entire at the base and coarsely toothed at the end. All the varieties are of the same character, and highly deserving of a situation in every collection. There is said to be a double white variety, which we doubt; it is not in artificial cultivation. *H. mutàbilis flòre plèno* is a splendid plant of strong growth, and will, when well established, flower abundantly, if the wood of last year is cut to within a few eyes of the wood of the previous year; the flowers are produced on the young wood, and come out a pale colour, and change to bright red, and about the size of a garden Provins rose; leaves downy, cordate, angular, five-lobed, accuminate, and slightly toothed. *H. lilliiflòrus*, is a new highly esteemed species; the flowers are various in colour, being pink, blush, red, purple, and striped. We have not seen it in flower, but had its character verbally, from a respectable cultivator. The leaves vary in character, but are generally cordate, crenate, accuminate; the petioles are brown, and the whole slightly hirsute; is deciduous, and requires to be kept in the warmest part of the house.

Hóyas, Wax-plant, seven species. All of them are climbing succulents, requiring plenty of heat and little water. *H. carnòsa* is the finest flowering species of the genus, and known in our collections as the wax plant; the leaves are green and fleshy; the flowers are mellifluous, five parted, and in pendulous bunches, slightly bearded, and have every appearance of a composition of the finest wax; of a blush colour. *H. crassifòlia* has the best looking foliage, and the flowers are white. The former will keep in the Green-house, but will not flower so profusely.

Hernándias, Jack-in-a-box. The species are rare, except *H. sonòra*, which is an elegant looking plant, when well grown; the leaves are peltate, cordate, accuminate, smooth; flowers white, and in panicles; the fruit a nut. The English name is said to have been given, in allusion to the small flowers and large leaves of the plant. A great heat is required to grow it well.

Ipomæas, a genus of tropical climbing plants, nearly allied to *Convolvúlus*, but of greater beauty. *I. paniculàta* has large purple flowers in panicles, with large palmated smooth leaves. *I. Jálapa* is the true jalap of the druggists, but not worthy of any other remark. *I. grandiflòra*, large white flowers, with acute petals; leaves large, cordate, ovate. *I. pulchélla* has flowers of a handsome violet colour. They are all easily cultivated. It is said that *I. tuberòsa* is much used in the West Indies to cover arbours, and will grow three hundred feet in one season; the flowers are purple striped with yellow, leaves palmated. We are not certain but the roots of this kind may be kept like the sweet potato, and become a useful ornament to our gardens.

Ixòras, a genus of fine flowering plants, and does extremely well in our collections in comparison to the state they are grown in England. The genus specifically is much confused amongst us, either from error originating with those who packed them for this country, or after they have arrived. *I. purpùrea*, leaves oblong, ovate, blunt; flowers crimson; it is now called *I. obavàta*. *I. crocàta*, leaves oval, lanceolate, narrowing towards the stem, smooth, underside of the leaf the nerves are very perceptible; flowers saffron coloured. *I. ròsea*, leaves large, regular, oblong, a little acute, very distant on the wood, centre nerve strong; flowers rose coloured in large corymbs, branching: *I. Bandhùca*, leaves very close to the stem, ovate, accuminate; nerves straight, middle nerve stronger than any other of the genus; flowers scarlet, corymbs crowded. *I. Blánda*, leaves small, lanceolate, ovate; flowers blush, cymes branching in three. *I. dichotìma*, leaves largest of the genus, ovate, accuminate, undulate, footstalk 3/8 of an inch long; whereas none of the leaves of the other species has footstalks of any length. It is now called *I. undulàta*, flowers are white. *I. grandiflòra*, leaves ovate, elongate, sessile; flowers in crowded corymbs, and scarlet; is called, *I. coccìnea* in the Botanical Magazine, by which it is known in our collections, and is the same as *I. strícta*. *I. flámmea* and *I. speciòsa*, leaves oblong, subsessile; flowers scarlet, in round spreading dense corymbs. *I. fúlgens*, same as *I. longifòlia* and *I. lanceolàta*; foliage glossy; flowers scarlet. *I. Pavétta*, the flowers are white, and said to be sweet-scented, the leaves of all the species are opposite; there are a few other species that we are not thoroughly acquainted with, but have been thus explicit to prevent error as far as possible in this beautiful genus. They are all evergreen, low growing shrubs; the plants grow best in Jersey black sandy earth, but flower most abundantly with half loam.

Jacarándas, a genus of beautiful shrubs, containing five species, with *Bignônia*-like blue or purple flowers. *I. mimòsifolia* and *I. filicifòlia* are the finest. The former has blue, and the latter purple flowers; in loose branching panicles. They are evergreen, and easy of culture.

Jambòsas, about twelve species, which have been principally taken from *Eugènia*, and contain its finest plants, and is a splendid genus of evergreen shrubs. *E. Jámbos* is now *Jambòsa vulgàris*, which flowers and fruits freely in our Hot-houses. The fruit is about an inch in diameter, eatable, and smelling like a rose, hence called "Rose Apple.' The petals of all the species are simple, and may rather be considered the calyx; the beauty of the flowers is in the many erect spreading stamens, either straw, white, rose, or green colour. *J. malaccénsis*, Malay Apple, is greatly esteemed for the delightful fragrance of its fruit. We frequently see *J. purpuráscens*, which is a native of the West Indies, going under *J. m.* which is an Asiatic species, with white flowers and entire oblong leaves; whereas the leaves of *J. p.* are small, ovate, accuminate, young shoots and leaves purple. *J. macrophylla*, white, and *J. amplexicaùlis*, green, have very large oblong, lanceolate leaves, and is of a strong woody habit. They are all easy of culture.

Jasmìnum, Jasmine, is a favourite genus of shrubs, for the exquisite fragrance of its flowers, of which none are more delightful than *J. Sàmbac* or Arabian Jasmine. There are two other varieties of it, *J. S. múltiplex*, semi-double; and *J. S. trifòliatum*, Double Tuscan Jasmine. The latter requires a great heat to make it grow and flower freely. We suspect there is another variety in cultivation. *J. hirsùtum* has cordate downy leaves; flowers many, in terminale, sessile umbels. *J. paniculàtum*, white, flowering in terminale panicles from March to November; leaves smooth, oval, obtusely accuminate; *plant scarce*. *J. simplicifòlium* is in our collections under the name of *J. lucidum*; plant spreading; leaves oblong and shining. There are several other species, all with white flowers, and generally easy of culture.

Játropha, Physic-nut, is a genus of six strong growing shrubs, natives of the West Indies. *J. multifida* and *I. panduræfòlia* have the handsomest foliage, and both have scarlet flowers; the appearance of the foliage of this genus is the only object; the flowers are small, in coarse disfigured panicles, and several of the species have not been known to flower in artificial cultivation. The seeds of *J. cúrcas* are often received from the West Indies; the leaves are cordate, angular, and smooth. *J. manihot*, now *Manihot cannabìna*, is the Cassada root, the juice of which, when expressed, is a strong poison. They are all easy of culture: want of strong heat in winter will make them cast their leaves, but do them no other injury.

Justícia. A few species of this genus are fine showy hot-house plants. *J. coccínea* has large terminale spikes of scarlet flowers, blooming from December to March, and a very desirable plant, of easy culture, and should be in every collection; it is apt to grow spindly, if not kept near the glass. *I. picta*, with its varieties; *I. lúcida* and *I. formósa*, are fine shrubby species. *I. speciòsa* is a beautiful purple flowering herbaceous plant.

Kæmpfèria, an Asiatic genus of tuberose rooted plants; none of them in our collections, except *K. rotúnda*; the flowers come up a few inches above the pot, without the leaves, in April and May and frequently sooner; they are purple and light blue, partially streaked and spotted; leaves large, oblong, purplish coloured beneath. The roots when dormant ought to be kept in the pot without watering, otherwise they will not flower freely. No bulbs or strong tuberose rooted plants, will flower in perfection if kept moist when they are not growing.

Lantàna, a genus of twenty species, all free flowering shrubs; the flowers are small, in round heads blooming from the axils, in yellow, orange, pink, white, and changeable colours; the plants are of such a rough straggling growth, that they are not esteemed. There are four or five species in our collections. They will not bear a strong fumigation; therefore, when the Hot-house is under that operation, they must be set down in the pathway, or other low part in the house.

Latànias. This genus contains three species of handsome palms. *L. borbònica* is one of the finest of the *Palmæ*, not growing to great magnitude; the leaves or fronds are plaited flabelliform, leaflets smooth at the edge, footstalk spiny, and the plant spreading. *L. rùbra*, fronds same as the former, but leaflets more divided and serrulate; footstalk unarmed; foliage reddish. *L. glaucophylla*, same as *L. rùbra*, only the foliage glaucous. They are all valuable plants, and are obtained by seed from the East Indies. They require plenty of pot room.

Laúrus. This genus, though of no beauty in flower, is generally admired in collections for its fine evergreen foliage, and aromatic or spicy flavour, and several trees are important in medicine. The most esteemed are given to a genus named *Cinnamòmum*, as has been observed in the Green-house, (see *March.*) *L. Chloróxylon* is the Cogwood of Jamaica. *L. Pérsea* is now *Pérsea gratíssima*, Alligator-pear, a fruit about the size of a large pear, and greatly esteemed in the West Indies. The plant is generally known in our collections. *C. vérum* is the true Cinnamon of commerce.

The part taken is the inside of the bark when the tree is from five to eighteen years old. The leaves are three-nerved, ovate, oblong; nerves vanishing towards the point, bright green above, pale beneath, with whitish veins. This plant ought to be kept in the warmest part of the Hot-house. C. *cássia*, is frequently given under the former name, but when compared may be easily detected by the leaves being more lanceolate, and a little pubescent. They both make handsome plants, but require great heat. Drain the pots well of the delicate sorts.

Magnífera, Mango tree. There are two species. *M. índica* is in our collections, and bears a fruit which is so highly esteemed in the East Indies, as to be considered preferable to any other except very fine pine apples. The leaves are lanceolate, and from six to eight inches long, and two or more broad. The flowers are produced in loose bunches at the end of the branches, but of no beauty, and have to be artificially impregnated, or it will scarcely produce fruit. The shell is kidney-shaped, and of a leathery, crustaceous substance. They contain one seed, and in their indigenous state are more juicy than an apple. Drain the pots well, as the roots are apt to get sodden from moisture. The other species goes under the name of *oppositifòlia*, but we question if it is not only a variety, for it has every character of the one just described.

Melàstoma, was once an extensive genus, on which the natural order *Melastomaceæ* is founded; but is now much divided into other genera contained in the natural tribe *Micomeæ*. There are about thirteen species remaining in the genus. They now display great unity of character, and many of them may be considered very ornamental. The finest are *M. malabáthrica*, rose-coloured; *M. sanguínea*, lilac; *M. decémfida*, purple; *M. pulverulénta*, red; and *M. áspera*, rose. There is a plant in several of our collections known as *M. purpùrea* and *M. tetragòna*, which is *Ossæa purpuráscens*; leaves ovate, lanceolate, accuminate, five-nerved, pilose; the footstalk and nerves underside of the leaf covered with brown hairs; stem four-sided; flowers purple. All the species are easy of culture. *M. nepalénsis* is a Green-house plant.

Malpíghia, (Barbadoes-cherry,) about eighteen species, all beautiful evergreen trees or shrubs. They are easily distinguished by having bristles on the under side of the leaves. These bristles are fixed by the centre, so that either end of it will sting. We are not aware of any other plant being defended in the manner. *M. ùrens* has oblong ovate leaves with decumbent stiff bristles; flowers pink. *M. aquifòlia* has lanceolate, stiff, spiny leaves, and we think the most beautiful foliage of the genus. *M. fucàta* has elliptical shining leaves, with lilac flowers. *M. glábra*, leaves ovate, entire, smooth; flowers purple. They all have five rounded clawed petals. The last species is cultivated in the West Indies for its fruit. The pots must be well drained.

Márica, a genus of Hot-house plants, closely allied to Iris, between which there is no distinction in the leaves. The flowers of *M. cærùlea* are beautifully spotted with light and dark blue, the scape many flowered. M. *Sabìni* has flowers similar, but not so dark in colour. M. *Northiàna* has splendid white and brown spotted flowers, spathe two flowered. These plants when growing require a liberal supply of water, and to be greatly encouraged by frequent potting to flower well.

Mùsa (Plantain-tree), contains eight species, and is greatly esteemed in the East and West Indies for the luscious sweet flavour of its fruit, which can be converted into every delicacy in the domestic cookery of the country. M. *paradisìæa* is the true plantain tree, has a soft herbaceous stalk, 15 or 20 feet high, with leaves from 5 to 7 feet long, and about 2 feet wide. M. *sapiéntum* is the true Banana-tree; habit and character same as the former, except it has a spotted stem, and the male flowers are deciduous. The pulp of the fruit is softer, and the taste more luscious. M. *rosàcea*, M. *coccínea*, and M. *chinènsis*, are most esteemed in artificial cultivation for their flowers, and being smaller in growth. They all require a very liberal supply of water when growing. They do best to be planted in the soil, where there can be a small corner of the Hot-house set apart for the purpose. They will be ornamental, but if kept in pots they will never attain any degree of perfection.

Nepénthes (Pitcher plant). There are two species of this plant. *N. distillatòria* is an esteemed and valuable plant in European collections. The leaves are lanceolate and sessile; from their extremity there is a spiral, attached to which are lublar inflated appendages that are generally filled with water, which appears to be confined within them by a lid, with which the appendages are surmounted; hence the name of pitcher plant. We have never observed these lids close again when once open. Writers have called it a herbaceous plant, but it is properly a shrub, never dying to the ground, having a continuation of extension. The pot in which it grows should be covered with moss, and the roots liberally supplied with water every day. It delights to be in a marshy state. The flowers are small and in long spikes.

Pancràtium is a genus of Hot-house bulbs, and now only contains five species. They are all free-flowering. Several of them are handsome and fragrant. P. *Marítimum* and P. *verecúndum* are the finest; the flowers are white, in large umbels; petals long, recurved, and undulate. P. *littoràlis*, P. *speciòsum*, and P. *caribæum*, are now given to the genus *Hymenocállis*, and are fine flowering species. Care must be taken not to give them much water while dormant. The soil ought at that time to be in a half dry state. They are in flower from May to August.

Polyspòra axillàris, once called *Camèllia axillàris*, though in appearance it has no characteristic of a *Camèllia*, and has been frequently killed in the Green-house by being too cold for its nature; leaves oblong, obovate, towards the extremity serrulate. The leaves on the young wood are entire. Flowers white; petals a little notched. It is worthy of a situation in every collection.

Passiflòra, "Passion-Flower, so named on account of its being supposed to represent in the appendages of its flower the Passion of Jesus Christ." There are about fifty species, all climbing plants, that belong to the Hot-house. Many are of no ordinary beauty; a few species are odoriferous; others bear edible fruits, though not rich in flavour. P. *alàta* is in our collections, and greatly admired; the flowers are red, blue, and white, beautifully contrasted, and flower profusely in pots. P. *racemòsa*, has red flowers, and one of the most profuse in flowering. P. *cærùleo-racemòsa*, purple and red, and by many thought to be the finest of the genus. P. *quadrangulàris* has beautiful red and white flowers. The plant is in several collections, but has seldom flowered; it requires to be planted in the ground to make it flower freely, and it will also produce fruit. P. *filamentòsa* is white and blue, and a good flowerer. P. *picturàta* is a scarce and beautiful variously coloured species. There are many other fine species, but these are the most esteemed sorts; and when well established will flower profusely from May to

August. They are desirable in every collection, and will take only a small space to hold them, by training the vines up the rafters of the Hot-house.

Pandànus, Screw Pine. There are above twenty species in this genus, several of them very interesting, but none so greatly admired as P. *odoratíssimus*. The leaves in established plants are from four to six feet long, on the back and edges spiny; are spreading, imbricated, and embracing the stem, and placed in three spiral rows upon it. The top soon becomes heavy when the plant throws out prongs one two, or three feet up the stem in an oblique descending direction, which take root in the ground, and thus become perfectly supported. It is cultivated in Japan for its delightful fragrance, and it is said, "of all the perfumes, it is by far the richest and most powerful." P. *ùtilis*, red spined. We question this species, and are inclined to believe that it is the former, only when the plants are newly raised from seed, the spines and leaves are red, changing to green as they become advanced in age. The plants are easy of culture, and will grow almost in any soil.

Pterospérmum, five species of plants that have very curiously constructed flowers, of a white colour, and fragrant; the foliage is of a brown rusty nature, and before expansion silvery-like. P. *suberifòlium* is in several of our collections, and esteemed. P. *semisagittàtum* has fringed bractæa; leaves oblong, accuminate, entire, sagittate on one side.

Plumèrias, above twenty species. Plants of a slow growth, robust nature, and are deciduous. The foliage is greatly admired. The plants are shy to flower, but are brilliant in colour. P. *acuminàta*, has lanceolate, acute leaves; flowers corymbose and terminale. P. *trícolor* has oblong, acute, veiny leaves; corolla red, yellow, and white. This and P. *rùbra* are the finest of the genus. They ought not to get any water while not in a growing state.

Phœnix, Date-palm, about eight species, principally Asiatic plants. The foliage is not so attractive as many others of the palm family, but it is rendered interesting by producing a well known fruit called Date. P. *dactylífera* will do very well in a common Green-house. In Arabia, Upper Egypt, and Barbary, it is much used in domestic economy. P. *paludósa* has the most beautiful foliage, and the best habit. The flowers are diœcious.

Roscòea. A genus of about five species, all pretty, but not much known. *R. purpùrea* has been introduced into our collections, and is the finest of the genus. The flowers are light purple, large, and in terminale sheaths at the top of the stem. *R. spicàta* and *R. capitàta* are both fine species, with blue flowers. They are all herbaceous, with strong half tuberous roots, requiring little water while dormant, and a liberal supply when growing.

Ruéllia. There are a few species, very pretty free flowering plants, of easy culture. *R. formòsa*, flowers long, of a fine scarlet colour; plant half shrubby. *R. fulgída* has bright scarlet flowers on axillary long stalked fascicles. *R. persicifòlia*, with unequal leaves, and light blue flowers, is now called *R. anisophylla*; and the true one has oblong, wavy, leaves, deeply nerved, petioles long; flowers yellow, sessile, in axillary and terminale heads, stem erect. One healthy plant will be frequently in flower from January to June. This species ought to be in every collection, both for its beauty of flower and foliage.

Rhápis, a genus of palms, that will grow very freely with heat, and room at the roots. *R. flabellifórmis* is an erect growing palm, with a spreading head. It is a native of China.

Thunbérgia, a genus containing six climbing plants, of a half shrubby nature. Some of them have a fragrant odour. *T. coccínea*, red; *T. grandiflòra*, blue; *T. fràgrans*, sweet-scented; *T. alàta*, has pretty buff and purple flowers, which are in great profusion. We are not certain but the latter will make a beautiful annual in the Flower-garden. It seeds freely, and from the time of sowing until flowering is about two months, if the heat is brisk. If sown in May, they will bloom from July until killed by frost.

Sàgus, Sago-palm. We are of opinion that the true palm from which the sago of the shops is produced, has not been introduced into our collections. It is very rare in the most extensive collections of Europe, but is not so fine as the one we have under the Sago, which is placed in the natural order of *Cycadeæ*; and Sagus is in that of *Palmæ*. The finest of this genus is *S. vinífera* and *S. Rúmphii.* They grow to a great height; even in artificial cultivation they may be seen from ten to twenty-five feet. We have not introduced them here for their beauty, but to prevent error.

Solándra, a genus of four species, remarkable for the extraordinary size of their flowers, and are considered beautiful. *S. grandiflora* and *S. viridiflòra* are the two best. The plants will bloom best if they are restricted in pot room, and are only introduced as being worthy of cultivation. If they are repotted once in two or three years, it is sufficient, except where the plants are small and want encouragement.

Strophánthus, a small genus of beautiful tropical shrubs. The segments of the corolla are curiously twisted before expansion. *S. divérgens* is a neat spreading shrub, with yellow flowers, a little tinged with red; the petals are about four inches long, undulate, lanceolate. *S. dichótomus* is rose coloured, corolla funnel shaped. The plants will flower freely in a strong moist heat. Drain the pots well.

Swietènia (mahogany-tree), the wood of which is celebrated in cabinet-work. *S. Mahógoni*, common. This tree varies much in general appearance according to soil and situation. The leaves are pinnated in four pairs; leaflets ovate, lanceolate; flowers small, white, in axillary panicles. *S. fubrifùga*, leaves pinnated, in four pairs; leaflets elliptical; flowers white, in terminale panicles. The wood of the last is the most durable of any in the East Indies. They are fine plants, and require heat and pot room to produce flowers.

Tecòma, a genus of plants closely allied to *Bignònia*, and are free-flowering; several of them much esteemed. *T. móllis*, *T. digitata*, and *T. splèndida*, are the most beautiful of those that belong to the Hot-house. They have large orange coloured, tubular, inflated, ringent flowers, in loose panicles. There is a plant known in our collections as *Bignònia stáns*, which is now *T. stàns*; has pinnated leaves, with oblong, lanceolate, serrated, leaflets; flowers in simple terminale, raceme, and of a yellow colour, and sometimes known by Ash-leaved *Bignònia*. It will always have a sickly aspect, if not well encouraged in light rich soil. Drain the pots well, as much moisture disfigures the foliage.

Tabernæmontána, a genus of little beauty, except for one or two species. A plant known in some collections as *Nèrium coronàrium*, is now, and properly, *T. coronària*. The variety, *flòre plèno*, is the one most deserving of culture, and will flower profusely from May to August; the flowers are double white, fragrant, and divaricating. The plant will lose its foliage if not kept in a strong heat; therefore place it in the warmest part of the Hot-house. *T. densiflòra* is a fine species, but very rare. Drain all the plants well, and keep them in the shade during summer.

Thrinax parviflòra, is a fine dwarf palm of the West Indies, with palmated fronds, plaited with stiff, lanceolate segments. The plant is of easy cultivation, and will grow in any soil.

Zàmia, a genus of plants in the natural order of *Cycadeæ*. Several species of them are admired. *Z. média*, *Z. furfuràcea*, *Z. ténuis*, *Z. integrifòlia*, are the most showy that belong to the Hot-house. The whole genus is frequently kept in this department. They are all plants of a slow growth, and the beauty is entirely in the pinnated fronds, with from ten to forty pairs of leaflets. The pots must be well drained.

Those genera of plants which we have enumerated under the head of repotting in this or next month, are composed of the finest Hot-house plants that have come under our observation. There are perhaps a few of them that are not to be found in the United States, or even on our continent; but the great object, in a choice collection of plants, is to have the finest from all parts of the known world. There are many plants whose nature does not require much support from soil, which is frequently observed in those that are mentioned. And there are many hundreds of plants desirable for beauty, ornament, and curiosity, which are not specified, our limits not permitting such an extended detail. Those whose nature agrees better with repotting at other periods, shall be noticed, especially those that are in the collections of the country. We have previously observed, that plants ought not to be flooded with water when newly potted, as it saturates the soil before the roots have taken hold of it; and that the best draining for pots is small gravel or potshreds broken fine. We wish it to be understood that when plants are repotted, any irregular branch or shoot should be lopped off, that cannot be tied in to advantage. And repotting may take place either before or after the plants are exposed to the open air, according to convenience.

OF BRINGING OUT THE HOT-HOUSE PLANTS.

Where the Hot-house is very crowded with plants, the best method to have them exposed without danger is, to take out those of the hardiest nature first, that have no tender shoots upon them, thereby thinning the house gradually. This may be done from the 16th to the 20th of the month, which will admit of a free circulation of air amongst those that remain. All may be exposed from the 24th to the 28th of the month. This is a general rule, though in some seasons there maybe exceptions. Having previously given all the air possible to the house, that no sudden transition take place, which would make the foliage brown, and otherwise materially injure the plants, choose calm days for the removing of them.

There are few plants while in pots that agree with the full sun upon them; or if the plants receive the sun, the pots and roots ought not. The best situation for them is on the north side of a fence, wall, house, or other building, where they are excluded from the mid-day sun, and they should stand on boards or gravel, with the tallest at the back, firmly, tied to a rail or some other security, to prevent them from being overturned by high winds. A stage erected, where it is practicable, for the reception of the smaller plants, and they set thinly and regularly thereon, is preferable to crowding them with the taller sorts. And it may be desired to have some of the plants plunged in the garden through the flower borders. Of those that are so treated, the pots must be plunged to the brim, and regularly turned round every two weeks, to prevent the roots from running into the earth. If the roots were allowed to do so, it might for the present strengthen the plant, but ultimately would prove injurious.

Where a sufficiency of shade cannot be obtained, it would be advisable to go to the expense of a very thin awning, that would not exclude the light, but merely the powerful rays of the sun, attending to roll it up every evening. Plants will keep in beautiful order by the above method, which amply repays for the trouble or expense. Avoid putting plants under trees; comparatively few thrive in such situations.

When they are thus all exposed to the open air, it will be very little trouble to give them a gentle syringing every evening when there is no rain, and continue your usual examinations for insects: when they appear resort to the prescribed remedies. *Green-fly* will not affect them, but perhaps the thrips. Give regular supplies of water to their roots every evening, and some will require it in the morning, especially small pots.

SUCCULENTS.

These plants are habituated to exposed dry, hot, situations in their indigenous state; and an aspect, where they would have the full influence of the sun, is the best, giving them water two or three times a week.

Green-House.

MAY.

About the first of the month, all the small half hardy plants may be taken out of the green house, and those that are left will be more benefited by a freer circulation of air, which will enure them to exposure. The *Geraniums* ought to stand perfectly clear of other plants, while in flower and growing, or they will be much drawn and spindly.

WATERING.

We have advanced so much on this subject, another observation is not necessary; except as to succulents, which are frequently overwatered about this period. Before they begin to grow, once a week is sufficient.

OF BRINGING OUT THE GREEN-HOUSE PLANTS.

Those trees or plants of *Orange*, *Lemon*, *Myrtle*, *Nerium*, &c. that were headed down with the intention of planting them into the garden, to renovate their growth, should be brought out and planted in the situations intended for them. A good light rich soil will do for either, and the balls of earth might be a little reduced, that when they are lifted they might go into the same pot or tub, or perhaps a less one. This being done, the plants, generally in a calm day from the 12th to the 18th of the month, should be taken out, carrying them directly to a situation shaded from the sun, and protected from the wind. In regard to a situation best adapted for them during summer, see *Hot-house* this month, which will equally apply to Green-house plants, except *Dáphne odòra*, *Dáphne hybrida*, and the Green-house species of *Coronílla*, which must be shaded from every ray of the sun, and even from dry parching winds. All Primroses and Polyanthus delight in shade. The reason of so many plants of the *D. odòra*[H] dying is from the effects of the sun and water.

[H] On examining these plants, when the first appearance of decay affected them, the decayed part was without exception at the surface of the soil, which was completely mortified, while the top and roots were apparently fresh. This led us to conclude that the cause was the effect of sun and water on the stem. We have since kept the earth in a conical form round the stem, thereby throwing the water to the sides of the pot, and kept them in the shade. Previous to doing this, we had quantities died every year, and now no plants thus treated die with us.

The large trees may be fancifully set either in a spot for the purpose, or through the garden. Put bricks or pieces of wood under the tubs to prevent them from rotting, and strew a little litter of any description over the surface of the soil to prevent evaporation, or about one inch of well decayed manure, which will from the waterings help to enrich the soil. A liberal supply of water twice or three times a week is sufficient. A large tree will take at one time from two to four gallons. We make this observation, for many trees evidently have too limited a supply. Continue to syringe the plants through the dry season every evening, or at least three times per week. All the tall plants must be tied to some firm support, because the squalls of wind frequently overturn them, and do much harm by breaking, &c. Keep those that are in flower as much in the shade as will preserve them from the direct influence of the sun.

REPOTTING PLANTS.

After the following mentioned plants, or any assimilated to them, are brought out of the house, and before they are put in their respective stations, repot them where they are required to grow well. *Aloes.* These plants so varied in character, have been divided into several genera. These are *Gastèria*, *Pachidéndron*, *Riphidodéndron*, *Howárthia*, and *Apicra*. Of these there are above two hundred species and varieties. To enter into any specific detail, would be beyond our limits; but the catalogue at the end of the work will contain the finest species.

Amaryllis. This is a genus of splendid flowering bulbs containing about eighty species, and one hundred and forty varieties. They are natives of South America, but more than one half of them are hybrids grown from seed by cultivators. They are generally kept in the Hot-house, but in our climate will do perfectly well in the Green-house;

and we have no doubt that in a few years many of them will be so acclimated, as to keep as garden bulbs, planting about the end of April, and lifting them in October. As the beauty of these plants is in the flowers, it will be proper to give a small description of a few of them. *A. striatifòlia*, has a stripe of pure white in the centre of each leaf, the flowers are purple and white, an esteemed species. *A. Johnsòni*, the flowers are a deep scarlet, with a white streak in the centre of each petal, four bloom on a stem of about two feet, each flower about six inches diameter; a bulb well established has two stems. *A. regìna*, Mexican Lily, has large scarlet pendant flowers, tube of the flower fringed-like, with three or four on the stem. *A. vittàta* is an admired species with scarlet flowers, striped with a greenish white. There are two or three varieties of it; corolla campanulate, three or four on the stem, about five inches diameter; petals a little undulate. *A. fùlgida*, flower scarlet, large tube striped, petals acute, two flowers on the stem. *A. áulica* is one of the most magnificent, has four flowers about seven inches diameter, erect on a stem about two and a half feet high; six petals, strongly united to the capsule, bottom of the petals green, connected with spots of dark crimson, which spread into fine transparent red, covered with rich tints, nerves very perceptible, anthers bold. It is called crowned *Amaryllis*. *A. psittácina*, Parrot Amaryllis, is scarlet striped with green, two flowers on the stem, each about five inches diameter. There are several varieties of it; the best that we have seen are *cowbèrgia* and *pulverulènta*. A bulb known in our collections as *A. purpùrea* is *Ballóta purpùrea*, has beautiful erect scarlet flowers, three or four on the stem, each about five inches in diameter. There are three varieties of it, differing only in habit. *A. longifòlia* is now *Crìnum capénse*, and is perfectly hardy; flowers pink, inclining to white, in large umbels, leaves long, glaucous, and is a desirable garden bulb.

There are many other superb Amaryllis, especially the hybrid sorts; from *Johnsòni* there are above twenty cultivated varieties; from *formòsa* above twelve; and from *Griffìni* about ten, all of them esteemed. Where they have been kept in the earth in which they were grown last year, the ball ought at this repotting to be reduced; when the bulbs are done flowering, they ought to have little water, so that they may be perfectly ripened, which will cause them to produce their flowers more freely.

Araucària. This noble genus contains four species, which are without exception the handsomest plants we are acquainted with, for the beauty of their foliage, and symmetry of their growth, that belong to the Green-house. *A. excélsa*, Norfolk Island Pine, has leaves closely imbricated as if with a coat of mail, and are imperishable. *A. imbricàta*, Chile Pine, is one of the grandest of trees, and is the hardiest of the genus; the leaves are also closely imbricated. The other two species are rarely seen even in European collections. The foliage of either of the species will adhere to the wood many years after the plant is dead. They are all highly valued, the pots must be well drained; for if the plants get much water while dormant, the foliage becomes yellow, and never attains its beautiful green colour again; otherwise they are easily grown.

Chamærops. There are about seven species of these palms: four of them belong to this department, and are the finest of those that will keep in the Green-house. They all have large palmated fronds, and require large pots or tubs to make them grow freely, and are tenacious of life if kept from frost.

Gardènia. This is an esteemed genus of plants, especially for the double flowering varieties, which are highly odoriferous, and have an evergreen shining foliage. *G. flòrida flòre-plèno*, Cape Jasmine, is a plant universally known in our collections, and trees of it are frequently seen above seven feet high and five feet in diameter, blooming from June to October. *G. rádicans*, dwarf Cape Jasmine, *G. longifòlia*, and *G. latifòlia*, are also in several collections, but not so generally known; the flowers are double, and all equally fragrant. We are inclined to think they are only varieties of *G. flòrida.* Any of the above will keep in the coldest part of the Green-house, and even under the stage is a good situation for them, where the house is otherwise crowded during winter. They must be sparingly watered from November to March. Much water while they are dormant, gives the foliage a sickly tinge, a state in which they are too frequently seen. *G. Rothmànnia* and *G. Thunbérgia* are fine plants, but flower sparingly; the flowers of the former are spotted, and are most fragrant during night.

Mesembryànthemum. A very extensive genus, containing upwards of four hundred and fifty species, and varieties, with few exceptions natives of the Cape of Good Hope. They are all singular, many of them beautiful, and some splendid; yet they have never been popular plants in our collections. The leaves are almost of every shape and form; their habits vary in appearance. Some of them are straggling, others insignificant, and a few grotesque. When they are well grown, they flower in great profusion; the colours are brilliant, and through the genus are found of every shade; yellow and white are most prevalent. Each species continues a considerable time in flower. The flowers are either solitary, axillary, extra axillary, but most frequently terminale; leaves mostly opposite, thick, or succulent, and of various forms. They are sometimes kept in the Hot-house, but undoubtedly the Green-house is the best situation for them. They must not get water above once a month during winter, but while they are in flower and through the summer, they require a more liberal supply, and they seldom need to be repotted; once in two years is sufficient.

Strelítzia, a most superb genus of evergreen perennial plants. They are greatly esteemed and highly valued in our collections. The finest flowering species are *S. reginæ* and *S. ováta*; the former is the strongest of the two, but in respect to the beauty of their flowers there is no difference. The scape arises about three feet, headed with a sheath which lies horizontal before the flowers burst forth. The sheath contains three, four, or five flowers, according to the strength of the plants. These arise erect, and pass in a few days to the bottom of the sheath, the one before the other. *S. hùmilis* is another fine species, but the most rare are *S. agústa*, which has a leaf nearly like the plantain; *S. jùncea*, *S. parvifòlia*, and *S. farinòso*. The flowers of all these are yellow and blue, except those of *S. agústa*, which are white, and it flowers sparingly. A few species of these plants ought to be in every Green-house: they are vulgarly called Queen plant. While in flower they should be liberally supplied with water, but while dormant very sparingly. They will suffer sooner from the effects of too much, than too little water. The roots are strong tubers, and require plenty of pot room, and will thrive exceedingly where they can be planted in the soil.

CAMELLIAS.

These plants, when they are brought from the Green-house, ought to be set in a situation by themselves, that they may be the more strictly attended to in watering and syringing. An airy situation where the sun has no effect upon them is the best. They should be syringed every evening when there has been no rain through the day. After heavy rains examine the pots, and where water is found, turn the plant on its side for a few hours to let the water pass off, and then examine the draining in the bottom of the pots, which must be defective.

CAPE BULBS.

As soon as these are done flowering, and the foliage begins to decay, cease watering, and turn the pots on their sides, until the soil is perfectly dry; then take out the bulbs and preserve them dry until the time of planting, which will be about the end of August or first of September.

MAY.

It is highly desirable to have all the scientific operations as much advanced in the beginning of this month as is practicable, that at all times immediate attention may be given to the destroying of weeds wherever they appear.

ANNUALS, HARDY AND TENDER.

By the first of the month finish sowing all hardy Annuals and Biennials; and about the middle of the month all those that are tropical. The weather being now warm, they will vegetate in a few days or weeks. Attend to thinning of those that are too thick, giving gentle waterings to such as are weak in dry weather. Those that have been protected in frames should be fully exposed therein night and day; take the first opportunity of damp cloudy days to have them transplanted into the borders or beds, after the 10th, lifting them out of the frame with as much earth as will adhere to their roots.

CARE OF HYACINTHS, TULIPS, &c.

For the treatment of these while in bloom, see last month. The best time to take them out of the ground is about five weeks after they are done flowering, or when the stem appears, what may be termed half decayed. The best method to dry them is to place the roots in rows, with bulb to bulb, the stems laying north and south, or east or west. Give the bulbs a very thin covering of earth, merely to exclude the sun, so that they may not dry too rapidly, being thereby liable to become soft. When they have thoroughly dried in this situation, which will be in eight or ten days in dry weather, (and if it rains cover them with boards,) take them to an airy dry loft or shade, clearing off the fibres or stems, and in a few weeks put them in close drawers, or cover them with sand perfectly dry, until the time of planting, for which see October.

It is not advisable to allow any of the bulbs of either Hyacinths or Tulips to seed, as it retards their ripening, and weakens the root, except where there are a few desired for new varieties. The small offsets must be carefully kept in dry sand, or immediately planted.

ANEMONES AND RANUNCULUS.

These while in bloom should be carefully shaded from the sun by hoops and thin canvass, or an erect temporary awning; and as soon as they are done flowering, they must be fully exposed, and the waterings given up.

DAHLIAS, TUBEROSES, AND AMARYLLIS,

That are not planted, should now be done. For full directions see last month. In many seasons, any time before the twelfth is quite soon enough; but nothing ought to be delayed when the season will permit it to be done. It is necessary to have them properly labeled.

AURICULAS, POLYANTHUS, AND PRIMROSES.

They will now be done flowering, but still must be carefully kept in a cool, shady situation, and all decayed leaves cut off as soon as they appear. Examine them carefully and frequently, in case slugs of any description be preying upon them. A dusting of hot lime will kill them, or they may be otherwise destroyed. Some have recommended to repot and slip those plants when done flowering, "or they will contract a destructive disease;" which disease is a loss of verdure, and is induced by too much heat and drought, and a few other causes from inattention; but if attended to as above until September, when they should be fresh potted, they will have time to be sufficiently established before winter, which is the most judicious time to take off slips, for two reasons, viz.—they do not need so much nursing through the most precarious season of the year (summer) for these plants, and they begin to grow, and will root afresh sooner.

DOUBLE WALL-FLOWERS.

As these are very seldom grown from seed, and are semi-biennials, art has to be used to preserve or renew them. About the end of this month take shoots of this year about three inches long, cutting them carefully off, and smoothing the cut end with a sharp knife; from this cut the lower leaves off about one inch and a half, and then put it in the ground; choose a very shady spot, mixing the soil with a little sand and earth of decayed leaves. Sprinkle them three times a day until they have taken root, which will be in a few weeks. Keep the cuttings about four inches apart.

GENERAL OBSERVATIONS.

We do not consider that it is essential every month to repeat the necessity of tying up plants, saving seeds when ripe, cutting down weeds, raking, &c. with many other similar observations. We have already been full on these subjects, and expect these to be remembered through the season. Particular care, however, is required to *carnations*, *pinks*, or any plants that have heavy heads and slender stems. If carnations are desired to flower strongly, cut off all the buds except three, leaving the uppermost and any other two of the largest. All climbing plants should have timely support, and tied securely every week while they are growing.

Rooms.

MAY.

All the plants will be able to withstand exposure, in the general state of the seasons, about the 10th of the month. Begin about the first to take out the hardiest, such as *Laurestínus*, *Hydrángeas*, *Roses*, *Primroses*, *Polyanthus*, &c. and thus allow the others to stand more free, and become hardened to exposure. The reason that plants are so often seen brown, stunted, and almost half dead, is from the exposed situation they are placed in, with the direct sun upon them, and too frequently from being so sparingly watered. There are no shrubby plants cultivated in pots that are benefited by the hot sun from this period to October. A north aspect is the best for every plant, except *Càctus*, *Aloe*, *Mesembryànthemum*, and such as go under the name of succulents. Where there are only a few, they should be conveniently placed, to allow water from a pot with a rose mouth to be poured frequently over them, which is the best substitute for the syringe. *Dáphne*, *Coronílla*, *Fúchsia*, *Camèllia*, *Primrose*, and *Polyánthus*, do not agree with a single ray of the sun, through the summer. There has been a general question what is the cause of the death of so many of the *Dáphne odòra*. It may be observed, that the first place that shows symptoms of decay, is at the surface of the soil, and this takes place a few weeks before there are evident effects of it. The cause is from the effect of heat or sun and water acting on the stem at least. If the soil is drawn in the form of a cone round the stem, to throw off the water to the edges of the pot, that the stem may be dry above the roots, mortification does not take place, neither do they die prematurely, when thus treated. For further remarks, see Green-house, this month.

CAPE BULBS.

Any of these that are done flowering, such as *Ixia*, *Oxalis*, *Lachenàlia*, &c. as soon as the foliage begins to decay, turn the pots on their sides, which will ripen the roots, and when perfectly dry, clear them off the soil, wrap them up in paper, with their names attached, and put them carefully aside until the time of planting.

REPOTTING.

Where it is required, repot *Cáctus*, *Aloe*, *Mesembryánthemums*, and all other succulents, with any of the *Amaryllis* that are required to be kept in pots, also Cape Jasmines. For description of the above, see Hot-house and Green-house of this month, under the same head.

Hot-House.

JUNE AND JULY.

As the plants of the Hot-house are all exposed to the open air, the directions will include both months. If the repotting is over, as recommended last month, all the attention they will require until the end of August, is the administering of water at the roots, and by the syringe over head. It will be impossible to say how great are their wants, that depending entirely upon the nature of the plant, the situation, and the season; but never neglect to look over them every evening, and after very dry nights they will need a fresh supply in the morning, observing to give to none except they are becoming a little dry. Make weekly examinations for insects of any description, and when they appear, have them instantly destroyed.

Always after heavy rains look over the pots, in case water should be standing in them, which would injure the roots. Where any is found, turn the pot on its side, and in a few hours examine the draining which is defective; small pots in continued rains should be turned likewise.

Tie up all plants and shoots to prevent them from being destroyed by the wind, and be attentive to pick all weeds from the pots. Turn round all the plants occasionally, to prevent them from being drawn to one side by the sun or light.

Green-House.

JUNE AND JULY.

The plants being out of the house, there need be little added under this head. Their treatment is in the general, and the required attention is in giving water according to their different constitutions and habits. Where there are not rain or river water, it should stand at least one day in butts or cisterns, to take the chilly air from it, and become softened by the surrounding atmosphere. This is more essential to the health of the plants than is generally supposed. The small plants in dry weather will need water evening and morning. Continue regular syringings as directed last month. There are frequently rains continuing for several days, which will materially injure many plants, if they are not turned on their sides until the rain is over, especially small plants. The syringings should never be done till after the waterings at the roots, and they should never be seldomer than every alternate evening. Turn all the plants frequently to prevent them from being drawn to one side by the sun or light. Carefully look over them at these turnings, to detect any insects. And observe that the tuberose rooted geraniums, such as *Ardéns*, *Bicòlor*, *Trístum*, &c. are not getting too much water, they being now dormant.

Flower Garden.

JUNE AND JULY.

HOLLAND BULBS.

The lifting of these will be general in June. For directions see *May*. It is not advisable to take up *Jonquils*, *Fritillària*, *Crocus*, and *Iris*, oftener than every alternate year; *Jonquils* may stand three years. *Anemones* and *Ranunculus* should be carefully lifted after their leaves begin to fade. Do not expose them to the sun, but cover slightly with earth or sand until they are perfectly dry, when they may be sifted out of the earth, and put into drawers carefully labeled. Some recommend to soak these roots in soap-suds, to destroy a worm that they are frequently attacked with. We know not how far this may be carried, nor the good or bad effects, never having practised it.

AUTUMN FLOWERING BULBS.

These are *Amaryllis lùtea*, now called *Sternbérgia lùtea*; *A. Belladónna*, now *Belladónna purpuráscens*; and *Neríne sarniénsis*. This is a beautiful flowering bulb, and requires the protection of a frame during winter. The old bulb seldom flowers oftener than two succeeding years, and then decays, but the off-sets will flower the second year; therefore when the old bulbs are lifted, they ought to be immediately planted, and receive every encouragement to strengthen them for flowering. *Crôcus satìvus*, *C Pallàsii*, *C. serotìnus*, and *C. nudiflòrus*, and all the species of *Cólchicum*, with species of several other genera not introduced into the country. They should all be lifted as soon as the foliage is decayed, and kept only a few weeks out of the ground, and then again replanted in fresh soil. The economy of the genus *Cólchicum* in regard to its bulbs, flowers, and seeds, is altogether singular, and may be termed an anomaly of nature. In producing the new bulbs or off-sets in a very curious manner, the old one perishes. The flowers which arise with long slender tubes from the root die off in October, without leaving any external appearance of seeds. These lie buried all the winter within the bulb, in spring they grow upon a fruit stalk, and are ripe about the first of June. How beautiful and admirable is this provision! The plant blooming so late in the year, would not have time to mature its seeds before winter; and is, therefore, so contrived that it may be performed out of the reach of the usual effects of frost, and they are brought above the surface when perfected, and at a proper season for sowing.

CARNATIONS AND PINKS.

In order to make the former flower well, if the weather is dry, give them frequent waterings at the root, and tie them up neatly to their rods. The criterion of a fine carnation is—the stem strong and straight, from thirty to forty inches high, the corolla three inches diameter, consisting of large round well formed petals, but not so many as to crowd it, nor so few as to make it appear thin or empty; the outside petals should rise above the calyx about half an inch, and then turn off in a horizontal direction, to support the interior petals, they forming nearly a hemispherical corolla. The interior petals should decrease in size toward the centre, all regularly disposed on every side; they should have a small degree of concavity at the lamina or broad end, the edges perfectly entire. The calyx above one inch in length, with strong broad points in a close and circular body. The colours must be perfectly distinct, disposed in regular long stripes, broadest at the edge of the lamina, and gradually becoming narrower as they approach the unguis or base of the petal, there terminating in a fine point. Those that contain two colours upon a white ground are esteemed the finest.

Of a double pink—the stem about twelve inches, the calyx smaller but similar to a carnation; the flowers two inches and a half in diameter; petals rose edges; colour white, and pure purple, or rich crimson; the nearer it approaches to black it is the more esteemed; proportions equal as in carnation. Those that are very tasteful with these flowers are attentive to the manner of their opening. Where the calyx is deficient in regular expansion to display the petals; that is, where there is a tendency to burst open on one side more than on the other, the opposite side in two or three different indentions should be slit a little at several times with the point of a small sharp knife, taking care not to cut the petals, and about the centre of the calyx tie a thread three or four times round to prevent any farther irregularity. Some florists and connoisseurs place cards on them. This is done when the calyx is small. Take a piece of thin pasteboard, about the size of a dollar; cut a small aperture in its centre to admit the bud to pass through. When on tie it tight to the rod, to prevent the wind from blowing it about; and when the flower is expanded, draw up the card to about the middle of the calyx, and spread the petals one over the other regularly upon it. When these plants are in flower, their beauty may be prolonged by giving them a little shade from the mid-day sun by an awning of any simple description. Where they are in pots, they can be removed to a cool shady situation, (but not directly under trees.)

OF LAYING CARNATIONS AND PINKS.

This is a necessary and yearly operation to keep a supply of plants, and likewise to have them always in perfection. As the process of laying, though simple, may not be known to all who are desirous of cultivating these plants, we will give an outline of the mode of operation. Provide first a quantity of small hooked twigs (pieces of *Asparagus* stems are very suitable) about three inches long, for pegging the layers down in the earth. Select the outward strongest and lowest shoots that are round the plant, trim off a few of the under leaves, and shorten with the knife the top ones even, and then applying it at a joint about the middle of the under-side of the shoot, cut about half through in a slanting direction, making an upward slit towards the next joint, near an inch in extent; and loosening the earth, make a small oblong cavity one or two inches deep, putting a little fresh light earth therein. Lay the stem part where the slit is made into the earth, keeping the cut part open, and the head of the layer upright one or two inches out of the earth; and in that position peg down the layer with one of the hooked twigs, and cover the inserted part to the depth of one inch with some of the fresh earth, pressing it gently down. In this manner proceed to lay all the proper shoots of each plant. Keep the earth a little full round the plant, to retain longer the water that may be applied. Give immediately a moderate watering, with a rose watering pot, and in dry weather give light waterings every evening. Choose a cloudy day for the above operation. In about two months they will be well rooted.

PRUNING ROSES.

The best time to prune what are termed "Garden roses" is immediately after flowering, which is generally about the middle of

June. Cut out all old exhausted wood, and where it is too thick and crowded, shortening those shoots which have flowered to a good fresh strong eye, or bud, accompanied with a healthy leaf, but leaving untouched such shoots as are still in a growing state, except where they are becoming irregular. Such should be cut to the desired shape. There is not a better period of the year for puting these bushes in handsome order, which ought to be studied. All wood that grows after this pruning will ripen perfectly and produce fine flowers next year.

Our reasons for doing so at this period are these: The points of the shoots of the more delicate sorts of roses are very apt to die when pruned in winter or spring; hence the consequences of this evil are avoided. The stronger the wood of roses is made to grow, the flowers will be the larger and more profuse, and this effect is but produced by cutting out the old and superfluous wood; at least it prevents any loss of vegetative power, which ought always to be considered.

OF BUDDING OR INOCULATION OF ROSES.

According to what we have previously hinted in regard to having roses as standards, where such are desired, the month of July is a proper time for the operation of budding. The kinds to be taken for stocks should be of a strong free growth. Such as *Ornamental parade*; *Dutch tree*; *R. vilòsa*; *R. canína*; and frequently the French *Eglantine*, are taken. Be provided with a proper budding-knife, which has a sharp thin blade adapted to prepare the bud, with a tapering ivory haft made thin at the end for raising the bark of the stock. For tieings use bass strings from Russia mats, which should be soaked in water to make them more pliable. The height of the stock or stem at which the bud is to be inserted, is to be determined by the intended destination of the tree, (as it may be properly called.) Choose a smooth part of the stem, from one to three years old. Having marked the place, prune away all the lateral shoots about and underneath it. With the knife directed horizontally, make an incision about half an inch long in the bark of the stock, cutting into the wood, but not deeper; then applying the point of the knife to the middle of this line, make a perpendicular incision under the first, extending from it between one and two inches. Having a healthy shoot of the growth of this year provided of the kind that is desired, begin at the lower end of this shoot, cut away all the leaves, leaving the footstalk of each. Being fixed on a promising bud, insert the knife about half an inch above the eye, slanting it downwards, and about half through the shoot. Draw it out about an inch below the eye, so as to bring away the bud unimpaired with the bark, and part of the wood adhering to it; the wood now must be carefully detached from the bark. To do this insert the point of the knife between the bark and wood at one end, and holding the bark tenderly, strip off the woody part, which will readily part from the bark if the shoot from which the piece is taken has been properly imbued with sap.[I] Look at the inner rind of the separated bark, to see if that be entire; if there be a hole in it, the eye of the bud has been pulled away with the wood, rendering the bud useless, which throw away; if there be no hole, return to the stock, and with the haft of the knife gently raise the bark on each side of the perpendicular incision, opening the lips wide enough to admit the prepared slip with the eye. If the slip is longer than the upright incision in the stock, reduce the largest end. Stock and bud being ready, keep the latter in its natural position, introduce it between the bark and wood of the stock, pushing it gently downwards until it reaches the bottom of the perpendicular incision. Let the eye of the bud project through the centre of the lips; lay the slip with the bud as smooth as possible, and press down the raised bark of the stock. The bud being deposited, bind that part of the stock moderately tight with bass, beginning a little below the incision, proceeding upward so as to keep the eye uncovered, finishing above the incision. In a month after the operation, examine whether the bud has united with the stock. If it has succeeded, the bud will be full and fresh; if not, it will be brown and contracted. When it has taken, untie the bandage, that the bud may swell, and in a few days afterwards cut the head of the stock off about six inches above the inoculation, and prevent all shoots from growing by pinching them off. This will forward the bud, which will push and ripen wood this season; but it must be carefully tied as it grows to the remaining head of the stock. Some do not head down the stock until the following spring, thereby not encouraging the bud to grow, which if winter sets in early is the safest method.

[I] We once budded three eyes of the white moss rose, after they had by mistake been carried in the pocket of a coat three days. The shoot was soaked six hours in water, and two of the buds grew. From this we infer that shoots, if properly wrapped up, may be carried very great distances, and grow successfully.

OF WATERING.

If the season is dry, look over the late planted shrubs, and give them frequent copious waterings; and a few of the finest annuals that are wanted to flower perfectly should be attended to. *Dahlias* suffer very much in dry seasons, therefore it is advisable to water the most beautiful (or all) of them two or three times per week, and be careful to tie up their shoots to any support that is given to them, in case of high winds breaking or otherwise destroying the flower stems.

JUNE AND JULY.

The only attention requisite to *these* plants, is in giving water, keeping them from being much exposed to either sun or high winds, and preventing the attack of insects. Water must be regularly given every evening, when there has not been rain during the day. Where they are in a growing state, they are not liable at this season of the year to suffer from too much water, except in a few instances, such as the Lemon-scented Geranium, and those kinds that are tuberose rooted, as *Ardèns*, *Bicòlor*, *Tristúm*, &c. which should have moderate supplies.

All the plants ought to be turned round every few weeks to prevent them from growing to one side, by the one being more dark than the other, and keep those of a straggling growth tied neatly to rods. Wherever insects of any description appear, wash them off directly. Give regular syringings or sprinklings from the rose of a watering pot. Be particularly attentive in this respect to the *Caméllias*, which will keep the foliage in a healthy state, and prevent the effects of mildew.

If the foliage of *Lílium longiflòrum*, or *japónicum*, has died down, do not water them while dormant, as they are easily injured by such treatment.

AUGUST.

The plants of the Hot-house that were repotted in May and June, according to the directions therein given, will at present be in an excellent state of health, provided they have got at all times the requisite supplies of watering. And as we already have been very explicit on that subject, more remarks now would be merely repetition.

REPOTTING.

If any of the repottings were neglected, during May or June, let it be done about the first of this month. Let young plants that are growing freely, where the roots have filled the pots, and the plants required to grow, have pots one size larger. In turning out the ball of earth, keep it entire, not disturbing any of the roots.

OF PAINTING, REPAIRING, AND CLEANSING THE HOUSE.

The necessary repairs of the Hot-house are too often put off to the last day or week; and then with hurry are superficially attended to. Previous to the first of September, have all the wood-work painted; which ought to have one coat every year, and the glass all repaired. Have the flues and furnace examined, and all rents plastered over, or any deficiency made good. Give the flue a thick coat of lime white-wash, and properly white-wash the whole interior stages and shelves to destroy any larvæ of insects; or, what is preferable for the latter, use oil paint. If there is a tan bed, have that renewed; take out what is most decayed, and add new tan. Wash out the floor perfectly clean, so that all may be in readiness for the plants next month.

Green-house.

AUGUST.

Any of the *Myrtles*, *Oranges*, *Lemons*, *Oleanders*, &c. that were headed down in April or May, will be pushing many young shoots. The plant must be carefully examined, to observe which of the shoots ought to be left to form the tree. Having determined on this, cut out all the others close to the stem with a small sharp knife; and if the remaining shoots are above one foot long, pinch off the tops to make them branch out.

The trees that were entirely headed down, should not have above six shoots left, which will, by being topped, make a sufficient quantity to form the bush or tree.

GERANIUMS.

These plants, about the first of the month, require a complete dressing. In the first place collect them all together, and with a sharp knife cut off the wood of this year to within a few eyes of the wood of last year. *Citriodórum* and its varieties do not need pruning. The plants grown from cuttings during the season, that have flowered, cut them to about four inches from the pot. This being done, have the earth all prepared with potshreds or fine gravel for draining the delicate kinds. And in a shaded situation turn the plants progressively out of the pots they are in, reducing the balls of earth so that the same pots may contain them again, and allow from half an inch to two inches, according to the size of the pot, of fresh soil around the ball, which press down by a thin piece of wood cut for the purpose. Finish by leveling all neatly with the hand. Give very gentle waterings from a pot with a rose mouth, for a few weeks, until they have begun to grow, protecting them entirely from the sun, till that period, then take the opportunity of a cloudy day to expose them. After this repotting, the following kinds are liable to suffer from too much water: *Pavonínum*, *Davey[)a]num*, *fúlgens*, *ardens*, *citriodórum*, *rubéscens*, *florabùndum*, *ardèscens*; with those of a similar habit, and these species do not require so much encouragement at the root as the strong growing sorts. The tuberous rooted and deciduous species must be very moderately supplied. Be careful when watering that the new soil does not become saturated with water, as, though allowed to dry again, it will not be so pure. When they shoot afresh, turn them regularly every two weeks, to prevent them growing to one side.

ORANGES, LEMONS, &c.

As it is frequently very inconvenient to shift these trees into larger tubs in the months of March and April, this month is a period that is suitable both from the growth of the trees, and their being in the open air. It would be improper to state the day or the week, that depending entirely on the season. The criterion is easily observed, which is when the first growth is over, these trees making another growth in autumn. When they are large, they require great exertion, and are frequently attended with inconvenience to get them shifted. Where there is a quantity of them, the best plan that we have tried or seen adopted is as follows: Have a strong double and a single block trimmed with a sufficiency of rope; make it fast to the limb of a large tree, or any thing that projects, and will bear the weight, and as high as will admit of the plant being raised a few feet under it. Take a soft bandage and put around the stem, to prevent the bark from being bruised; make a rope fast to it, in which hook the single block. Raise the plant the height of the tub, put a spar across the tub, and strike on the spar with a mallet, which will separate the tub from the ball. Then with a strong pointed stick probe a little of the earth from amongst the roots, observing to cut away any that are affected by dry-rot, damp, or mildew, with any very matted roots. Having all dressed, place a few potshreds over the hole or holes in the bottom of the tub; measure exactly the depth of the ball that remains around the plant, and fill up with earth, pressing it a little with the hand, until it will hold the ball one inch under the edge of the tub. If there is from four to six inches of earth under it, it is quite enough. Fill all around the ball, and press it down with a stick, finishing neatly off with the hand. Observe that the stem of the tree is exactly in the centre. This being done, carry the tree to where it is intended to stand, and give it water with a rose on the pot. The earth will subside about two inches, thus leaving three inches, which will at any time hold enough of water for the tree. Trees thus treated will not require to be shifted again within four or five years, having in the interim got a few rich top-dressings.

Frequently in attempting to take out of the tubs those that are in a sickly state, all the soil falls from their roots, having no fibres attached. When there are any such, after replanting, put them in the Green-house, and shut it almost close up, there give shade to the tree, and frequent sprinklings of water, until it begins to grow, when admit more air gradually until it becomes hardened. These trees should be put in very small tubs, and a little sand added to the soil. Give very moderate supplies of water, merely keeping the soil moist. Tubs generally give way at the bottom when they begin to decay, and in the usual method of coopering after this failure they are useless, the ledging being rotten, and will not admit of another bottom. The staves should be made without any groove, and have four brackets nailed on the inside, having the bottom in a piece by itself that it can be placed on these brackets, and there is no necessity of it being water tight. Then when it fails, it can be replaced again at a trifling expense. A tub made this way will last out three or four bottoms, and is in every respect the cheapest, and should be more wide than deep. *Large Myrtles* and *Oleanders* may be treated in the same manner as directed for the above.

OF PRUNING ORANGES, LEMONS, &c.

These trees will grow very irregularly, especially the *Lemon*, if not frequently dressed or pruned. Any time this month look over them all minutely, and cut away any of the small naked wood where it is too crowded, and cut all young strong straggling shoots to the bounds of the tree, giving it a round regular head. It is sometimes necessary to cut out a small limb, but large amputations should be avoided. Cover all wounds with turpentine or bees-wax, to prevent the bad effects of the air.

OF REPOTTING PLANTS.

Any of the plants enumerated in March under this head, may be now done according to directions therein given, and which apply to all sizes. This is the proper period for repotting the following:—

Cálla, a genus of four species. None of them in our collections, and in fact are not worth cultivation, except *C. æthiòpica*, Ethiopian Lily, which is admired for the purity and singularity of its large white flowers, or rather spatha, which is cucullate, leaves sagittate. It is now called *Richárdia æthiópica*. The roots which are tubers should be entirely divested of the soil they have been grown in, breaking off any small offsets, and potting them wholly in fresh earth. When growing they cannot get too much water. The plant will grow in a pond of water, and withstand our severest winters, provided the roots are kept at the bottom of the water.

Cyclamen. There are eight species and six varieties of this genus, which consists of humble plants with very beautiful flowers. The bulbs are round, flattened, and solid, and are peculiarly adapted for pots and the decorating of rooms. *C. côum*, leaves almost round; flowers light red; in bloom from January to April. *C. pérsicum*, with its four varieties, flower from February to April; colour white, and some white and purple. *C. hederæfòlium*, Ivy-leaved; colour lilac; there is a white variety; flowers from July to September. *C. Europæum*, colour lilac, in bloom from August to October. *C. neapolitànum*, flowers red, in bloom from July to September. These are all desirable plants. When the foliage begins to decay, withhold the accustomed supplies of water, keeping them in a half dry state; and when growing they must not be over watered, as they are apt to rot from moisture. Keep them during the summer months in the shade. The best time for potting either of the sorts is when the crown of the bulb begins to protrude. If the pots are becoming large, every alternate year they may be cleared from the old soil, and put in smaller pots with the crown barely covered. When the flowers fade, the pedicles twist up like a screw, inclosing the germen in the centre, lying close to the ground until the seeds ripen, from which plants can be grown, and will flower the third year.

Lachenàlia, a genus of about forty species of bulbs, all natives of the Cape of Good Hope, and grow remarkably well in our collections. The most common is *L. trícolor*. *L. quadrícolor*, and its varieties, are all fine; the colours yellow, scarlet, orange, and green, very pure and distinct; *L. rùbida*. *L. punctàta*, *L. orchoídes*, and *L. nervòsa*, are all fine species. The flowers are on a stem from a half to one foot high, and much in the character of a hyacinth. The end of the month is about the time of planting. Five inch pots are large enough, and they must get very little water till they begin to grow.

Oxalis, above one hundred species of Cape bulbs, and like all other bulbs of that country, they do exceedingly well in our collections, in which there are only comparatively a few species, not exceeding twelve. *O. rubèlla*, branching, of a vermilion colour; *O. marginàta*, white; *O. elongàta*, striped; and *O. amœna*, are those that require potting this month. The first of September is the most proper period for the others.

This genus of plants is so varied in the construction of its roots, that the same treatment will not do for all. The root is commonly bulbous, and these will keep a few weeks or months out of the soil, according to their size. Several are only thick and fleshy: these ought not to be taken out of the pots, but kept in them, while dormant; and about the end of this month give them gentle waterings. When they begin to grow, take the earth from the roots, and pot them in fresh soil. In a few years the bulbs are curiously produced, the original bulb near the surface striking a radical fibre downright from its base, at the extremity of which is produced a new bulb for the next year's plant, the old one perishing.

Ornithógalum, Star of Bethlehem, about sixty species of bulbs, principally from the Cape of Good Hope. Many of them have little attraction. The most beautiful that we have seen are *O. lactéum*, which has a spike about one foot long of fine white flowers; and *O. aùreum*, flowers of a golden colour, in contracted racemose corymbs. These two are magnificent. *O. marítimum* is the officinale squill. The bulb is frequently as large as a human head, pear-shaped, and tunicated like the onion. From the centre of the root arise several shining glaucous leaves a foot long, two inches broad at base, and narrowing to a point. They are green during winter, and decay in the spring; then the flower-stalk comes out, rising two feet, naked half way, and terminated by a pyramidal thyrse of white flowers. The bulb ought to be kept dry from the end of June till now, or it will not flower freely.

GENERAL OBSERVATIONS.

Watering, and other practical care of the plants, to be done as heretofore described. Frequently the weather at the end of this month becomes cool and heavy. Dew falling through the night will in part supply the syringing operation, but it must not be suspended altogether. Three times a week will suffice. Any of the plants that are plunged should be turned every week. In wet weather observe that none are suffering from moisture.

FLOWER-GARDEN

AUGUST.

EVERGREEN HEDGES.

These always make two growths in the season, and the best time to perform the clipping or dressing of them is before the plants begin their second growth. Choose if possible dull and cloudy days for the operation. The general practice in forming these, is to have the sides even, and the top level, forming a right angle on each side. However neat in appearance this may be considered, it certainly is stiff and formal. We never approve of shearing where it can be avoided, and when adopted, nature ought to be imitated. We consider that all hedges and edgings ought to be narrowed at the top.

CARNATIONS AND PINKS.

If layed about the end of June, and been properly attended, they will by the end of this month be well rotted and fit for transplanting. Clear away the earth lightly, and cut them clean off from the parent plant, nearer the stool than the original slit. Raise them neatly out of the earth, with as many of the root-fibres as possible; cut off the naked part of the stem close to the fibrous roots, and trim away the straggling leaves. Plant the finest sorts in four inch pots, and those more common three plants in five inch pots, in the form of a triangle, which can be separated in spring to plant in the garden. Any of the principal stools should be (if in the ground) lifted and put into seven inch pots to be preserved: the others may be allowed to stand through the winter, covering them with a few dry leaves. Keep them in the shade a few weeks, when they may be fully exposed. Give gentle and frequent sprinklings of water until they have taken fresh root; or if in want of pots, mark out a bed that can be covered with a frame, preparing the soil therein properly. Plant them from four to six inches apart. Shade them from the sun until they begin to grow, giving sprinklings of water over the foliage every evening.

BULBOUS ROOTS.

Look over the bulbs that are out of the ground, and examine those that require planting. *Fritillària*, about twenty species, but few of them generally cultivated, except *F. imperiàlis*, Crown Imperial; and *F. pérsica*. These will require planting, and ought not to be lifted oftener than every third year. There are four or five varieties of the above, showy flowers, and singular in appearance. They require a deep rich loamy soil, and if in beds, plant them from three to four inches deep, and one foot apart. They will grow under shade of trees, or any situation where the soil is adapted for them. No imbricated or scaly bulb ought to be retained long out of the ground. When any of these are lifted, and the young bulbs taken off, they should be planted at once. See particularly on bulbous roots in general next month.

SOWING SEEDS OF BULBOUS ROOTS.

Where any seeds of these are saved, with the intention of sowing, let it be done this month. Procure boxes about seven inches deep, and in size proportioned to the quantity to be sown. Put five inches of light sandy soil in the box, level it smoothly, and sow the seeds separately and thickly; cover with half an inch of light sandy loam, with a portion of earth from the woods. Keep the box or boxes in a sheltered situation, giving frequent sprinklings of water to keep the earth damp, which must be protected with a frame, or covered with leaves during winter. The plants will appear in spring, and must be watered and kept in the shade: when the leaves decay in June, put one inch more soil upon them, and the second year they can be planted with the small offsets in the garden, and treated as other bulbs. They must be carefully marked every year. Tulips require many years of trial before their qualities are known; and a poor soil is best to produce their characters after the first bloom.

SOWING AND SAVING SEEDS.

About the end of this month or first of next, is an advisable period to sow seed of *Delphínum Ajácis flòreplèno*, or Double Rocket Larkspur. This plant does not flower in perfection except it is sown in autumn, and grown a little above ground before winter, when a few leaves can be lightly thrown amongst them, but not to cover them entirely, as that would cause damp, and they would rot off. *Coreópsis tinctòria*, which is now *Callíópsis tinctòria*, and a beautiful plant, should likewise be sown. Be attentive in saving all kinds of seeds, many of which will keep best in the capsule. Name them all correctly, and with the year in which they were grown.

Rooms.

AUGUST.

For the kinds of plants that require potting, we refer to the Green-house for this month. All that are therein specified are peculiarly adapted for rooms, and we would call attention to the genus *Cyclamen*, which has not been generally introduced into the collections of our ladies; as, from the character and beauty of the flowers, they are very attracting and highly deserving of culture. Attend to the Geraniums as there directed, and be particular in having them cut down, and repotted, as there fully described. The *Oranges*, *Lemons*, *Oleanders*, and *Myrtles*, that are kept in cellars or rooms, should have the same attention in this month as directed in the Green-house, which to repeat here would be occupying space unnecessarily.

Réseda odoráta, or Mignonette, is one of the most fragrant annuals. To have it in perfection, the seed should be sown about the end of this month, or beginning of next, into pots of fine light earth, and sprinkled with water frequently. When it comes up the plants must be thinned out or transplanted; the former method is preferable. Keep them from frost during winter, and always near the light.

This will equally apply to the Green-house.

Hot-House.

SEPTEMBER.

DRESSING THE PLANTS.

Having last month put the house in complete order, all that remains necessary to be attended to, is the state of the plants and pots, which should be regularly examined, and of those where the roots fill the soil, a little may be taken off the top, supplying its place with fresh earth, thereby giving what is called a top dressing. Give each a sufficient rod that requires it, tieing the plant neatly thereto; minutely scrutinise each for insects, and where they are detected, have them eradicated.

Finally, wash all contracted foulness from off the pots, at the same time pick off any decayed leaves; thus all will be in perfect order to take into the house. If any plants have been kept in the Hot-house during summer, they must likewise go through the same operations.

OF TAKING IN THE PLANTS.

From the 16th to the 24th, according to the season, is the proper time to take in the Hot-house plants. It is preferable to have them what might be deemed a few days too early, than have them in the slightest affected by cold.

Commence by housing the largest first, and those that stand farthest in the house, observing to place the most tender sorts nearest the heat or warmest part of the house. For observations on them, see *May*: in regard to arrangement, that must be according to the taste of the operator. We may observe that in a small collection it is better to have them in a regular than in a picturesque form. A dry shelf is indispensable in this department for placing on it all herbaceous plants, such as *Cánna*, *Hedychium*, *Zíngiber*, *Kæmpféria*, &c. the watering of which from this time should be gradually suspended, that they may have their required cessation to make them flower well. This shelf may be in any situation; one in darkness, where other plants will not grow, will answer perfectly well. If there is a bark bed, do not, until the end of December, plunge any of the pots therein.

GENERAL OBSERVATIONS.

The plants being now all under protection, they must have as much air as possible admitted to them every day, by opening the doors, front and top sashes, closing only at night. The syringings must be continued, and care taken that plants of a deciduous or herbaceous nature are not over watered. *Alstrœmèrias* are apt to rot while dormant when they are supplied with water. The tuberous species might be kept almost dry. Some practical men of sound science repot these plants in this month into fresh soil, and allow them to stand till January almost without water. We have never adopted this method with any description of plants, but do not doubt of its success with that genus.

See that the ropes and pullies of the sashes are in good order, and fit to stand all winter.

SEPTEMBER.

During this month every part of the Green-house should have a thorough cleansing, which is too frequently neglected, and many hundreds of insects left unmolested. To preserve the wood work in good order, give it one coat of paint every year. Repair all broken glass, white-wash the whole interior, giving the flues two or three coats, and cover the stages with hot-lime, white-wash, or oil-paint; examine ropes, pullies, and weights, finishing by washing the pavement perfectly clean. If there have been any plants in the house during summer, be sure after this cleansing that they are clean also, before they are returned to their respective situations.

OF WATERING.

The intensity of the heat being over for the season, the heavy dews during night will prevent so much absorption amongst the plants. They will, in general, especially by the end of the month, require limited supplies of water comparatively to their wants in the summer months. Be careful amongst the *Geraniums* that were repotted in August, not to water them until the new soil about their roots is becoming dry. Syringing in this month may be suspended in time of heavy dews, but in dry nights resort to it again.

The herbaceous plants and those of a succulent nature must be sparingly supplied. The large trees that were put in new earth will require a supply only once a week, but in such quantity as will go to the bottom of the tubs.

PREPARING FOR TAKING IN THE PLANTS.

About the end of the month all the plants should be examined and cleaned in like manner as directed for those of the Hot-house last month, which see. From the 1st to the 8th of October is the most proper time to take them into the Green-house, except those of a half hardy nature, which may stand out till the appearance of frost. All the

Geraniums that were put in the shade after shifting, may after the 10th be fully exposed, which will in some degree prevent them from being weak. Turn them in such a manner as will make them grow equally. Always endeavour to have these plants short and bushy, for they are unsightly otherwise, except where a few very large specimens are desired for show. All Myrtles and Oleanders that were headed down, if the young shoots are too crowded, continue to thin them out, and give regular turnings, that all the heads may grow regularly.

STOCKS AND WALL-FLOWERS,

That are wanted to flower in the Green-house (where they do remarkably well) and are in the ground, have them carefully lifted before the end of the month, and planted in six or seven inch pots, with light loamy soil. Place them in the shade till they take fresh root, and give them frequent sprinklings of water. As soon as the foliage becomes erect, expose them to the full sun, and treat as Green-house plants.

CHRYSANTHEMUMS.

These very ornamental plants blooming so late, and at a period when there are few others in flower, one of each variety (or two of some of the finest) should be lifted and put in 8 inch pots, in light loamy soil, and treated as above directed for Stocks, &c. These will flower beautifully from October to December, and when done blooming the pots may be plunged in the garden, or covered with any kind of litter, until spring, when they can be divided and planted out.

CAPE AND HOLLAND BULBS.

About the end of this month is the period for all of these that are intended for the Green-house to be potted. We specified some of the former last month, and will here enumerate a few others.

Babìana, a genus of small bulbs, with pretty blue, red, and yellow flowers. *B. distíca*, pale blue flowers in two ranks. *B. stricta*, flowers blue and white. *B. tubiflòra* is beautiful, colour white and red. *B. plicàta* has sweet-scented pale blue flowers. There are about twenty species of them, and they grow from six to twelve inches high. Four inch pots are sufficient for them.

Gladìolus, Corn-flag, a genus of above fifty species. There are several very showy plants amongst them, and a few very superb. *G. floribúndus*, large pink and white flowers. *G. cardinàlis*, flowers superb scarlet, spotted with white. *G. byzantìnus*, large purple flowers. *G. blándus*, flowers of a blush rose colour, and handsome. *G. cuspidàtus*, flowers white and purple. *G. psittácinus* is the most magnificent of the genus, both in size and beauty of flower; the flowers are striped with green, yellow, and scarlet, about four inches diameter, in great profusion, on a stem about two feet high, and though rare in Europe may be seen in some collections in this country. The beauty of this genus is all centred in the flowers; the leaves are similar to *Iris*.

Ixia, a genus containing about twenty-five species of very free-flowering bulbs. *I. monadélpha*, flowers blush and green. *I. leucántha*, flowers large, white. *I. capitàta*, flowers in heads of a white and almost black colour. *I. cònica*, flowers orange and velvet. *I. columellàris* is beautifully variegated with purple, blush, and vermilion colours. The flower stems are from six to twenty-four inches high.

Sparáxis, a beautiful genus of twelve species, closely allied to the last, but more varied in colour. *S. grandiflòra striàta* is striped with purple ground blush. *S. versícolor*, colours crimson, dark purple, and yellow. *S. anemonæflòra* is of various colours, and very similar to *Anemòne*.

Tritònia, a genus of about twenty-five species. Few of them deserve culture in regard to their beauty. *T. crocàta* is in our collections, as *I. crocàta*, which is amongst the finest, and *T. zanthospìla* has white flowers curiously spotted with yellow.

Watsònia, a genus containing several species of showy flowers, several of which are in our collections, under the genus *Gladíolus*, but the most of the species may easily be distinguished from it by their flat shell formed bulbs. *W. iridifòlia* is the largest of the genus, and has flowers of a flesh colour. *W. ròsea* is large growing, the flowers are pink, and on the stem in a pyramid form. *W. humilis* is a pretty red flowering species. *W. fúlgida*, once *Antholyza fúlgens*, has fine bright scarlet flowers. *W. rùbens* is an esteemed red flowering species, but scarce.

These six genera are in general cultivation. There are several of others of merit that our limits will not admit of inserting. We have no doubt there are some splendid species that have not come under our observation, and others which may be obtained from the Cape of Good Hope not known in any collection. Many hundreds of superb bulbs indigenous to that country, and of the same nature and habit of the above, have not been seen in collections. The flowers of those which we have specified are from one to four inches in diameter, ringent, tubular, or campanulate. Pots from four to seven inches diameter, according to the size of the roots, will be large enough. Give them very little water until they begin to grow; then supply moderately, and keep them near the light. Of the Holland or Dutch bulbs, the *Hyacinth* is the favourite to bloom in the Green-house. A few of the *Tulip*, *Narcissus*, *Iris*, and *Crocus*, may for variety be also planted with any other that curiosity may dictate. When these are grown in pots, the soil should be four-eighths loam, two-eighths leaf mould, one-eighth decomposed manure, one-eighth sand, well compounded; plant in pots from four to seven inches, keep the crown of the bulb above the surface of the soil, except of the Tulip, which should be covered two inches. When these roots are potted, plunge them in the garden about three inches under ground; mark out a space sufficient to contain them; throw out the earth about four inches deep, place the pots therein, covering them with earth to the above depth, making it in the form of a bed. Leave a trench all round to carry off the rain. By so doing, the bulbs will root strong, the soil will be kept in a congenial state about them, and they will prove far superior than if done in the common method. Lift them from this bed on the approach of frost, or not later than the second week of December, wash the pots and take them to the Green-house.

OF REPOTTING.

Vibúrnum. This is a good period to repot all the flowering plants of this genus. For a full description of them, see *Green-house, March*. The repotting is only intended for young plants that are wanted to grow freely. When the *V. tìnus* is much encouraged, it does not flower profusely.

Lìlium, Lily. There are four species of this splendid genus kept in the Green-house. It has always been our practice to repot them when they begin to grow, though it is said by some that, when removed at that time, they will not flower perfectly. They will not do to be kept above a few weeks out of the ground, and we think they ought never to be kept out any period. We place them here, that a choice may be made by the cultivator of either of the periods, which is not material; observing in either case, that excess of moisture is injurious while they are dormant. *L. longiflòrum* grows about one foot high, with one or more flowers. *L. longiflòrum suavèolens*, is sweet-scented, and has only one flower. *L. japònicum* is the most magnificent, grows about two feet high, with three or more flowers on one stem. *L. lancifòlium*; we incline to class this with *L. speciòsum*, there being no apparent distinction in any character. The flowers are all of the purest white. They require from five to seven inch pots.

SEPTEMBER.

OF DAHLIAS.

See that all these plants are supported with proper stakes, rods, &c., that the wind may have no effect in breaking down or otherwise destroying the flower stems. Strictly observe their respective heights and colours, that they may be duly disposed and interspersed next year, if not done so this. If the early part of the month is dry, give them liberal supplies of water.

GENERAL CARE OF PLANTS IN POTS.

All the flowers that are in pots, and intended to be kept in frames during winter, should have a top-dressing, and a general preparation for their winter quarters, by tieing up, &c. The carnation and pink layers that were lifted and potted last month must be brought from the shade as soon as they begin to grow; and those that are not lifted, have them done forthwith, that they may be rooted afresh before the frost sets in. All Wall-flowers and Stocks should be lifted this month, and planted in five to seven inch pots, and treated as directed for carnation layers last month, until they begin to grow, when they must be fully exposed.

PREPARE BEDS AND BORDERS FOR BULBOUS ROOTS.

Bulbous roots of every character delight in deep free soil; consequently, wherever they are desired to be planted, due attention must be paid to put the soil in proper order, to have them in perfection. Where there are a quantity intended to be planted, to have them in beds is the general and preferable method. These ought to be dug from eighteen inches to two feet deep, at the bottom of which place three or four inches of decayed manure. Where the soil is poor it should be enriched with well decomposed manure and earth from the woods, incorporating both well with the soil, breaking it all fine. This being done, allow it to stand until the middle of next month, which see for farther directions.

GENERAL OBSERVATIONS.

Tie up carefully all the *Chrysánthemums*, *Tuberoses*, &c. Clear away the stems or haulm of any decayed annuals or herbaceous plants, that nothing unsightly may appear. Be attentive to the collecting of all kinds of seeds.

SEPTEMBER.

Where there is a quantity of plants to be kept in these apartments, they should be disposed to the best effect, and at the same time in such a manner as will be most effectual to their preservation. A stage of some description is certainly the best, and, of whatever shape or form, it ought to be on castors, that it may, in severe nights of frost, be drawn to the centre of the room. The shape may be either concave, a half circle, or one square side. The bottom step or table should be six inches apart, keeping each successive step one inch farther apart, to the desired height, which may be about six feet. Allowing the first step to be about two feet from the floor, there will be five or six steps, which will hold about fifty pots of a common size. A stage in the form of half a circle will hold more, look the handsomest, and be most convenient. We have seen them circular, and when filled appeared like a pyramid. These do very well, but they must be turned every day, or the plants will not grow regularly. With this attention it is decidedly the best. Green is the most suitable colour to paint them.

GENERAL OBSERVATIONS.

The directions given for the Green-house this month are equally applicable here. The *Tasseled White Chrysanthemum*, and a few other late blooming sorts, are particularly adapted for rooms. If there is no convenience to plunge the pots with Dutch bulbs in the garden, as described in the Green-house of this month, give them very little water until they begin to grow.

Hot-House.

OCTOBER.

Very few directions remain to be given to the department of the Hot-house. The supplies of water for this and the two preceding months are, according to the state and nature of tropical plants, more limited than at any other period of the year. This is the first month of what may be called their dormant state. Observe the herbaceous plants, that they are, as soon as their foliage decays, set aside, in case of being too liberally supplied with water. Airing is highly essential about this period, that the plants may be gradually hardened; but guard against injuring them. The temperature should not be under fifty degrees; when the days are cool, and the wind chilling, airing is not necessary; and when air is admitted, always close up early in the afternoon, whilst the atmosphere is warm, to supersede the necessity of fire as long as possible. If at any time you have recourse to it in this month, use it with great caution.

Examine all the shutters and fastenings, and see that they are in good substantial order, and where deficient repair them instantly, that they may be in readiness. Remove all leaves, and give syringings twice a week. Clear off, sweep out, and wash clean, that every part may be in the neatest order.

OCTOBER.

OF TAKING IN AND ARRANGING THE PLANTS.

As observed in the previous month, let the housing of Green-house plants now be attended to. Have all in before the eighth of the month, except a few of the half hardy sorts, which may stand until convenient. Begin by taking in all the tallest first, such as *Oranges*, *Lemons*, *Myrtles*, *Oleanders*, &c. Limes ought to be kept in the warmest part of the house, otherwise they will throw their foliage. In arrangement, order is necessary to have a good effect; and in small houses it ought to be neat and regular, placing the tallest behind, and according to their size graduating the others down to the lowest in front. Dispose the different sorts in varied order over the house, making the contrast as striking as possible. Having the surface of the whole as even as practicable, with a few of the most conspicuous for shape and beauty protruding above the mass, which will much improve the general appearance, and greatly add to the effect. All succulents should be put together. They will do in a dark part of the house, where other plants would not grow, studying to have the most tender kinds in the warmest part, and giving gentle waterings every three or four weeks. When all are arranged, give them a proper syringing, after which wipe clean all the stages, *benches*, &c. sweeping out all litter, and wash clean the pavement, which will give to all a neat and becoming appearance.

Let the waterings now be done in the mornings, as often and in such quantities as will supply their respective wants, examining the plants every day.

During the continuance of mild weather, the circulation of air must be as free as possible, opening the doors and front and top sashes regularly over the house. But observe in frosty nights, and wet, cloudy weather, to keep all close shut. Be attentive in clearing off decayed leaves and insects.

Any plants of *Lagerstræmia*, *Sterculia*, *Hydrángea*, *Pomegranate*, and others equally hardy, that are deciduous, may be kept perfectly in a dry, light, airy cellar, giving frequent admissions of air.

OF REPOTTING.

Anemònes. Where *A. nemoròsa flòre plèno* and *A. thalictròides flòre plèno* are kept in pots in the Green-house, they should be turned out of the old earth, and planted in fresh soil. They are both pretty, low growing, double white flowering plants, and require a shaded situation. The latter is now called *Thalíctrum anemonoídes.*

Dáphne, is a genus of diminutive shrubs, mostly evergreens, of great beauty and fragrance. Very few species of them are in our collections. *D. odòra*, frequently called *D. índica*, is an esteemed plant for the delightful odour of its flowers, and valuable for the period of its flowering, being from December to March, according to the situation; leaves scattered, oblong, lanceolate, smooth; flowers small, white, in many-flowered terminale heads. *D. hybrida* is a species in high estimation at present in Europe, but little known here, being only in a few collections; flowers rose-coloured, in terminale heads, and lateral bunches in great profusion, and very similar to the former in habit and shape of flower; blooms from January to May, and is of a peculiar fragrance. *D. oleoídes* is what may be termed "ever-blooming;" flowers of a lilac colour; leaves elliptic, lanceolate, smooth. *D. laurèola*, Spurge laurel; *D. póntica*, *D. alpìna*, and *D. Cneòrum*, are all fine species, and in Europe are esteemed ornaments in the shrubbery, but we are not certain if they will prove hardy in our vicinity.

Prímula. There are a few fine species and varieties in this genus, adapted either for the Green-house or Rooms. All the species and varieties will keep perfectly well in a frame, except the China sorts. Having previously observed a few of the other species and varieties, we will observe the treatment of these. *P. sinénsis*, now *prænitens*, known commonly as China Primrose; flowers pink, and in large proliferous umbels, flowering almost through the whole year, but most profusely from January to May. Keep them in the shade, and be careful that they are not over-watered during summer. As the stems of the plant become naked, at this repotting a few inches should be taken off the bottom of the ball, and placing them in a larger pot will allow the stems to be covered up to the leaves. *P. p. albiflòra*, colour pure white and beautiful. *P. p. dentiflòra*. There is also a white variety of this, both similar to the two former, only the flower indented. All these require the same treatment. As they only live a few years, many individuals, to propagate them, divide the stems, which in most cases will utterly destroy them. The best, and we may say the only method to increase them, is from seed, which they produce in abundance every year.

Pæonia, is a magnificent genus. There are four varieties of them, half hardy and half shrubby. They will bear the winter if well protected, but are better in the Green-house. These are *P. moután*, Tree Pæony; the flower is about four inches in diameter, of a blush colour, and semi-double; *P. M. Bànksii* is the common Tree Pæony, and called in our collection *P. Moutàn*; it has a very large double blush flower, and is much admired. *P. M. papaveràcea* is a most magnificent variety; has large double white flowers, with pink centres; *P. M. ròsea* is a splendid rose-coloured double variety, and is scarce. These plants ought not to be exposed to the sun while in flower, as the colours become degenerated, and premature decay follows.

If the Dutch bulbs intended for flowering during winter are not potted, have them all done as soon as possible, according to directions given last month.

CAMELLIAS.

These plants ought to have a thorough examination, and those that were omitted in repotting before they commenced growing, may be done in the early part of this month; but it is not adviseable, except the roots are matted round the ball of earth, which should be turned out entire. Examine all the pots, stir up the surface of the earth, and take it out to the roots, supplying its place with fresh soil. Destroy any worms that may be in the pots, as they are very destructive to the fibres. Look over the foliage and with a sponge and water clear it of all dust, &c. Frequently the buds are too crowded on these plants, especially the *Double white* and *Variegated*. In such case pick off the weakest, and where there are two together, be careful in cutting, so that the remaining bud may not be injured.

This is the best period of the year to make selections of these, as they now can be transported hundreds of miles without any material injury, if they are judiciously packed in close boxes. In making a choice of these, keep in view to have distinctly marked varieties, including a few of those that are esteemed as stocks for producing new kinds, which are undoubtedly indispensable; and will reward the cultivator in a few years with new sorts. Besides, it will afford unbounded gratification to behold any of these universally admired ornaments of the Green-house improving by our assistance and under our immediate observation. There is nothing to prevent any individual from producing splendid varieties in a few years. Mr. Hogg correctly observes, "It is very probable in a few years we shall have as great a variety of Camellias, as there are of Tulips, Hyacinths, Carnations, Auriculas, &c."

It has been often said that these plants are difficult of cultivation. This is unfounded, indeed they are the reverse if put in a soil congenial to their nature. When highly manured soils are given, which are poisonous to the plants, sickness or death will inevitably ensue; but this cannot be attributed to the delicacy of their nature. We can unhesitatingly say there is no Green-house plant more hardy or easier of cultivation, and they are equally so in the parlour, if not kept confined in a room where there is a continuance of drying fire heat, their constitution not agreeing with an arid atmosphere.

Flower-Garden

OCTOBER.

OF PLANTING VARIOUS BULBOUS FLOWER ROOTS.

From the middle of October to the beginning of November is the best period for a general planting of Dutch bulbs.

Cròcuses are the earliest in flower, and may be planted about six inches off the edgings, about four inches apart and two deep, or in beds four feet wide; the varieties selected and planted across the bed in rows of distinct colours, they flowering so early, and in that manner have a grand effect. There are above sixty varieties to be had.

Hyacinths. The ground that was prepared for these last month, should be all divided into beds four feet wide, leaving between each alleys of twenty inches. Skim off three inches of the surface of the former into the latter, level the bed smoothly with the rake, and mark it off in rows eight inches apart. Plant the roots in the row eight inches asunder. Thus they will be squares of eight inches, and by planting the different colours alternately the bed will be beautifully diversified. Press each root gently down with the hand, that in covering up they may not be displaced. Put about four inches of earth over the crowns, which will make the beds from two to three inches higher than the alleys. The beds before and after planting should be gently rounded from the middle to each side to let the rain pass off. Finish all by raking evenly, straighten the edgings with the line, and clear out the alleys or pathways.

Tulips like a lighter and richer earth than Hyacinths. Prepare the beds in the same manner, and so as the roots will stand nine inches apart each way; cover them five inches deep, as the new bulbs are produced above the old.

If it is intended to screen either of these while in flower, the beds should be made wider. Where two beds are to be shaded under one awning, make the alleys alternately two or three feet wide; the one two feet wide to be under the awning.

Polyanthus and Italian Narcissus, may be planted in every respect as *Hyacinths*, only they require a lighter and richer soil.

Jonquils. Plant these in the same soil as *Tulips*, six inches apart, and cover three inches deep. They do not flower so well the first year as in the second and third, therefore should only be lifted every third year.

Anemones and Ranunculuses. These roots like a fresh rich, well pulverized, loamy soil. In light sandy soils they will languish in early droughts, and sometimes do not show their flowers fully. Cow manure is the best to use for enriching the soil. The whole should be well mixed and incorporated to the depth of eighteen or twenty inches. The roots may be planted in four-foot beds, or in such a manner as a low frame of boards can be placed over them, when the winter sets in very severe. If intended to be shaded while in flower, leave a sufficiency of space in the alleys as directed for Tulips and Hyacinths. Do not raise the beds above one inch higher than the alleys, and form the surface level, in order to detain rather than throw off moisture. Then draw drills exactly two inches deep and six inches apart across the bed. In these place the roots, claws down, about four inches distant from each other. The roots of the Anemones are flat, and the side on which there are small protuberances, is that from which the stems proceed. Press each root a little down with the hand, and cover all carefully so as not to displace them. Smooth the surface with the rake, leaving the bed quite level.

Many other bulbous flowers might be added to the above; but as their culture is so similar, it would be superfluous to say more of them. They should be allowed space and depth according to the size of the bulb; a covering of two inches for the smallest, and five for the largest, will generally answer, and the intermediate roots in proportion. We will enumerate a few of the different kinds, *Starch* and *Musk Hyacinths*; of *Narcissus*, the *Paper*, *Grand Monarque*, and *Nodding*, with the two previously mentioned, are the most profuse in flower. Some of them will have above twelve flowers on one stem. Of *Lilies*, all the varieties of *Mártagon*, *Tigrìnum* and *Chalcedónicum*, with our native species and varieties. Of *Iris*, *Lusitánica*, two varieties, yellow and blue;

Xiphioídes, or *Ziphioídes*; and *Pérsica*, are the finest of the bulbous sorts. Snow-drop with several other minor bulbs.

All of these flowering bulbs may be advantageously planted in patches through the garden by taking out about one square foot of earth. Break it well, and if poor enrich it. Plant four bulbs in each of the same colour, and the clumps that are contiguous to contain different colours.

PLANTING AND TRANSPLANTING.

This is a very proper period to plant the beautiful and early flowering *Pyrus japónica*, now called *Cydónia japónica*. The blossoms are of a rich scarlet colour. It is the earliest flowering shrub of the garden, and deciduous, though said by some to be "an evergreen." The plant is bushy, and well adapted for single plants in grass plats, or forming low ornamental hedges. There is likewise *C. j. álba*, a fine white variety of the same habit, and both are of the hardiest nature—also for the various species of *Anemònes* and all the herbaceous *Pæonias*.

Of the latter there are above nineteen species and twenty-two varieties, a few of which are particularly esteemed, and exceedingly handsome. *P. èdulis whitlíji* is a splendid large double *P èdulis* white; *P. Hùmei* is a beautiful large double dark blush; *P. èdulis fràgrans* is a fine large double scarlet, rose-scented variety. These three plants ought to be in every garden. The flowers are full in the centre, and frequently above six inches in diameter; *P. álba chinènsis* is said to be the largest and finest of the herbaceous sorts; colour pure white, with pink at the bottom of the petals—it is a scarce variety; *P. paradóxa fimbàtria*, fringed double red, and esteemed; *P. officinális rúbra* is the common double red. There are several other very fine single species and varieties, the flowers of which are principally red or blush, but none so magnificent as the above mentioned. This is perhaps a more favourable period to plant *Dodecátheon* than March; for its character see that month of this department. *Asclèpias tuberòsa* should now be planted.

Double Primroses, *Polyanthus*, *Daisies*, &c. Any of these that were planted in shaded situations in spring, and have been preserved through the summer, should have for their farther protection a bed well sheltered from the north west, in which they should be planted four inches apart. Give them a few sprinklings of water in the morning, and have a temporary frame of rough boards put together to place over them during the severity of winter. The frame may be covered with the same in place of glass, which must be kept over them while they are in a frozen state.

Any other plants that are in the ground, which are intended to be protected with frames through the winter, ought to be immediately lifted and potted; and treated as directed for all new potted plants.

GRASS AND GRAVEL WALKS.

The former should be trimly cut and well rolled this month, that they may appear neat all winter. Never allow decayed leaves to lay any time upon them, as they are apt to rot out the grass. The latter should be divested of every weed, and receive a firm rolling. Clear them at all times of leaves and other litter. These, if on a declivity, and have not a firm substantial bottom, will be subject to be cut up with every heavy rain. A break should be put in every twenty, forty, or eighty feet, to throw off the water. A strong plank will answer perfectly well, but in such situations we would prefer grass-walks.

PLANTING EVERGREENS.

This month is the best period in autumn to plant these shrubs, and where there is a great extent to be planted it would be advisable to do a part of it now; but we give the preference to April, which see for directions.

GENERAL OBSERVATIONS.

When the plantings of bulbs, &c. are finished, every part of the garden should have a thorough cleaning. All annual flowers will have passed the season of their beauty; therefore, remove the decayed flower stems or haulm, and trim off the borders. Dig all vacant ground, especially that intended to be planted with shrubs in the ensuing spring, which ought to be dug from one to two feet deep. Roses delight in a deep light soil.

OCTOBER.

Have a stage or stages, as described last month, in the situations where they are intended to remain all winter; place the plants on them from the first to the eighth of this month, beginning with the tallest on the top, graduating to the bottom. It is desirable to place flats or saucers under each, to prevent the water from falling to the floor, and the water should be emptied from the flats of all except those of *Cálla* and *Hydrángea.* The latter while dormant should be kept only a little moist.

Previous to taking in the plants, they should be divested of every decayed leaf, insects, and all contracted dust, having their shoots neatly tied up, and every one in correct order. Every leaf of the *Caméllias* ought to be sponged, and the plants placed in a cool airy exposure, shaded from the direct rays of the sun. If the flower buds are too crowded, picking off the weakest will preserve the remainder in greater perfection, and prevent them in part from falling off. Do not on any occasion keep them in a room where there is much fire heat, as the flower buds will not expand in an arid atmosphere. See Greenhouse this month more largely on this subject.

OF BULBOUS ROOTS.

Those that are intended to flower in glasses, should be placed therein this month and kept in a cool room. After the fibres begin to push a few shoots, the glasses may be taken to the warmest apartments to cause them to flower early. Bring a few from the coldest to the warmest every two weeks, and thus a succession of bloom may be kept up from January to March. Where the roots intended for pots are still out of the ground, the sooner they are planted the better. (See last month for directions.)

Cape Bulbs. All that are unplanted and offering to grow, should be put in pots forthwith. Ample directions are given for the planting of these in the two preceding months.

Repot *Rùbus rosæfòlius*, or Bramble-rose. They should have pots one size larger than those they are now in. To make them flower profusely, when done blooming in May, divide them and put only a few stems in one pot, and repot them in this month, as above directed.

GENERAL OBSERVATIONS.

Any herbaceous plants in the collection ought to be set aside, and the water in part withheld. When the stems and foliage are decayed, the plants may be put in a cool cellar, where they will not be in danger of frost, and be permitted to remain there until they begin to grow; then bring them to the light, and treat as directed for these kinds of plants. Deciduous plants may be treated in a similar manner.

NOVEMBER.

The essential points to be attended to in the Hot-house during this month, are *fire*, *air*, and *water*. The former must be applied according to the weather, observing not to allow the temperature to be under fifty degrees, and it ought not to continue long at that degree; fifty-two degrees being preferable. The shutters should be on every night when there is any appearance of frost, and taken off early in the morning. Admit air in small portions every day that the sun has any effect, and the atmosphere mild, observing that the temperature of the house be above sixty degrees previous to admission. Shut all close early in the afternoon or when any sudden changes occur.

OF A CISTERN AND WATER.

In watering it is important to have the water of the same temperature in this department as the roots of the plants. To have this there are two kinds of cisterns, or tanks, that might be adopted; one may be sunk in the house under ground, either closely plastered, or lined with lead, and neatly covered up, having a small perpendicular pump therein, or placed so that the water could be lifted by hand. The other might, where convenience will admit, be placed over the furnace, either in the back shed, or inside of the house, and the water could be drawn off this by a stop-cock. These can be supplied in part with rain water by having spouts round the house to lead into the cisterns, supplying any deficiency from the pump. Thus water of a congenial temperature may always be at hand, which is of great importance to the healthful constitution of the plants. The water must now be given in moderate portions, examining the plants every day. Be careful in watering bulbs, as the smallest supply is sufficient for them at present. Succulents will require a little every two weeks, except they are over the flues, when they may have some every week.

Constantly clear off all decayed leaves, and carry them out of the house, which sweep and wash clean, and keep all in the neatest order.

NOVEMBER.

OF AIR AND WATER.

Airing the house should be strictly attended to. Every day that there is no frost it may be admitted largely, and in time of slight frosts in smaller portions, never keeping it altogether close when the sun has any effect on the interior temperature of the house, which should not be allowed to be higher than fifty degrees.

Water must be given in a very sparing manner. None of the plants are in an active state of vegetation, consequently it will be found that looking over them twice a week and supplying their wants will be sufficient. Succulents will need a little once in three weeks or a month. Give very moderate supplies to the *Amaryllis* that are dormant, and keep all of these bulbs in the warmest part of the house.

OF TENDER BULBS.

Where there are tropical bulbs in the collection, and there is not the convenience of a Hot-house; they may be very well preserved by shaking them clear of the soil. Dry them properly, and place them in a box of very dry sand, or moss, which also must be perfectly dry, and put them in a situation where they will be clear of frost, and free from damp. These can be potted about the first of April. Give no water till they begin to grow, then plant them in the garden about the middle of May, when they will flower during the summer season, if their age will permit.

GENERAL OBSERVATIONS.

If there are any of the half hardy plants exposed, have them taken into the house, or under the requisite protection, in frames, pits, cellars, &c. The autumn flowering Cape bulbs should be placed near the glass, and free from the shade of other plants. Cleanliness through the whole house and amongst the plants ought at all times to be attended to.

NOVEMBER.

Wherever there are any Holland bulbs remaining unplanted, have them put in as soon as possible, lest frost should set in. It is not advisable to keep them later out of the ground than the beginning of this month.

PROTECTION OF CHOICE BULBS.

On the appearance of the severity of winter, the finer sorts of these should have a simple protection, not because they will not do without such care, but to prevent the alternate thawing and freezing of the embryo of the bulb. To give them a covering three inches deep of any of the following substances, will do perfectly well,—saw-dust not resinous, old tan bark, half decayed leaves, or very rotten manure. The last is preferable, as it would in part enrich the soil.

Anemònes and *Ranunculus* ought to be protected by a frame; the foliage being above ground, none of the above will answer. It is not necessary that the frame should be covered with glass, close boards will answer perfectly, which must not be over them except during frost.

TUBEROSES, DAHLIAS, TIGRIDIAS, AND AMARYLLIS.

These tubers and bulbs, as soon as the frost has partly injured the foliage, should be taken up, and dried thoroughly, either in the sun or a room where there is fire heat, taking care at all times to keep them clear from frost. When they are dry, divest them of their foliage and fibres. When perfectly dry, pack them in boxes with dry sand, or moss. Store these away for the winter, either in a warm room or a dry cellar, where they will at all times be exempt from frost, the least touch of which would destroy them. We have kept them completely secure in the cellar.

ERYTHRINAS.

Where there are any plants of *E. herbàcea*, *E. laurifòlia*, or *E. crísta-gálla*, which are intended to be lifted, they should be carefully done and preserved in half dry earth, and kept beside the *Dáhlias*. We are not sure of the former agreeing with this treatment, but certain of the others, which are magnificent ornaments in the Flower-garden.

PRIMROSES, POLYANTHUS, AND DAISIES,

That were planted in a sheltered spot, as directed last month, should have a frame placed over them, and their covering in readiness for the approach of winter; giving the plants a light covering of leaves, which will preserve their foliage from the effects of frost.

CHOICE CARNATIONS, PINKS, AND AURICULAS,

That are in pots, should be placed in the frame intended for their abode during winter. If the pots are plunged to the rims in tan, half decayed leaves, or saw dust, it will greatly protect their roots from the severe effects of frost. Where glass is used for these frames, they should have besides a covering of boards, or straw mats; those that are in beds may be covered as above directed for Primroses, &c.

They ought not to be uncovered while in a frozen state. It is not altogether the intensity of cold that destroys these plants so much as the alternate thawing and freezing.

All half hardy plants, such as *Wall-flower*, *German stocks*, *Sweet-bay*, tender roses, with several others, should be protected as above directed for Carnations. Earth or tan should be put round the outside of these frames, which will be a partial shelter from the changing state of the atmosphere. Oak leaves answer the purpose very well, but they are a harbour for all kinds of vermin, especially rats and mice, which would destroy every thing. It may be useful to say a few words on the nature of tan or tanner's bark. Many suppose that the smallest quantity will produce heat, If three or four cart loads of it are put into one heap, and protected from the rain, it will ferment; and when the first fermentation is abated, by mixing it with leaves, a substantial hot-bed may be made. Or put it by itself into a pit, and where there is no pit, boards may be substituted to keep it together; either of these methods will produce a lasting heat. But in small quantities and exposed to rain, &c. no heat will be produced, but rather the contrary. It is excellent when dry in keeping out frost from any plants, being a body not easily penetrated, similar to dry sand, saw-dust, or dry leaves. Frequently the same opinion is held in regard to stable manure, small portions of which will never produce heat.

OF PROTECTING PLANTS IN THE GARDEN.

During this or next month, according to the state of the season, protect all the plants that are in the ground, which are not completely hardy. To avoid repetition, these will be designated in the general list. The coverings may be straw, Russia mats, canvass, boxes or barrels. The two latter must be perforated in the top, to let the damp air pass off, or the plant would become musty, or finally mortify. Those covered with straw or mats should have small stakes placed round the plants, and covering tied thereto, and remain so until the month of March or first of April. Herbaceous plants that are tender, may be covered with three or four inches of tan, saw-dust, or half decayed leaves, which will tend greatly to preserve their roots. These coverings must be carefully removed on the first opening of spring. The shrubs that are otherwise covered would be greatly benefited by having their roots protected in a similar manner as directed for herbaceous plants.

PROTECTION OF SEEDLING BULBS.

If any seeds of *Hyacinths*, *Tulips*, *Fritillària*, were sown in pots or boxes, let them be removed to a dry sheltered situation, and plunged level with the ground; or fill the spaces between them with dry leaves or tanner's bark, and cover the whole with new fallen leaves, laying over all a few boards to prevent the wind blowing them off. These form better coverings than straw or haulm, which is liable to become musty, and communicate the effect to the roots. The above covering is not required until the approach of severe frost.

OF PLANTING DECIDUOUS TREES AND SHRUBS.

It is not recommendable to make a general planting of these at this period of the year; the success entirely depending on the nature of the season and the state of the soil. If any are planted, let them be those of the hardiest nature, and in light and absorbent soil, not subject to be stagnated or over-flooded during winter. When this and next month are mild, autumn plantings are frequently as sure as those of the spring. But the precarious state of the seasons is not to be depended upon, therefore avoid largo plantings of any kind, and more especially of delicate roses, the roots of which are apt to rot off except they have been previously grown in pots. Nothing can be more injurious to a plant at this season particularly, than to bed its roots in mortar, by which the tender fibres either perish or are cramped ever afterwards. The soil at time of planting should be so friable as not to adhere to the spade, which is a good rule in planting at any season, or in any soil.

GENERAL OBSERVATIONS.

Carry out of the garden all decayed leaves and litter of every description, cutting down any weeds that remain. Collect all the stakes and rods that have been supporting plants; tie them up in bundles for the use of next year, and put them under cover. Look over every part of the garden, and see that nothing has been omitted in the way of covering or other protection. The sashes that are to be used on the frames should be perfectly whole, every interstice in the glass puttied, and all ready for use when occasion may require. Attend to all plants in pots, and give them gentle waterings as they stand in need; but never during the time the soil is frozen about their roots.

NOVEMBER.

GENERAL OBSERVATIONS.

The remarks and instructions that are given last month for these apartments will equally answer here. Where the Dutch bulbs were omitted to be placed in glasses, they ought not to be longer delayed. A few pots of those that were planted in September may be placed in a warmer situation. If they were plunged in the ground, the roots will be strongly fibred, and will produce large flowers, providing the bulbs are of a good sort.

Oxàlis. The autumn flowering species will now be in bloom, and must be kept in the sun to make them expand freely. The neglect of this is the principal reason that these plants do not flower perfectly in Rooms.

Camëllias. These plants, where there is a collection, flower from this period to April; and the general desire to be fully acquainted with the method of their culture has induced us to be liberal in our observations on every point and period through the various stages of their growth and flowering. We will here only remind the enquirer, that a pure air, a damp atmosphere, and giving the plants frequent sprinklings, are the present necessities, which only are conducive to their perfection.

Attend to the turning of Geraniums and other rapid growing plants, that all sides of them may have an equal share of light.

Hot-House.

DECEMBER.

The uncertainty of the weather in this month requires the operator to be constantly on guard, to ward off danger, either from frost, snow, or cutting winds. The temperature observed last month must be continued, but not exceeded, which would cause premature vegetation, of which the result and effects have already been frequently observed. Always kindle the fires in time, to prevent the heat from being lower than what has been mentioned, lest a severe frost should take, as then a considerable lapse ensues before the fire has any effect, and if the wind blows high, the result might be injurious, unless the house be very close.

OF SHUTTERS.

The benefit of these in severe weather is of material service, for the preservation of an even temperature in the house during the night, when changes are not observed, but they ought never to remain on through the day when the fire can be properly attended to. If the front and the lowest sash of the roof are covered with these, it is generally sufficient. They should be made of half inch boards, closely grooved together, having a cross bar in the centre, and one at each end with one at each side, which will make them substantial. If they are frequently painted with care, they will last many years. No snow ought to be allowed to lay on these while they are on the glass, for reasons that we have assigned. See *January* and *February*.

Some adopt double panes of glass to supersede the use of shutters, which, they think are attended with considerable labour, (at the most only ten minutes a day while in use.) The sash frame is made a little deeper, so as to allow half an inch between the panes of glass. The one is glazed from the out and the other from the inside. It appears to answer the purpose tolerably well, but the glass must be both fine and even in the surface, lest a lens should be produced, and cause a focus, which would evidently hurt some part of the plants. We are almost confident that we have seen this effect in some instances. There must be a small hole about an eighth of an inch in both ends of each row of glass to allow a current to dry up the moisture that may arise.

OF PLACING BULBS, &c. IN THE HOT-HOUSE.

If any *Hyacinths* or other Dutch roots are wanted to flower early, a few of them may be put in the Hot-house near the front glass, which will greatly tend to forward their time of flowering. By having some brought in every two weeks, a continued succession of bloom will be kept up.

Calceolàrias. Two or three plants of the fine blooming kinds may be placed in this department, towards the end of the month. Divide the roots as soon as they begin to grow, leaving only one stem to each root, which put in a four inch pot, enlarging it as soon as the roots extend to the outside of the ball, that by the month of May they may be in seven or eight inch pots, in which they will flower superbly. Give *Alstrœmèrias* the same treatment.

GENERAL OBSERVATIONS.

If there is a tan bed in the house, and it was renewed in September, the pots should now be plunged therein. The violent heat will partly be over, and the plants are not so liable to suffer at root in this as last month. It will in part prevent the plants from being affected by sudden changes of temperature. Be attentive in keeping all insects completely under. This is the period that these are most neglected, but by attending to the modes of their destruction, as already given, no species of them will either be hurtful or unsightly. Syringe the plants about twice a week, and always remember that decayed leaves or litter of any description do not beautify healthy plants, neither do they form a part of a well kept Hot-house.

Green-House.

DECEMBER.

The weather may probably be now severe, and it is at all times advisable to keep the temperature as steady and regular as possible. The thermometer should be kept in the centre of the house, and free from the effects of reflection. As noticed last month, sun heat may be as high as 50° in the house, and would not be hurtful, but it should not continue so for any considerable time without admission of air. The fire heat should not exceed 43°, and never be below 33°. It ought not to continue at that point—36° is the lowest for a continuation that with safety can be practised. So that no error may occur, the temperature ought to be known in the coolest and warmest part of the house, and the variation remembered. Then whatever part of the house the thermometer is placed, a true calculation of the heat of the whole interior can be made. We would recommend to the inexperienced to keep the thermometer in the coldest part of the house. A Green-house compactly and closely built, and the glass all covered with shutters, (which no house ought to be constructed without,) will seldom require artificial heat; but by being long kept close, the damp will increase. In such case give a little fire heat, and admit air to purify the house. In fresh mild weather, give liberal portions of air all over the house; and though there is a little frost, while mild, and the sun shining, the plants will be benefited by a small portion of air for the space of an hour, or even for half of that time.

Whatever state the weather may be through the winter, never keep the house long shut up. Thirty-six hours, or at most sixty, should be the longest time at once; rather give a little fire heat.

We are no advocates for keeping plants long in darkness, and never think that our plants are receiving justice, if kept longer in darkness than two nights and one day.

Respecting watering and other necessary operations, see next month particularly.

BULBOUS ROOTS.

Those that were plunged in the garden, if not lifted and brought under cover, should now be done without delay. Clean the pots, and stir up the surface of the soil. Hyacinths grow neatest by being kept very close to the top glass; the flower stems are thereby stronger and shorter. Water moderately until they begin to grow freely.

Flower Garden.

DECEMBER.

GENERAL OBSERVATIONS.

Having in the preceding month, under this head, given details for the protection of plants of a delicate nature, and the forwarding of necessary work, only a few remarks remain to be added. If there is any part therein described omitted, have it done forthwith; every day increases the danger of the effects of frost. If there is a doubt of any plants not standing without protection which are generally considered perfectly hardy, such as *Champney*, *Grevillii*, *Noisette*, and similar roses, tie straw or mats three or four feet up the stems of such, which will prevent all risk.[J] For valuable plants that are on walls, and in danger of being entirely destroyed, it is advisable to be at the expense of having a frame made to answer them, and cover the same with oil-cloth. The frame thus covered could be taken off in mild weather, and replaced again when necessary, causing very little trouble; and if properly taken care of, would last many years. Coverings of any construction and of the same material would answer for any part of the garden, and are the best in our opinion that could be adopted.

[J] In the winter of 1831-1832, some of these roses were cut to the ground, where strong plants of *Lagerstrœmia índica* received not the smallest injury.

DECEMBER.

As the trying season is now approaching for all plants that are kept in rooms, especially those that are desired to have a flourishing aspect through the winter, a few general instructions (although they may have been previously advanced) will perhaps be desirable to all those who are engaged in this interesting occupation, which forms a luxury through the retired hours of a winter season, and with very little attention many are the beauties of vegetative nature that will be developed to the gratification of every reflecting mind. The following is a routine of every day culture.

Do not at any time admit air (except for a few moments) while the thermometer is below 32° exposed in the shade.

In time of very severe frosts the plants ought to be withdrawn from the window to the centre of the room during night.

Never give water until the soil in the pots is inclining to become dry, except for Hyacinths and other Dutch bulbs that are in a growing state, which must be liberally supplied.

Destroy all insects as soon as they appear; for means of destruction see next month.

Give a little air every favourable opportunity, (that is, when the thermometer is above 33° exposed in the shade,) by putting up the window one, two or three inches, according to the state of the weather.

Clean the foliage with sponge and water frequently to remove all dust, &c. The water thus used must not exceed 96° or blood-heat, but 60° is preferable.

Turn the plants frequently to prevent them growing to one side.

Roses of the daily sort may be obtained early by having them in a warm room, that has a south window, and as soon as they begin to grow, admit air in small portions about noon every day that the sun has any effect. Such must be well supplied with water.

Caméllias, when in bud and flower, should never be allowed to become the least dry, neither confined from fresh air. The effects would be that the buds would become stinted, dry, and drop off. Therefore, to have these in perfection, attend strictly to watering. Give frequent airings, and wash the leaves once in two weeks with water. Never keep them above one day in a room, where there is a strong coal fire, and not above two days where wood is used as fuel. The most of *Caméllias* will bear 3° of frost without the smallest injury, so that they are easier kept than *Geraniums*, except when they are in bloom. In that state frost will destroy the flowers. The air of a close cellar is destruction to the buds.

Bulbs in glasses must be supplied with fresh water once a week, in which period they will inhale all the nutritive gas that they derive from that element, if they are in a growing state.

ON THE CONSTRUCTION OF A HOT-HOUSE.

There have been many plans devised and visionary projects offered to the public as the best for a well regulated Hot-house. As we intend forming one for practical purposes, we shall adopt a convenient size, have flues for the conveyance of heat, and coal or wood for fuel.

Site and Aspect.—The house should stand on a situation naturally dry, and if possible sheltered from the north west, and clear from all shade on the south, east and west, so that the sun may at all times act effectually upon the house. The standard principle as to aspect is to set the front directly to the south. Any deviation from that point should incline to east.

Dimensions.—The length may be from ten feet upwards; but if beyond thirty feet, the number of fires and flues are multiplied. The medium width is from twelve to sixteen feet. Our directions will apply to the two extreme points, viz. thirty feet by sixteen, and in height at back from twelve to eighteen feet; the height in front six feet, including about three feet in brick basement to support the front glass, which will be two and a half feet, allowing six inches for frame work.

Furnace and Flues.—It is of great importance to have these erected in such a manner as will effectually heat the house. The greatest difficulty is to have the furnace to draw well. As workmen are not generally conversant on the subject, nor yet understand the effect or distribution of heat in these departments, we will give minute details on their construction. The furnace should be outside of the house, either at back or end; the former is preferable, circumstances not always allowing it on the other plan. Dig out the furnace hole, or what is termed stock hole, about five feet deep. Let the door of the furnace be in the back wall of the house, thereby having all the heated building inside, that no heat may be lost. The brick work round the furnace should be from fifteen to eighteen inches thick, laying the inside with fire-brick. The furnace will require to be two and a half feet long, ten inches wide, and one foot high, before the spring of the arch and clear of the bars; leave one foot for an ash pit, then lay the bars. They should be sixteen inches long, one inch broad on the upper side, two inches deep, and two eighths broad on the lower side, and with the door and frame should be cast iron. Half an inch between each bar will be sufficient. The flue should rise from the furnace by a steep declivity of about two feet, and pass the door of the house (without a dip), when it must be elevated above the level of the floor of the house along the front, and at the opposite end of the house must dip to pass the door. The dip must not be lower than the top of the furnace, and should be of a concave form, (avoiding acute angles.) Lead it along the back to enter the wall over the furnace. When thus taken round the house, the heat will be expanded before it passes off, The inside of the flues should be about six inches wide and eight inches deep; plaster the bottom of it, but no other part, as plaster is partially a non-conductor. The above description is for burning anthracite coal, but where wood is to be the fuel, the furnace and flues must be one half larger. We have been particular in the description of furnace bars, as those generally used are miserable substitutes. Circumstances may cause the furnace to be placed at the end or front of the house. In either case the stock hole will not require to be so deep; or where there is only one door in the house a stock hole three and a half feet deep will be enough, which should be built like a cellar to keep out any under water. In all instances pass the first flue to the front of the house, over which have a close shelf eight inches clear, covered with two inches of sand, and by keeping it moist will afford a very congenial heat to young valuable plants. Likewise over the furnace have a frame in the same manner, which will be found valuable. Any part of the furnace or flue that is under the floor of the house, should have a vacuity on both sides to let the heat pass upward.

Bark Pit.—We consider such an erection in the centre of a Hot-house a nuisance, and prefer a stage, which may be constructed according to taste. It should be made of the best Carolina pine, leaving a passage round the whole to cause a free circulation of air. The back and end paths should be about two feet wide, and the front three feet. The angle of the stage should be parallel with the glass, having the steps from six inches to one foot apart.

Where there are some large plants, they may stand on the floor behind the stage, or on tressels, according to their height.

Angle of the glazed roof.—The pitch of the roof is usually varied to agree with the design of the house, and the size of the plants to be grown therein. Where pleasure and ornament are the principal objects, the angle should be about 43°, but a few degrees of inclination either way is of minor importance, the height and elevation being regulated by the size of the plants intended to be cultivated. It is not advisable to shingle any part of the roof on the south aspect.

Materials for glazed frames.—Carolina pine is the best material for the wood work, as it is not so subject to decay from moisture and heat as the other kinds of pine wood. The frames or sashes can be of any convenient length, not exceeding ten feet, and about three and a half or four feet wide, divided so as they can be glazed with glass six inches wide.

Of glazing. The pieces of glass should not exceed six inches by ten, the lappings about one quarter of an inch. The frames ought to have one coat of paint previous to glazing, and all under the glass puttied. Some prefer the lappings to be puttied also. It is our opinion that in a Hot-house these should not be puttied, but in the Green-house the closer they can be made the better.

Of Shutters.—These should be made of half inch white pine, and bound on both ends and sides, having a cross piece in the middle of the same. They ought to be painted once in three years.

ON THE CONSTRUCTION OF A GREEN-HOUSE.

In many respects, the construction of the Green*-house will be the same as the Hot-house, but might be made much more an ornamental object, and could be erected contiguous to the mansion-house, with large folding doors to open at pleasure, and be connected with the drawing-room or parlour. The extent may vary according to the collection to be cultivated.

It was formerly the practice to build these houses with glass only in front, and even to introduce between the windows strong piers of brick or stone: but this is now abolished, and has given way to a light and ornamental style, by which cheerfulness and the desired utility are better consulted. There should be conveniences in the back part of the house, that a free current of air may be obtained whenever desired, which is an essential point. Two or three dark windows will answer the purpose well, if made to open and shut at pleasure.

ON LAYING OUT A FLOWER-GARDEN.

Soil, situation, and ground—Plan.—A soil of common good qualities, moderately light and mellow, will grow most of the hardy herbaceous flowers, and the evergreen and deciduous ornamental shrubs. The situation should not be so low as to be damp and wet, or liable to be inundated, neither so high as to be scorched or dried up by the sun. The surface should be level or moderately sloping, and if unequal, parts of it may be transposed, so as to make gentle inclinations. In regard to form, it may be of any shape, and must be often adapted to local circumstances; but if it is so circumscribed that the eye can at once embrace the whole, it is desirable that it should be of some regular figure.

Of Fences.—Where domestic buildings do not serve as a boundary, either paling or hedge-fence has to be resorted to: we would prefer the former on the north or north-west side, which is of great advantage as a screen from cutting winds. For hedge-fences and their kinds, see page

210. The exotic observed there is *Thùja orientàlis*, Chinese Arbor-vitæ. The internal fences for shade or shelter to particular compartments, or to afford a diversity of aspect, may be made of *Sweetbriar*, *hardy China roses*, *Pyrus*, *red* and *white*, with a few others of a similar nature, all of which must be attended to, to have them in neat order.

Style of dividing the Ground.—This may vary with the extent of the ground, and the object of the cultivator.

The principal designs may be delineated, but one to answer every view and situation, we pretend not to give. In the first place, carry a boundary walk all round the garden, on one or two sides of which it may be straight, the others winding. The intersecting walks should (almost imperceptibly) lead to a centre, but not to cross at right angles, or to have parallel lines, as if divided or laid down by a mathematical scale, which is too formal for the diversification of nature. All walks through these pleasure departments should be winding and enlivening, not continuing any length in one direction.[K] The continuous view of a straight walk is dull and monotonous. The divisions should be highest about the centre, that whatever is planted therein may have effect; and to make a Flower-garden fully interesting, and render it a source of natural information, where free scope might at all times be afforded to employ the leisure hours in mental improvement, there should be a good system of arrangement adopted.

[K] Since writing the above we have seen the Flower-garden of J. B. Smith, Esq. and consider it a beautiful specimen, finely illustrating the taste of that gentleman.

The *Linnean* system is the most easily acquired. A small compartment laid out in beds might contain plants of all the twenty-four *classes*, and a few of all the hardy *orders*, which do not exceed one hundred. Or to have their natural characters more assimilated, the *Jussieuean* system could be carried into effect by laying down a grass plat, to any extent above one quarter of an acre, and cut therein small figures to contain the natural families, which of hardy plants we do not suppose would exceed one hundred and fifty. The difficulties of this arrangement are, that many of the characters are imperfectly known even to the most scientific. *Mr. John Lindley* has given additional light on the subject by his last publication. All the large divisions should be intersected by small allies, or paths, about one and a half or two feet wide. These may be at right angles, or parallel, for convenience and order, in making beds, &c. for the various Dutch roots and other flowers. Patches or plats of grass studded with shrubs, deciduous and evergreen, are indispensable, and perhaps one or two grass walks.

Of Walks.—These should have five or six inches of lime and brick rubbish, or broken stone in the bottom, covered with small pebbles, and firmly rolled with a heavy roller, over which lay two or three inches of fine gravel, giving the whole a complete rolling. Walks made on this method will stand well, and be always dry and firm. With regard to breadth, they must be made according to the extent of ground, and vary from three to thirty feet; from four to eight feet is generally adopted.

Plants described or mentioned in this Work

Linnæan Name.	*English Name.*
ACÀCIA 61, 219.	
1 móllis,	downy.
glaucéscens,	glaucescent.
verticiláta,	whorl-leaved.
florabùnda,	many-flowered.
diffùsa,	spreading.
prostràta.	
armàta,	armed.
var. pendùla,	weeping.
verniciflùa,	varnished.
decúrrens,	decurrent.
púbescens,	hairy-stemmed.
leucolòbia,	white-podded.
dealbàta.	
decípiens,	paradoxical.
fragràns,	scented.
pulchélla,	neat.
lophántha,	two-spiked.

Mimósa élegans.

myrtifòlia,	myrtle-leaved.
Catéchu,	Catechu.
véra,	true.
Arábica,	Arabian.

ANNESLÈIA 219.

1 Houstóni,	Houston's.
Acàcia Houstóni.	
grandiflòra,	large-flowered.
Acácia grandiflòra.	

ACMADÈNIA 86.

6 lávigata,	smooth.
púngens,	pungent.
tetragýnia,	four-sided.

AGATHÓSMA 86.

6 accuminàta,	taper-pointed.
hýbrida,	hybrid.
Thunbergiàna,	Thunberges.
imbricàta,	imbricated.
prolífera,	proliferous.
pátula,	spreading.

pulchélla,	pretty.
ciliáta,	profuse-flowering.

ADENÁNDRA 86.

6 speciòsa,	large-flowered.
umbellàta,	umbel-flowered.
álba,	white-flowered.
fragràns,	sweet-scented.
uniflòra,	one-flowered.

ANEMÓNE 134.	Wind-flower.
15 palmàta plèno,	double-yellow.
stellàta versícolor,	various.
pavonìna plèno,	scarlet.
narcissiflòra,	narcissus-flowered.
Hallèri,	Haller's.
alpìne,	alpine.
nemoròsa plèno,	double-leaved.
thalictròides "	common-double.

AMÓMUM 36.

ATRÀGENE 196.

alpìna,	alpine.
ÁPICRA 260.	
AMARÝLLIS 260, 271, 274.	
11 striatfòlia,	stripe-leaved.
Jonsòni,	Johnson's.
regìna,	Mexican-lily.
vittàta,	striped.
fùlgida,	fulged.
àulica,	crowned.
psittácina,	parrot.
" Cowbèrgia,	Cowberges'.
" pulverulènta,	powdered.
Griffìni,	Griffin's.
formòsa,	large.
ANTIRRHÌNUM 134,	Snap-dragon.
màjus,	large.
mólle,	soft.
Sículum,	Sicilian.
ASCLÈPIAS 134, 321,	Silk-flower.

tuberòsa,	tuberous.
rùbra,	red.
nívea,	white.
purpuráscens,	purple-coloured.
incarnàta,	fleshy-coloured.
ACONÍTUM 134,	Wolfe's-bane.
speciòsum,	showy.
anthòra,	wholesome.
neúrbergensis,	Syria.
am'ænum,	pretty.
napéllus,	monk's-hood.
venústum,	beautiful.
zoóctonum,	beast-bane.
pyramidále,	pyramidal.
lycóctonum	great-yellow.
albùm,	white.
versícolor,	three-coloured.
ÁLOE 219, 271.	
10 vulgàris,	common.
Barbadénsis,	Barbadoes.
oblíqua,	oblique.

dichótoma, smooth-stemmed.

lineàta, red-edged.

ADÓNIS 134.

vernális, spring.

ARISTÉA 125.

5 cyànea, blue.

ALSTRŒMÈRIA 18, 57, 229, 339.

10 flós-martína, san-martin.

pelegrìna, spotted.

pulchélla, pretty.

atro-purpùrea, dark.

AGROSTÉMMA 143.

flós-cucùla, ragged-robin.

Lychnìs flós-cucùla.

ARAUCÀRIA 261.

12 excélsa, Norfork-Island-pine.

imbricàta, Chile-pine.

APHÉLEXIS 88.

5 hùmilis, dwarf.

Elichrýsum spectábile.

AMÓRPHA 45.

ASTÉLMA 93.

8 exímia, beautiful.

spiràlis, spiral-leaved.

speciosíssimus, showy.

fruticàns, frutescent.

imbricàtum, imbricated.

ANGÓPHORA 107.

6 cordifòlia, heart-leaved.

híspida, hispid.

ALOÝSIA 123.

9 citriodòra, lemon-scented.

Verbéna tripfýlla.

AMPELÒPSIS 198.

hederàcea, Virginian creeper.

Císsus hederàcea.

ARISTOLÓCHIA 221.	Birth-wort.
9 labiòsa,	lipped.
ASTRAP'ÆA 221.	
12 wallíchii,	Wallich's.
ARÉCA 221.	Cabbage-tree.
12 cátechu,	catechu.
olerácea,	eatable.
montàna,	mountain.
ARDÍSIA 220.	
10 crenulàta,	crenulate.
solanàcea,	night-shade-leaved.
élegans,	elegant.
umbellàta,	umbel-flowered.
littoràlis.	
AGATHAÉA 82.	
12 cæléstus,	blue.

AGAPÁNTHUS 62.	African lily.
umbellàtus,	umbel-flowered.
var. variegàtus,	striped-leaved.
ALONSÒA 62.	
incisifòlia,	nettle-leaved.
Hemímeris urticifòlia.	
lineàris	
Hemímeris lineàris.	
AÙCUBA 63.	
4 japónica,	blotch-leaved.
ANAGÝRIS 63.	
4 fætida,	strong smelling.
AZÁLEA 63.	
5 índica,	Chinese.
" álba,	white.
" purpùrea,	double.
" phœnícea,	purple.
sinénse,	yellow.

AÒTUS 64.

1 villòsa, villous.

virgáta, slender.

ANDERSÒNIA 64.

6 sprengelioídes, sprengilia-like.

ÁRBUTUS 64. Strawberry-tree.

7 Unèdo, common.

" rùbra, red-flowered.

hýbrida hybrid.

serratifòlia, andrachnoides.

andráchne, oriental.

BÁNKSIA 64.

8 dentàta, tooth-leaved.

'æmula, deeply sawed.

serráta, saw-leaved.

undulàta.

latifòlia, broad-leaved.

grándis, great-flowered.

speciòsa, long-leaved.

cunninghàmii, Cunningham's.

spinulòsa,	spiny-leaved.
palludòsa,	marsh.
rèpens,	creeping
verticillàta,	whorl-leaved.

BLÈTIA 66.

9 hyacinthìna,	hyacinthine.
Cymbídium hyacinthìnum.	

BÒRONIA 66

5 pinnáta,	scented.
serruláta,	rose-scented.
aláta,	wing-leaved.

BARÓSMA 86.

6 serratifòlia,	saw-leaved.
pulchèlla,	blunt-leaved.
fœtidíssima,	strong-scented.
odoráta,	odoriferous.
dioíca,	dioecious.

BABÌANA 303.

11 distíca two-ranked.

strícta,	erect.
tubiflòra,	tube-flowered.
plicáta,	plaited.

BRUNSVÌGIA 222.

11 multiflòra,	many-flowered.
laticòma,	broad-headed.
Josephínæ,	Josephine's
falcáta,	falcate
margináta,	red-margined
cilliáris,	hairy-margined.

BAMBUSA 222.	Bamboo-cane.
14 arundinàcea,	reed-like.

BANISTÈRIA 223.

fúlgens,	fulgent.
chrisophýlla,	shining.
splèndens,	splendid.

BARRINGTÒNIA 223.

10 speciòsa,	showy.

BRÒWNEA 233.

10 coccínea,	scarlet.
ròsa,	Trinidad-rose.
grandicéps,	grandest.

BOUVÁRDIA 66.

7 triphýlla,	three-leaved.
Jacquínii,	shark-leaved.
Ìxora americána.	

BRACHYSÈMA 66.

5 latifòlium,	broad-leaved.
undulátum,	wave-leaved.

BURCHÉLLIA 67.

10 capénsis,	cape.
parviflòra,	small-flowered.

BEAUFÓRTIA 67.

8 decussáta,	cross-leaved.
spàrsa,	alternate-leaved.

BRÙNIA 67.

5 nodiflòra, imbricated.
languinósa, woolly.
comòsa, tufted.
abrotanoídes, southern wood-like.
formòsa, handsome.

BÓSEA 67. Golden-rod-tree.
5 yervamóra.

B'ÆCKIA 67.
6 camphoráta, camphor.
pulchélla, neat.
virgáta, slender.

BILLARDIÉRA 68. Apple-berry.
longiflòra, long-flowered.
mutàbilis, changeable.
scándens, climbing.
fusifórmis, long-fruited.

BÉLLIS 135. Daisy.
perénnís hortensis var. var. garden.

BALLÓTA 260.

11 purpúrea, purple-flowered.

Amarýllis purpúrea.

BELLADÓNNA 208.

11 purpuráscens, Belladonna Lily.

Amarýllis Belladónna.

BIGNÒNIA 197. Trumpet-flower.

crucígera, cross-bearing.

grandiflòra, large-flowered.

rádicans, rooting.

COTYLÉDON 39.

COLÙTEA 45.

CÝTICUS 45.

CÁLTHA 135.

palústris plèno, double yellow.

CHAM'ÆROPS 262. Dwarf-fan-palm.

12 sp. sp.

CÓRYPHA 232.	Large-fan-palm.
11 ambraculifera,	large.
talìera,	great.
CLÉMATIS 196, 138, 83,	Virgin's-bower.
12 integrifòlia,	entire-leaved.
angustifòlia,	narrow-leaved.
erécta,	erect-growing.
viticélla pulchélla,	double-blue.
flámmula,	sweet-scented.
virginiàna,	Virginian.
flòrida plèno,	double-white.
aristàta,	awned.
brachiàta,	armed.
COB'ÆA 83.	
scándens,	climbing.
CALLICÁRPA 229.	
CAROLINEA 229.	Cream-nut.

17 insignis,	great-flowered.
álba,	white-flowered.
prínceps,	digitated.
robústa,	robust.

CARYÓTA 229.

12 ùrens,	stinging.

CALÀTHEA 223.

zebrìna	Zebra-plant.
Maránta Zebrína.	

CÁNNA 224, 35.	Indian-shot.
3 gigántea,	tall.
limbàta,	bordered.
díscolor,	two-coloured.
iridiflòra,	nodding-flowered.

CÁCTUS 224, 271.

CÈRUS 225.

18 peruviànus,	Peruvian.
heptagònus,	seven-angled.

flagellifórmus,	creeping.
grandiflòrus,	night-blooming.
triangulàris,	triangular.
phyllanthoiídes,	rosy-flowered.
Cáctus Speciosus.	
Jenkinsòni,	Jenkinsons'.
Speciosíssimus,	showy.
Ackermánnia,	Ackerman's.
truncàtus,	truncated.

COREÓPSIS, 138.

tenuifòlia,	slender-leaved.
verticullàta,	whorl-leaved.
díscolor,	two-coloured.
trípteris,	three-leaved.

CALCEOLÁRIA 68, 17, 35, 338.,	Slipper-wort.
10 angustifòlia,	narrow-leaved.
integrifòlia,	entire-leaved.
plantagínea,	plantain-leaved.
corymbósa,	corymb-flowered.
purpùrea,	purple-flowered.
Hopiána,	Dr. Hopes'.

micàns,	fine.
hybrìda,	hybrid.
Fothergíllii,	Fothergill's.
arachnóidea,	cob-web.

CALOTHÁMNUS 68.

6 quadrífida,	four-cleft.
claváta,	club-leaved.

CAMÉLLIA 69, 80.,	Japan-rose.
11 víridis,	green-tea.
Bohèa,	black-tea.
sesánqua,	Lady Banks'.
oleífera,	oleiferous.
maliflòra,	pink-flowered.
Sesanqua rosea.	
kíssi,	nepaul.
reticulàta,	Capt. Rawes'.
japónica,	original.
rùbra,	common.
álba,	single-white.
semidúplex,	semidouble red.
rùbro pléno,	double red.

cárnea,	Middlemist's.
myrtifòlia,	myrtle-leaved.
involuta.	
myrtifolia,	minor.
hexanguláris,	six-sided.
atrorùbens,	Loddiges' red.
anemoniflòra,	red waratah.
" rósea,	rose war.
dianthiflòra,	carnation war.
blánda,	blush war.
pompónia,	Kew blush.
pæoniflòra,	pæony flowered.
Welbánkii,	Welbank's.
álba-plèno,	double white.
flavéscens,	ladies'-blush.
fimbriàta,	fringed white.
imbricàta,	imbricate petaled.
variegàta,	double striped.
crassinervis?	thick-nerved.
conchiflòra,	shell-flowered.
rubricáulis,	Lady Campbell's.
longifòlia,	long leaved.
chandlèrii,	Chandler's.

versìcolor.

Aitònia,	Aiton's.
althæflòra,	holly-hock flowered.
corallìna,	coral-flowered.
insígnis,	splendid.
anemoneflòra álba,	white anemone flowered.
heterophýlla,	various leaved.
Woódsii,	Mr. Wood's.
speciósa,	striped waratah.
fúlgens,	fulgent.
grandiflòra,	large flowered.
rósa-sinénsis,	bright pink.
intermédia,	new blush.
invíncible,	Press's.

punctàta.

pressíi.

rose-mundií,	streaked.
compàcta,	compact-white.
gloriòsa,	dark-red.
Róssii,	Ross's.

CALLICÒMA 80.

6 serratifòlia,	saw-leaved.

CARMICH'ÆLIA 81.

8 austrális, New-Zealand.

CUNÒNIA 81, Decandria-digynia.

2 Capénsis, Cape.

CLÉTHRA 81.

2 arbórea, tree.

" variegàta, variegated-leaved.

COTONEASTÈR 81.

2 denticulàta, toothed.

microphýlla, small-leaved.

CRÒWEA 81.

1 salígna, willow-leaved.

CHORIZÈMA 81.

5 nàna, dwarf.

ilicifòlia, holly-leaved.

CINERÀRIA 82, Cape-aster.

12 speciósa,	large-flowered.
amelloìdes,	blue.
purpûrea,	purple.
lanáta,	woolly.
CÍSTUS 82,	Rock-rose.
3 ladaníferus,	gum.
Monspeliénsis,	Montpelier.
sálignis,	willow-leaved.
populifòlius,	poplar-leaved.
undulàtus,	wave-leaved.
CAMPÁNULA 135,	Bell-flower.
persicifòlia,	peach-leaved.
" àlba-plèno,	double-white.
" cærùlea-plèno,	" blue.
urticifòlia,	nettle-leaved.
speciòsa,	spacious.
glomeràta,	headed-flowered.
versícolor,	three-coloured.
CHEIRÁNTHUS 136.	
chéiri-vulgaris,	Wall-flower.

" hæmànthus,	double-bloody.
mutàbilis,	changeable.

CHELONE 136.

glábra,	glabrous.
oblíqua,	oblique-leaved.
barbàta,	bearded-flowered.
atropurpùrea,	purple-flowered.
pulchélla,	pretty.
venústa,	showy.
speciòsa,	spacious.

CHRYSÁNTHEMUM 137.

sinénse,	variable-chinese.
" tubulòsum álbum,	quilled-white.
" supèrbum,	superb-white.
" díscolor,	large-lilac.
" fúlvum,	Spanish-brown.
" atropurpùreum,	early-crimson.
" involùtum,	curled-lilac
" fasciculàtum,	superb-yellow.
" serotìnum,	pale-purple.
" papyràceum,	paper-white.

" waratáh,	yellow-anemone-flow'd.
" versícolor,	two-coloured red.
" stellàtum,	starry-purple.
" verecúndum,	early-blush.
" mutábile,	changeable.
COCOLÒBA 229,	Sea-side-grape.
15 pubéscens,	downy.
latifòlia,	broad-leaved.
CÙPHEA 229.	
6 Melvílla,	Melvill's.
CRÒTON 230.	
pìctus,	painted.
variegàtus,	variegated.
" latifòlia,	broad-leaved.
CÉRBERA 230.	
17 thevètia,	linear-leaved.
ahoùai,	oval-leaved.
odállam,	spear-leaved.
mànghas,	blunt-leaved.

CÝCAS 230,	Sago-palm?
11 revolúta,	revolute.
circinàlis great.	
glaùca,	glaucous.
COMBRÈTUM 231.	
élegans,	elegant.
formòsum,	handsome.
purpùreum,	scarlet.
CRÀSSULA 231.	
CRÒCUS 275,	saffron.
satìvus,	garden.
Pallàsii,	Pallas'.
serotìnus,	late-flowered.
nudiflòrus,	naked-flowered.
CÓLCHICUM 275.	
CÁLLA 289.	
12 Æthiòpica,	Ethiopian-lily.

CORONÍLLA 83.

12 glaúca,	glaucous.
valentìna,	nine-leaved.
stipulàris.	
viminális,	slender.

CORRÈA 84.

5 álba,	white-flowered.
rúfa,	rusty-leaved.
pulchélla,	pretty.
speciósa,	showy.
virèns,	green-flowered.

CRAT'ÆGUS 84.

CUPRÈSSUS 85,	Cypress.
6 lusitánica,	cedar of Goa.
péndula,	pendulous.
juniperoídes,	African.

CALÁMPELIS 85.

11 scábra,	climbing.

Eccremocárpus scáber.

CELÁSTRIS 85.	Staff-tree.
4 pyracánthus,	red-fruited.
cymósus,	cyme-flowered.
multiflòrus,	many-flowered.
lúcidus,	shining.
COÒKIA 85.	Wampee-tree.
11 punctàta,	punctate.
CALLISTÀCHYS 85.	
6 lanceoláta,	lanceolated.
ovàta,	oval-leaved.
CHARLWÒODIA 234.	
11 strícta,	erect.
COFFÈA 227,	Coffee-tree.
17 Arábica,	Arabian.
CINNAMÓMUM 101.	
15 camphòra,	camphire-tree.

CLERODÉNDRON 124.

12 fràgrans múltiplex,	double.

CRINÙM 261, 232.

11 capénse,	cape.
Amarýllis longifòlia.	
cruéntum,	red.
scábrum,	scabrous.
amàbile,	showy.

CYRTÀNTHUS 232.

11 odòrus,	scented.
striátus,	striped.
oblíquus,	oblique-leaved.
vittàtus,	ribanded.

CARÝOPHYLLUS 233.

9 aromáticus,	aromatic.

CALLÌSTEMON 107.

6 salígnum,	willow-leaved.
lanceolàtum,	lance-leaved.

semperflòrens, ever-blooming

glaùcum, glaucous.

metrosidèros speciòsa.

CÝCLAMEN 290, 297.

11 Coúm, round-leaved.

Pérsicum, Persian.

hederæfòlium, ivy-leaved.

Europ'æum, round-leaved.

Neapolitànum, Neapolitan.

CENTRÀNTHUS 150.

Phù, garden.

Valeriána Phù.

rùbra, red.

Valeriána rùbra.

DION'ÆA 36.

5 mucípula, Venus-fly-trap.

DILLÈNIA 233.

7 speciòsa, spacious.

scàndens, climbing.

DRAC'ÆNA 233.	Dragon-tree.
11 férrea,	purple-leaved.
frágrans,	scented.
margináta,	margined.
dráco,	large
DÁPHNE 313, 258, 270.	
15 odòra,	sweet-scented.
índica.	
hýbrida,	daphine.
oleoídes,	olea-leaved.
laurèola,	spurg-laurel.
póntica,	pontic.
alpìna,	alpine.
cneòrum,	trailing.
DELPHÍNUM 138.	Larkspur.
grandiflòrum,	large-flowered.
intermèdium,	intermediate.
var. var.	
elàtum,	Bee-larkspur.
montànum,	tall-growing.

DIANTHUS 138.	Pink.
17 barbátus,	sweet-william.
" plèno,	double.
díscolor,	two-coloured.
chinènsis,	china.
alpínus,	alpine.
supérbus,	superb-red.
caryophýllus,	clove.
plumárius,	common.
frágrans,	sweet-scented.
DICTÁMNUS 139.	
fraxinélla,	red.
àlbus,	white.
DODECÀTHEON 321.139.	American cow-slip.
mèdia,	purple.
" àlba,	white.
DIGITÀLIS 140. FOX-GLOVE.	
leucoph`æa,	broad-lipped.
ferrugínea,	rusty-flowered.

ochroleùca,	large yellow.
purpuràscens,	blush-flowered.
erubéscens.	
purpúrea,	purple.
" àlba,	white.

DAVÌESIA 86.

6 ulicìna,	furze-like.
latifòlia,	broad-leaved.
aciculáris,	needle-leaved.
incrassáta,	thick-leaved.

DIÓSMA 86.

6 capitàta,	crown-flowered.
oppositifòlia,	opposite-leaved.
longifòlia,	long-leaved.
rùbra,	heath-leaved.
ericifòlia.	
treretifòlia,	round-leaved.

DRYÁNDRA 87.

6 nívea,	white-leaved.
formòsa,	apricot-scented.

floribúnda,	many-flowered.
armáta,	acute-leaved.
plumòsa,	feathered.
baxtèri,	Baxter's.
nervòsa,	nerve-leaved.
falcáta,	falcate-leaved.

DILLWÝNIA 87.

6 floribúnda,	close-flowered.
ericifòlia.	
teretifòlia,	round-leaved.
phylicoídes,	phylica-like.

DAMPIÈRA 87.

6 purpùrea,	purple-flowered.
unduláta,	wave-leaved.
stricta,	upright.

EDWÁRDSIA 88.

6 grandiflòra,	large-flowered.
chrysophýlla,	silver-leaved.
microphýlla,	small-leaved.

ELICHRÝSUM 88.

ENKIÁNTHUS 88.

6 quinqueflòrus,	Canton.
reticulàtus,	netted-leaved.

EPÁCRIS 88.

5 grandiflòra,	large-flowered.
pulchélla,	sweet-scented.
impréssa,	unpressed.
palludòsa,	marsh.
purpuráscens *rúbra*.	red.

ERÍCAS 89.	Heath.
6 mediterránea,	common.
5 aristáta,	awned.
bàccans,	arbutus-flowered.
bowieána,	Bowie's.
conférta,	crowded-flowered.
élegans,	elegant.
fasciculáris,	cluster-flowered.
florabùnda,	many-flowered.
glomeràta,	glomerate.

grandiflòra,	large-flowered.
inflàta,	inflated.
mammòsa,	nipple.
prégnans,	swelled.
pubéscens,	downy.
refúlgens,	refulgent.
regérminans	cluster-flowered.
rùbens,	red-flowered.
speciòsa,	specious.
spléndens,	splendid.
tenélla,	delicate.
triúmphans,	triumphant.
vestìta,	tremulous.
var. var.	
ventricòsa,	beautiful.
víscaria,	clammy-flowered.

ERÁNTHEMUM 234.

11 pulchéllum,	neat.
bícolor two-coloured.	

EUGÈNIA 234.

11 piménta,	Allspice.

Mýrtus Piménta.

frágrans,	scented.
EUPHÓRBIA. 234.	Spurg.
18 heterophýlla.?	
ERYTHRÌNA 235. 330.	Coral-tree.
13 corallodéndrum,	smooth.
speciòsa,	splendid.
pubéscens,	downy.
herbácea,	herbaceous.
laurifòlia,	laurel-leaved
crísta-gàlli,	Cocks-comb.
ERIABÒTRYA 107.	loquat.
11 japónica,	Japan.
ENTÈLIA 119.	
12 arboréscens,	tree.
ECHINOCÁCTUS 225.	
18 gibbòsus,	gouty.
crispàtus,	curled-ribbed.

recúrvus,	recurve-spined.

EUPATÓRIUM 91. 140.

10 élegans,	scented.
cœlestínum,	blue.
aromáticum,	aromatic.

EUTÁXIA 92.

6 myrtifòlia,	myrtle-leaved.
pùngens,	pungent.

EUCHÌLUS 92.

6 obcordáta.

ERÓDIUM 91,	Heron's-bill.
incarnàtum,	fleshy.
crassifòlium,	thick-leaved.
laciniátum,	laciniated.

EUCALÝPTUS 91.

6 cordàta,	Heart-leaved.
rostráta,	beaked.
radiáta,	rayed.

pulvigéra.

glóbifera, round-fruited.

pulverulénta, powdered.

resinífera, red-gum-tree.

EURCÚMA 36.

EÙCOMIS 24.

FURCHR'ÆA. 39.

FÚNKIA 96, 141.

11 álba.

Hemerocállis japónica.

cærùlea.

Hemerocállis cærùlea.

FERRÀRIA 40.

11 undulàta, curled.

antheròsa, variegated.

FRITILLÀRIA 295.

imperiàlis, Crown-imperial.

Pérsica,	Persian.
FÌCUS 236,	Fig-tree.
12 elástica,	gum-elastic.
brassiì,	brass.
religiòsa,	superstitious.
lùcida,	shining.
Bengalénsis,	Bengal.
nìtida,	glossy.
índica,	banyan-tree.
exasperàta,	very-rough.
costàta,	rib-leaved.
FÚCHSIA 92,	Ladies-ear-drop.
13 virgáta,	twiggy.
cònica,	conical-tubed.
coccínea,	scarlet.
microphýlla,	small-leaved.
arbórea,	tree.
gràcilis,	slender.
thymifòlia,	thyme-leaved.
GELSÈMIUM 93.	Carolina-jasmine.

5 nìtidum,	shining-leaved.

GNAPHÀLIUM 93.	(See *Astélma.*)

GOMPHOLÒBIUM 94.

5 barbigérum,	bearded-flowered.
polimórphum,	variable.

GEORGIÀNA 180.

Dáhlia supérflua.

dwarf-globe,	crimson.
pulla.	
Electa,	scarlet.
flamæa,	flame.
Zeno.	
Etna,	scarlet.
imperiosa.	
Cicero.	
cocade.	
Cambridge-surprise.	
Duchess-of-Wellington,	pink.
Countess-of-Liverpool.	
Barret's-Wm.-4th,	scarlet.

mountain-of-snow,	*true.*
Diana,	lilac.
crimson-bonnet,	glob.
eximia,	scarlet.
star-of-Brunswick,	pink.
Lafayette,	orange.
morning-star,	red.
Romulus,	scarlet.
Florabunda,	crimson.
speciosissima,	purple.
Veitches-triumphant,	purple.
coronation,	maroon.
Stephenia,	bloody.
feathered,	light crimson, *glob.*
dwarf,	crimson, *fine glob.*
striated buff,	*anemone-flowered.*
large-pink,	"
" rose,	"
spectabile,	"
painted-lady,	"
early-blood,	"

GLÓBBA 36.

GESNÉRIA 36.

10 bulbósa, bulbous.

GLORIÓSA 37.

10 supérba, superb.

GASTÈRIA 259.

GEÙM 141.

quéllyon, scarlet.

coccíneum.

hýbridum, hybrid.

urbánum, common.

GENTIÁNA 140.

lútea, yellow.

purpúrea, purple.

septémfida, crested.

acaúlis, dwarf.

GÆRTNÈRA 237.

12 racemòsa, climbing.

GEISSOMÉRIA 237.

2 longiflòra,	long-flowered.

GARDÈNIA 237, 262.

9 campanuláta,	bell-flowered.
am'æna,	neat.
costàta,	ribbed.
lúcida,	shining.
flòrida-pléno,	Cape-jasmine.
ràdicans,	dwarf.
longifòlia,	long-leaved.
latifòlia,	broad-leaved.
Rothmònnia,	spotted.
Thunbérgia,	Thunberg's.

GLADIÒLUS 303.	Corn-flag.
11 floribùndus,	many-flowered.
cardinàlis,	cardinal.
Byzantínus,	Turkish.
blándus,	fairest.
cuspidàtus,	sharp-pointed.
psittàcinus,	parrot.

GOMPHOLÒBIUM 94.

latifòlium,	broad-leaved.
grandiflòrum,	large-flowered.
venústum,	showy.

GENÍSTA 94.

1 Canariénsis,	Canary.
tricuspidáta,	three-pointed,
cuspidòsa,	sharp-pointed.
umbellàta,	umbelled.

GNÍDIA 94.

6 símplex,	flax-leaved.
serícea,	silky.
imbérbis,	smooth-scaled.
pinifòlia,	pine-leaved.

GOODÈNIA 94.

6 stellígera,	starry-haired.
suavèolens,	sweet-scented.
ovàta,	oval-leaved.
grandiflòra,	large-flowered.

GORTERIA 94.

6 personàta.

GAZÀNIA 94.

6 rìgens,	great.
Pavònia,	peacock.
heterophýlla,	various-leaved.

GREVÌLLEA 95.

6 punícea,	scarlet.
acanthifòlia,	acanthus-like.
coccínea,	pretty.
juniperìna,	juniper-like.
lineàris,	linear-leaved.

HÀKEA 95.

6 gibbòsa	gibbous-fruited.
nítida,	glossy.
salígna,	willow-leaved.
suavèolens,	sweet-scented.
conculàta,	conculate.
Lambérti,	Lambert's.

HEMEROCÁLLIS, 96.	Day-lily.
11 speciòsa,	spacious.
HERMÁNNIA 96.	
HELICHRÝSUM 93.	Everlasting.
8 grandiflòrum,	large-flowered.
arbòreum,	árborescent.
orientàle,	common.
fràgrans,	sweet-scented.
odoratìssimum,	odoriferous.
fruticàns,	shrubby.
fúlgidum,	splendid.
HIBBÉRTIA 96.	
12 grossulariæfòlia,	gooseberry-leaved.
dentàta,	toothed.
volùbilis,	twining.
fasciculàta,	bushy.
salígna,	willow-leaved.
pedunculàta,	long-pedicled.

HABRÁNTHUS 96.

2 Andersónii,	Anderson's.
versícolor,	three-coloured.
robústa,	robust.

HÒVEA 97.

6 lineàris	linear-leaved.
rosmarinifòlia,	rosmary-leaved.
longifòlia,	long-leaved.
Célsii,	Cels's.

HYDRÁNGEA, 97. 172.

14 horténsis,	variable.
hypéricum,	St. John's-wort.
10 monógynum,	three-styled.
baleàricum,	warted.
floribúndum,	many-flowered.
canariénse,	canaries.
ægyptìacum,	Egyptian.
cochinchinénse,	cochinchina.

HIBÍSCUS 238. 141. 27. 45.

9 Ròsa sinénsis plénus,	double red.

" " cárnea,	" salmon.
" " variegàtus,	" striped.
" " lútea,	" yellow.
palústris,	marsh.
ròseus,	rose-coloured.
militàris,	smooth.
speciòsus,	showy crimson.
grandiflòrus,	large flowered.
púngens,	pungent.
Syrìacus,	Althea.
var. var.	
mutábilis plènus,	double-changeable.
lilliiflòrus,	various.

HEDÝCHIUM 36.

HEMEROCÁLLIS 141.	Day lily.
fúlva,	copper-coloured.
gramínea,	grass-leaved.

HÉDERA 198.

Hèlix,	Irish-ivy.

HERITÉRIA 238.	Looking-glass-plant.
11 littoràlis,	large-leaved.
HOWÁRTHIA 260.	
HÓYA 239.	wax-plant.
carnòsa,	common.
crassifòlia,	thick-leaved.
HERRNÁNDIA 239.	Jack-in-a-box.
Sonòra,	peltate-leaved.
ÌXORA 240.	
5 obovàta,	purple.
purpùrea.	
crocàta,	saffron-coloured.
ròsea,	rose-coloured.
bandhùca,	stem-clasping.
blànda,	charming.
undulàta,	waved.
dichotíma.	
coccínea,	scarlet.
grandiflòra, strícta, flámmea, speciòsa.	

fúlgens,	glossy.
longifòlia, *lanceolàta*.	
pavètta,	scented.
ÍRIS, 142, 320.	Flower-de-luce.
subiflòra,	sub-flowered.
nepalénsis,	Nepaul.
Pallàsii,	Pallas'.
pállida,	pale.
cristáta,	crested.
arenària,	sand.
furcàta,	forked.
germánica,	German.
florentìna,	florentine.
vérna,	spring.
susiàna,	chalcedonian.
lusitánica,	Portuguese.
var. var.	
Hiphioídes,	great bulbous.
Pérsica,	Persian.
ÍXIA, 203.	
11 monadélphia,	monadelphus.

leucántha,	white flowered.
capitàta,	headed.
cònica,	orange-coloured.
colamelàris,	variegated.

IPOMAÈA 240.

9 paniculáta,	panicle-flowered.

ÌLEX 98.	Holly.
15 aquifòlium,	European.
var. var.	
cassìne,	cassine-like.
vomitòria,	south-sea tea.

ILLÍCIUM 99.	Anniseed-tree.
floridànum,	purple-flowered.
parviflòrum,	small-flowered.
anisàtum,	anise-scented.

INDIGÓFERA 99.	Indigo-tree.
denudàta,	smooth-leaved.
am'æna,	pretty.
austrális,	round-stemmed.

angulàta, angular-stemed.

cándicans, white-leaved.

filifòlia, filiform-leaved.

ISOPÒGON 99.

9 formòsus, handsome.

anemonefòlious, anemone-leaved.

attenuàtis, attenuated.

polycéphalus, many-headed.

jálapa, Jalap.

grandiflòra, large-flowered.

pulchélla, pretty.

tuberòsa, tuberous.

JUSTÍCIA 99. 243.

nìgricans, spotted.

orchioídes, orchis-like.

adhàtoda, Malabar-nut.

coccínea, scarlet.

pícta, painted.

lúcida, shining.

form`osa, handsome.

speciòsa, showy.

JACKSÒNIA 100.

6 scopària,	broom-like.
da,	horrid.
reticulàta,	netted.

JUNÍPERUS 210.	Juniper.
virginiàna,	red-cedar.

JÁTROPHA 242.	Physic-nut.
17 multífida,	multifid.
panduræfòlia,	fiddle-leaved.
cúrcas,	angular-leaved.

JACARÁNDA 241.

9 mimosifòlia,	mimosa-leaved.
filìcifòlia,	fern-leaved.

JAMBÒSA 241.	Rose-apple.
11 vúlgáris,	common.
malacénsis,	Malay-apple.
purpuráscens,	purple-flowered.
macrophýlla,	large-leaved.

amplexicaùlis,	stem-clasping.
JASMÌNUM 242.	Jasmine.
3 sámbac,	Arabian.
" multiplex,	semi-double.
hirsútum,	hairy-stemmed.
paniculàtum,	panicled.
simplicifòlium,	simple-leaved.
lucídium	shining.
odoratíssimum 3,	Azorian.
revolùtum	revolute-leaved.
grandiflòrum,	Catalonian.
officinàle,	common.
KALOSANTHUS 231,	
18 coccínea,	scarlet.
Crassùla coccínea.	
versícolor,	changeable.
Crassùla versícolor.	
odoratíssima,	sweet-scented.
KÆMPFÈRIA 243, 36.	
17 rotúnda,	round-rooted.

KENNÈDIA 100.

5 monophýlla,	simple-leaved.
rubicúnda,	dingy-flowered.
prostráta,	trailing.
Glýcine coccínea.	
coccínea,	many-flowered.
comptoniána,	comptonian.
inophýlla,	few-leaved.

LAGERSTR'ÆMIA 129. 172.

índica,	crape-flower.

LAMBÉRTIA 100.

6 formòsa,	handsome.
echinàta,	lobe-leaved.
uniflòra,	one-flowered.
inérmis,	unarmed.

LASIOPÈTALUM 100.

LAVÁNDULA 101.	Lavender.
7 dentáta,	toothed.

formòsa,	handsome.
pinnàta,	pinnated.
LAÚRUS 101. 244.	Laurel.
15 f'ætens,	til.
aggregàta,	clustered.
glaùca,	glaucous.
scàbra,	rough.
vérum,	true.
cássia,	false.
chloróxylon,	cogwood.
LANTÀNA 244.	
LANTÀNIA 244.	Dwarf-palm.
12 borbònica,	borbon.
rùbra,	red.
glaucophýlla,	glaucous.
LÌATRIS 142.	Gay-feather.
squarròsa,	squarrose.
élegans,	elegant.
paniculáta,	paniculate.

spicáta.

macróstachya, large-spiked.

LÝCHNIS, 143. 104.

9 chalcedònica, chalcedonian.

fúlgens, fulgent.

flós-jòvis, umbelled.

Agrostéma flós-jòvis.

coronáta, crowned.

LÝTHRUM 143.

alàtum, erect-growing.

virgàtum, twiggy.

diffùsum, diffuse.

lanceolàtum, lance-leaved.

LOMÀTIA 103. (See errata.)

6 silaifòlia, cut-leaved.

dentàta, toothed.

ilicifòlia, holly-leaved.

LACHENÀLIA 291.

11 trícolor, three-coloured.

quadrícolor,	four-coloured.
rùbida,	dotted-flowered.
punctàta,	spotted-flowered.
orchoídes,	orchis-like.
nervòsa,	nerved-leaved.

LILÌUM 32. 35. 306.

11 màrtagon,	red.
tygrìnum,	spotted.
chalcedònicum,	Chalcedonian.
speciòsum?	showy.
longiflòrum?	
japónicum.	Japan.

LOBÈLIA 102.

6 tùpa,	mullein-leaved.
speciòsa,	specious.
spléndens,	splendid.
fúlgens,	fulgent.
cærùlea,	blue.
Thunbérgii,	Thurberg's.
corymbòsa,	corymbose.
pyramidàlis	pyramidal.

ilicifòlia,	holly-leaved.
LOPHOSPHÉRMUM 103.	
12 scándens	climbing.
LACHN'ÆA 103.	
1 glaùca,	glaucous.
conglomeràta,	clustered.
eriocéphala,	wooly-headed.
LEONÒTIS,	Lion's-ear.
7 intermédia,	intermediate.
LEONÙRUS,	narrow-leaved.
LEUCOSPÉRMUM 103.	
9 formòsum,	handsome.
grandiflòrum,	tomentose.
cándicans,	hoary.
LIPÀRIA 104.	
sph'ærica,	crowned.
tomentòsa,	downy.

villósa,	hairy.
serícea,	silky.

LYSINÈMA 104.	
5 pentapétalum,	five-petaled.
conspícum,	conspicuous.
róseum,	rose-coloured.

LÝCHNIS 104.	
9 coronàta,	crowned.

LEPTOSPÉRMUM 104.	South-Sea-Myrtle.
6 baccàtum,	berry-fruited.
péndulum,	pendulous.
juníperinum,	juniper-leaved.
ovátum,	ovate-leaved.
stellàtum,	starry-flowered.
grandiflórum,	large-flowered.
scopàrium,	New-Zealand-tea.

LEUCADÉNDRON 105.	Silver-Tree.
9 argentéum,	silvery.
Pròtea argentéa.	

squarròsum,	squarrose.
stellàtum,	starry
Pròtea stellàris.	
tórtum,	twisted.
seríceum,	silky.
marginàtum,	margined.
plumòsum,	feathered.
Pròtea parviflòra.	

MAGNÓLIA 105.

9 fuscàta,	rusty.
annonæfòlia,	annonæ-leaved.
pùmila,	dwarf.
conspícua,	youlan.
purpùrea,	purple.

MELALÈUCA 106.

6 elíptica,	eliptic.
fúlgens,	fulgent.
decussàta,	cross-leaved.
hypericifòlia,	hypericum-leaved.
squarròsa,	square-set.
linarifòlia,	linear-leaved.

incàna, hoary.

telragònia, four-sided.

thymifòlia, thyme-leaved.

MAURÁNDIA 106.

6 Barclàyana, Barclay's.

semperflòrens, ever-blooming.

MÝSINE 106, Cape-Myrtle.

4 retùsa, erect.

rotundifòlia, round-leaved.

MÉSPILUS 107. Medlar.

METROSIDÈROS.

6 flòrida, many-flowered.

umbellàta, umbel-flowered.

angustifòlia, narrow-leaved.

lanceolàta, lance-leaved.

MÁNIHOT 243.

17 cannabìna, cassada root.

MESEMBRÝANTHEMUM 263. 271.

18 sp. sp.

MÝRTUS 108.	Myrtle.
12 commùnis,	common
múltiplex,	double.
leucocàrpa,	white-fruited.
itálica variegàta,	variegated.
maculàta,	blotch-leaved.
tomentòsa,	downy.
tenuifòlia,	slender-leaved.

MIMÙLUS 143.	Monkey-flower.
lùteus,	yellow.
rivulàris,	dark-spotted.
moschàtus,	musk-scented.

MONÁRDA 143.	
dídyma,	Oswego-tea.
kalmiána,	pubescent-flowered.
Russeliàna,	Russells'.
punctàta,	spotted.

MATHÍOLA 144.	Stock-gilly.
simplicicáulis,	Brompton-stock.
var. var.	
incàna,	queen-stock.
var. var.	
ánnua,	annual.
var. var.	
glàbra,	wall-leaved.
MAMILLÀRIA 224.	
18 coccínea,	scarlet-flowered.
símplex,	small-red-spined.
pusílla,	starry.
cònica,	cone-headed.
MELOCÁCTUS 225.	
18 commùnis,	Turk's-cape.
macránthus,	large-spined.
pyramidàlis,	pyramidale.
MELÀSTOMA 245,	
1 Malabáthrica,	Malabar.
sanguìnea,	bloody.

decémfida,	ten-cleft.
pulverulénta,	powdered.
áspera,	rough.
nepalénsis,	Nepaul.

MALPÍGHIA 246.	Barbadoes-cherry.
17 ùrens,	stinging,
aquifòlium,	holly-leaved.
fucáta,	painted.
glábra,	smooth.

MÁRICA 246.	
12 *cærùlea*,	*blue.*
Sabìni,	Sabin's.
northiána,	spotted.

MÙSA, 247,	Plantain-tree.
15 paradisìaca,	common.
sapiéntum,	banana-tree.
rosàcea,	rose-coloured.
coccínea,	scarlet-coloured.
chinénsis,	Chinese.

MANGÍFERA 245,	Mango-tree.
11 índica,	common.
oppositifòlia?	opposite-leaved.
NANDÌNA 108,	Nandin.
1 doméstica,	common.
NINTÒOA.	
longiflòra,	long-flowered.
Lonicéra-japónica.	
NÉRIUM 108,	Oleander.
12 oleánder,	common.
" spléndens,	double-rose.
" elegantìssimum,	variegated.
" álba,	white.
" " pleno?	double-white.
ŒNOTHÈRA 144,	Evening-primrose.
macrocárpa,	broad-leaved.
média,	intermediate.
latiflòra,	broad-flowered.
Frazèri,	Frazer's.

speciòsa,	handsome.
pállida,	pale.
odoràta,	sweet-scented.

ÒLEA 109,	Olive-tree.
11 europæa,	common.
" longifòlia,	long-leaved.
" latifòlia,	broad-leaved.
capènsis,	Cape.
verrucòsa,	warted.
fràgrans,	scented.
paniculàta,	panicled.

OXYLÒBIUM 110.

obtusifòlium,	blunt-leaved.
retùsum,	retuse-leaved.
ellípticum,	elliptic-leaved.

ÓXALIS.

11 rubèlla,	red.
marginàta,	margined.
elongàta,	striped-flowered.
am'æna,	neat.

OSS'ÆA 246.	
1 purpurásscens,	purple.
Melàstoma-purpùrea.	
ORNITHÓGALUM 292.	Star-of-Bethlehem.
11 lactéum,	white.
aùreum,	golden.
marítimum,	squill.
OPÚNTIA 227.	
18 cochinillìfera,	cochineal-fig.
ficus-índica,	Indian-fig.
PELARGÒNIUM 110, 273,	Stork's-bill.
Geràniium.	
12 álbum.	
macrànthum.	
grandiflòrum.	
Navarino.	
Longstrethium.	
Jacksonium.	
Lucretia.	

Leopold.

Lafayette.

triumphans.

Jeffersoniaum.

Franklinium.

Queen-Adelaide.

Simsium.

obovatum.

Pepperium.

Philadelphicum.

foliosum.

Dutchess-of-Gloucester.

verecundum.

Lady Clifford.

Delaware.

marianum.

urbanum.

dissimilum.

Royal-George.

Washington.

Scotiaum.

banburyensis.

florabundum.

19 pavoninum.

Waterloo.

ignescens.

Lord-Yarborough.

decorum.

Sherwoodium.

doubreyanum.

Effi-Deans.

Lord-Byron.

Glorianum.

Chandler's-grand-purple.

Princess-Augusta, *new*.

Lord-Brougham.

Websterium.

ardescens.

Russellianum.

succulentum.

Rob-Roy.

Davyanam.

[The above begin with the lightest, and end with the darkest colours]

The following are various fancy sorts.

Lemon-scented.

apple-scented.

rose-scented.

peppermint-scented.

oak-leaved.

ardens.

bicolor.

tristum.

pulchellum.

nutmeg-scented.

PHÓRMIUM 112,	New-Zealand.
7 tenàx,	flax.

PHÝLICA 113.	
5 horizontàlis,	spreading.
plumòsa.	
squarròsa,	squarrose.
imbricàta,	imbricated.
myrtifòlia,	myrtle-leaved.
callòsa,	callous-leaved.
bícolor,	two-coloured.
ericoídes,	heath-like.

PIMÈLEA 113.

5 decussàta,	cross-leaved.
ròsea,	rose-coloured.
linifòlia,	flax-leaved.
spicàta,	spike-flowered.
drupàcea,	berry-bearing.

PITTOSPÓRUM 113.

13 tobìra,	Chinese.
undulàta,	wave-leaved.
coriàceum,	leather-leaved.
revolùtum,	revolute.
fúlvum,	yellow.
ferrugíneum,	rusty.

PHRÝNIUM 36.

PACHIDÉNDRON 259.

PÌNUS 210.

Canadénsis,	hemlock-spruce.

PERIPLÓCA 198.	Silk-vine.
gr'æca,	Virginian.
PHÆNÀCOMA 88.	
5 prolífera,	many-headed.
PHOTÍNIA 84.	
10 serrulàta,	serrulate.
arbutifòlia,	arbutus-leaved.
PÉRSEA 244.	Alligator-pear.
11 gratíssima,	common.
Laúrus-pérsea.	
PUNÍCA 172,	Pomegranate.
PULSATÍLLA 134,	Pasque-flower.
vernàlis,	spring.
PERÍSKIA 228,	Barbadoes-gooseberry.
18 aculeàta,	prickly.
PÝRUS 320.	

japònica,	red.
" álba,	white.

PÓÆNIA 321, 315, 151.

èdulis-whitlìjii,	white.
" fràgrans,	scented.
" hùmea,	crimson.
chinènsis-álba,	double-white?
paradòxa-fimbriàta,	fringed.
officinàlis-rúbra,	common.
15 moután,	tree.
" bànksii,	common.
" papaverácea,	white.
" rosèa,	rose-coloured.

POTENTÍLLA 147.

nepalénsis,	Nepaul.
formòsa.	
atropurpùrea,	dark-purple.
Russelliàna,	Russell's.
Hopwoodiàna,	Hopwood's.
spléndens,	splendid.

PLATYLÒBIUM 113,	Flat-pea.
5 formòsum,	handsome.
ovàtum,	ovate-leaved.
triangulàre,	triangular-stock.
PISTÀCIA 113.	
2 terebínthus,	turpentine-tree.
lentíscus,	mastic-tree.
vèra,	true.
reticulàta,	netted-leaved.
PLUMBÀGO 114,	Lead-wort.
trístis,	red-leaved.
Capénsis,	Cape.
PSORÀLEA 114.	
6 odoratíssima,	sweet-scented.
spicàta,	spike-flowered.
aculeàta,	prickly.
argéntea,	silvery.
tomentòsa,	downy.
PODALÝRIA 114.	

serícea,	silky.
styracifòlia,	storax-leaved.
corúscans,	glittering.
argéntea,	silvery.
laparioídes,	liparia-like.
subiflòra,	netted-leaved.

PERSOÓNIA 114.

6 hirsùta,	hairy-leaved.
móllis,	soft-leaved.
teretifòlia,	round-leaved.
lùcida,	shining-leaved.

PRÓTEA 115.

9 cynaroídes,	artichoke-flowered.
speciòsa,	splendid.
" rùbra,	red.
umbonàlis,	embossed.
longifòlia.	
melaleùca,	black-fringed.
grandiflòra,	large-flowered.
coccínea,	scarlet-flowered.
cenocárpa.	

pállens.

formòsa, handsome.

magnífica, magnificent.

mellífera, honey-bearing,

PULTEN'ÆA 115.

5 villòsa, villous.

obcordàta, heart-leaved.

argéntea, silvery-leaved.

plumòsa, feathered.

fléxilis, fragrant.

cándida, white-leaved.

strìcta, erect-growing.

PHLÓX 145.

paniculàta, panicled.

acuminàta, cross-leaved.

intermèdia, intermediate.

odoràta, odoriferous.

pyramidàlis, pyramid-flowered.

" álba, white.

suavèolens, sweet-scented.

refléxa, reflex-leaved.

stolonífera,	creeping.
pilòsa,	hairy.
divaricáta,	early-flowering.
nivàlis,	snowy-white.
subulàta,	awl-leaved.
PRÍMULA 146, 314,	Primrose.
vulgàris,	English-primrose.
elàtior,	ox-lip.
var. var.	polyanthus.
aurícula,	auricula.
var. var.	
cortusoídes,	cortuso-like.
dentiflòra,	jagged-flowered.
suavèolens,	sweet-scented.
decòra,	pretty.
scótica,	Scotch.
farinòsa,	bird's-eye.
vèris,	cowslip.
2 sinènsis,	China.
" alba,	white.
dentiflòra,	ragged.

PANCRÀTIUM 248.

11 maritímum,	sea-daffodil.
verecúndum,	narcissus-leavad.
littoràlis,	sea-side.
speciòsum,	showy.
carib'æum,	Caribbean.

POLYSPÒRA 248.

axillàris,	axil-flowered.

Caméllia axillàris.

PASSIFLÒRA 248,	Passion-flower.
13 alàta,	winged-stalked.
racemòsa,	racemose.
cærulea "	blue
quadrangulàris,	square-stalked.
filamentòsa,	thready.
picturàta,	pictured.

PANDÀNUS 249,	Screw-Pine.
13 odoratíssimus,	scented.

utilis? red-spined.

PTEROSPÉRMUM 250.	
13 suberifòlium,	various-leaved.
semisagittàtum,	half-sagittate.
PLUMÉRIA 250.	
11 acuminàta,	acuminate.
trícolor,	three-coloured.
rùbra,	red-coloured.
PH'ŒNIX 250,	Date-Palm.
12 dactylìfera,	common.
paludòsa,	marsh.
RÉSEDA 297,	Mignonette.
11 odoràta,	scented.
RÒCHEA 231.	
18 falcàta.	sickle-leaved.
Crussùla fulcáta.	
RHÚS 45.	
ROBÍNIA 45.	

ROSCÒEA 251.

purpùrea,	purple.
spicàta,	spike-flowered.
capitàta,	crown-flowered.

RUÉLLIA 251.

10 formòsa,	handsome.
fulgída,	shining.
anisophýlla,	unequal-leaved.
persicifòlia.	
persicifòlia.	peach-leaved.

RHÁPIS 251.

11 flabellifòrmis,	creeping-rooted.

RHODODÉNDRON 115,	Rose-tree.
16 arbòreum,	tree.
" álbum,	white-flowered.
" supérbum,	superb.
" purpùreum,	purple-flowered.
" álte-clárance,	large.
campanulàtum,	bell-flowered.

anthopògon, bearded-flowered.

cinnamòmeum, cinnamon-coloured.

ROÉLLA 116.

5 cilliáta, cilliate.

spícàta, spiked-flowered.

pedunculàta, peduncled.

RIPHIODÉNDRON 260.

RÙBUS 325.

3 rosæfòlius, Bramble-rose,

RÒSA 172, China-Rose,

12 índica.

" mínor.

animated.

Bengal elongata.

Belle-Chinese.

La-tendere-japonica.

belle-vibert.

odorata, tea-scented.

" alba, white-tea.

Florence, scarlet-tea.

Bengal, yellow-tea.

Venella.

Belle-de-monza.

amaranthe.

Clintonia.

semperflòrens-plèno.

Otaheite.

sanguinea-purpurea.

Grandvil.

Indica-alba, white-China.

magnifier.

Florabunda-multiplex.

Flamæa.

Hibbertia.

Jacksonia.

Adamsonia.

Websteria.

gigantea.

Washington.

calyxifòlia.

Montezuma.

Hortensia.

ROSA 156,	common Moss, Garden-rose.
blush	"
crimson	"
white	"
scarlet	"
Clinton	"
Damask	"
mottled	"
sweet-briar	"
de-Meaux	"
Lee's-crimson-perpetual.	
unique, or white-Provence.	
tricolor.	
spinosíssima,	Scotch.
gàllica,	officinale.
centifòlia,	Provins.
Damacène,	damask.
álba,	white.
rubiginósa,	sweet-briar.
white-monthly,	
red "	
striped "	

Black-Tuscany.

Sponge's-provins.

favourite-mignone.

champion.

fair-maid.

rouge-superb.

red-and-violet.

Pomonia.

black-fringe.

royal-provins.

royal-virgin.

royal-bouquet.

Great-Mogul.

striped-nosegay.

paragon.

ornament-de-parade.

York-and-Lancaster.

mundii.

Flanders.

delicious.

ROSA 189, Climbing.

Champneyàna, pink-cluster.

blush-noisettia.	
red-noisettia,	scarlet-cluster.
white-cluster or musk.	
superb " "	
aralie-noisettia.	
" purple.	
Bourbon.	
Boursault.	
Lisle.	
microphýlla.	
Franklin,	cluster-tea.
Banksiæ,	white.
"	yellow.
multiflòra,	
"	white.
"	scarlet.
"	purple.
Grevíllii,	many-coloured.
arvensis multiplex.	
sempervírens pléno.	
bracteàta plèno,	Macartney.

SÀGUS 252, Sago-Palm.

11 vinìfera, prickly-leaved.
Rumphii, Rumphius'.

SOLÁNDRA 252.
7 grandiflòra, large-flowered.
viridiflòra, green-flowered.

STROPHÁNTHUS.
divérgens, spreading.
dichótomus, forked.

SWIETÉNIA 253, Mahogany-tree.
15 mahógoni, common.
febrifùga, febrifuge.

SÁLVIA 117.
12 spléndens, splendid.
cærúlea, blue-flowered.
coccínea, scarlet-flowered.
aùrea, yellow-leaved.
paniculàta, panicle-flowered.
índica, Indian.
élegans, elegant.

SENÈCIO 117.	ground-sel.
12 grandiflòrus,	large-flowered.
venústus,	wing-leaved.
cineràscens,	gray.
élegans plèno,	elegant.
SCHÓTIA 118.	
1 speciòsa,	spacious.
aláta,	wing-leaved.
latifòlia,	broad-leaved.
Omphalòbium schótia.	
tamarindifòlia,	Tamirand-leaved.
SWAISÒNA 118.	
1 galegifòlia,	red-flowered.
coronillæfòlia,	purple-flowered.
astragalifòlia,	white-flowered.
SCÒTTIA 118.	
6 dentáta,	toothed.
angustifòlia,	narrow-leaved.
trapezifòrmus,	trapeziforum.

SPARRMÁNNIA 119.

12 africàna, African.

SPHÆROLÒBIUM.

6 vimíneum, yellow-flowered.

médium, red-flowered.

SPRENGÉLIA 119.

6 incarnáta, flesh-coloured.

STYLIDÍUM 120.

6 graminifòlium, grass-leaved.

fruticòsum, shrubby.

laricifòlium, larch-leaved.

adnátum, adnate.

STYPHÌLIA 120.

6 tubiflòra, tube-flowered.

triflòra, three-flowered.

adscéndens, ascending.

longifòlia, long-flowered.

SALPIGLÓSSIS 120.

13 pícta,	painted.
atropurpùrea,	dark-purple.
sinuáta,	crimson.

STRELÍTZIA 263.

19 regìnæ,	Queen.
ováta,	oval-leaved.
hùmilis,	dwarf.
agústa,	large-leaved.
jùncea,	rush-leaved.
parvifòlia,	small-leaved.
farinòsa,	mealy-stalked.

SPARÁXIS 304.

grandiflòra striáta,	striped.
versícolor,	various.
anemonæflòra,	anemone-flowered.

STERNBÉRGIA 274.

11 lútea,	yellow.
Amarýllis lútea.	

SPREIKÈLIA 207.

11 formosíssima, Jacobea-lily.

Amarýllis formosíssima.

SAPONÀRIA 147, Soap-wort.

officinális plèno, double.

cæspitòsa, tufted.

SILÈNE 147, Catch-fly.

viscósa, clammy.

" plèna, double.

SAXÍFRAGA 147, Saxifrage.

hirsùta, hairy.

crassifòlia, thick-leaved.

granolata multiplex, double.

umbròsa, London-pride.

sarmentòsa, sarmentose.

pulchélla, pretty.

pyramidális, pyramidal.

SPIR'ÆA 148,

ulmária multiplex, double meadowsweet.

filipéndula "	drop-wort.
lobàta lobe-leaved.	
STÁTICE 148.	Thrift.
vulgáris,	common.
Armèria vulgáris.	
speciòsa,	showy.
latifòlia,	broad-leaved.
maritìma,	sea-side.
TAGÈTES 120.	
11 lúcida,	sweet-scented.
TESTUDINÀRIA 221,	Hottentot's bread.
elephántipes,	Elephant's-foot.
montàna,	mountain.
TÁXUS 121.	Yew.
14 nucífera,	nut-bearing.
TELOPÈA 121.	
19 speciosíssimus,	showy.

TEMPLETÒNIA 122.

6 retùsa,	erect.
gláuca,	glaucous.

TRISTÀNIA 122.

1 neriifòlia,	oleander-leaved.
confertá,	crowded.
suavèolens,	scented.

TECÒMA 253, 65.

10 móllis,	soft.
digitàta,	digitated.
splèndida,	splendid.
capènsis,	cape.
stáns,	ash-leaved.
Bignònia stáns.	

TABERNÆMONTÁNA

11 coronària plèno,	double-white.
Nèrium coronàrium plèno.	
densiflòra,	dense-flowered.

THRÌNAX 254.

11 parviflòra, small-flowered.

TAXÁNTHEMA 149.

tatàrica, Tartarean.

Státice tatàrica.

latifòlia, broad-leaved.

conspícua, conspicuous.

THOMÀSIA 101.

1 solanàcea, night-shade-leaved.

quercifòlia, oak-leaved.

TRITÒNIA 304.

11 crocàta, crocus-leaved.

Ixìa crocàta.

xanthosphìla, yellow-spotted.

THUNBÉRGIA 251.

1 coccínea, scarlet.

grandiflòra, large-flowered.

fràgrans, scented.

alàta, wing-leaved.

TRÓLLIUS 149,	Globe-flower.
Europ'æus,	European.
Asiàticus,	Asiatic.
THÙJA 210.	American arbor-vitæ.
accidentalis,	western.
orientàlis,	eastern.
TIGRÍDIA 208.	Tiger-flower.
11 pavònia,	peacock.
conchiiflòra,	yellow-spotted.
TETRAMÈRIUM 228.	
17 odoratíssimum,	scented.
Coffèa occidentàlis.	
VERBÉNA 122,	Vervain.
chamædryfòlia,	scarlet.
melíndres.	
Lambértii,	Lambert's.
pulchélla,	pretty.
VIBÚRNUM 123, 306, 45.	

17 tìnus,	laurestinus.
lùcidum,	shining.
odoratíssimum,	scented.
hirsútum,	hairy.
strìctum,	erect.
variegàtum,	variegated.

VEMINÀRIA 124.

6 denudàta,	half-naked.

VIRGÍLIA 124.

capènsis,	cape.

VOLKAMÈRIA 124.

VERÓNICA 149.	Speed-well.
officinàlis,	officinal.
cham'ædrys,	Germander.
mèdia,	long-spiked.
incàna,	hoary.
élegans,	elegant.
spícàta,	spiked.
grándis,	large white.

incarnàta,	flesh-coloured.
cárnea,	pale red.
leucántha,	white-flowered.
bellidioídes,	daisy-leaved.
vérna,	vernal.
am'œna,	fine-blue.
pulchélla,	neat.
VALERÌANA 149.	
dioíca,	dioicious.
VÌOLA 150.	Violet.
odoràta,	sweet-scented.
" plèno álba,	double-white.
" " purpùrea,	" purple.
WITSÈNIA 125.	
8 corymbòsa,	corymbose.
WESTRÍNGIA 125.	
1 rosmariniفórmis,	rosemary-leaved.
longifòlia,	long-leaved.

WACHENDÓRFIA 24.

WHALÉNBERGIA 136.

7 grandiflòra, large-flowered.

Campánula grandiflòra.

WATSÒNIA 304.

11 iridifòlia, iris-leaved.

ròsea, rose-coloured.

hùmilis, dwarf.

fúlgida, scarlet.

Antholýza fúlgens.

rúbens, red-spotted.

WISTÈRIA 197.

frutéscens, shrubby.

Glýcine frutéscens.

chinéusis, Chinese.

Glýcine chinénsis.

YÚCCA 150. Adam's-needle.

supérba, superb.

Gloriòsa.

aloifòlia,	aloe-leaved.
angustifòlia,	narrow-leaved.
acuminàta,	tapering-flowered.
serrulàta,	saw-leaved.
filamentòsa,	thready.

ZÀMIA 125, 254.

11 hórrida,	horrid.
púngens,	pungent.
spíralis,	spiral.
latifòlia,	broad-leaved.
média,	intermediate.
furfuràcea,	chaffy.
ténuis,	slender.
integrifòlia,	entire-leaved.

ZÍNGIBER 36. Ginger.

CPSIA information can be obtained
at www.ICGtesting.com
Printed in the USA
LVHW011241061021
699678LV00001B/36

9 789355 116352